PALAZZI
OF ROME

Original title: Ville e palazzi di Roma
© 1998 by Magnus Edizioni SpA, Udine

© 1998 for the English-language edition:
Könemann Verlagsgesellschaft mbH
Bonner Str. 126, D-50968 Köln

Translation from Italian: Janet Angelini
Editor of the English-language edition: Sharon Herson
Proofreader: Shayne Mitchell
Typesetting: Goodfellow & Egan
Project coordinator: Stephan Küffner
Production manager: Detlev Schaper
Assistant: Nicola Leurs
Printing and binding: Mladinska knjiga tiskarna d.d.
Printed in Slovenia

ISBN 3-8290-1348-5

10 9 8 7 6 5 4 3 1

PALAZZI OF ROME

Text by
CARLO CRESTI AND CLAUDIO RENDINA

Photography by
MASSIMO LISTRI

KÖNEMANN

ACKNOWLEDGEMENTS

The publisher would like to thank the following
individuals and institutions: His Excellency Paolo
Pires Do Rij, ambassador of Brazil to Italy, His
Excellency Philippe Cuvillier, former ambassador
of France to Italy, Monsignore Claudio Celli and
the office-holders of the Order of St. John of
Malta, particularly the late Don Giovan Pietro dei
Duchi Caffarelli, Claudio Strinati, Soprintendente
per i Beni Artistici e Storici di Roma, Francesco
Buranelli Reggente della Direzione of the Vatican
Museums, Count Paolo Tournon, Luigi Borgia,
Doimo Frangipane, Antonio Zanardi Landi,
Baroness Chiara Barracco, Guido Cornini,
Barbara Jatta of the Biblioteca Apostolica
Vaticana, Annamaria Torroncelli of the Biblioteca
Casanatense, Sergio Guarino of the Capitoline
Pinacoteca, Giuseppe Mazzella, Professor Arsenio
Scalambrin, Guido Ceriotti, and the staff of the
Ufficio del Servizio del Patrimonio at the
Quirinal, the Presidenza del Consiglio at Palazzo
Chigi, the Segreteria del Cerimoniale del
Ministero degli Affari Esteri at Villa Madama, the
Académie de France, the Accademia dei Lincei,
the Soprintendenze for historic buildings, and
Rome museums, libraries, superintendencies,
and galleries.

CONTENTS

The Architecture of Roman Palazzi:
Splendor and Pride

The Domus Aurea and the Farnese *Dado*:
   The Custom of "Thinking Big"   p. 10

Palazzo, Street, and Piazza   »   13

Courtyards and Gardens   »   22

Sumptuous Interiors: Decorations,
   Furnishings, and Picture Galleries   »   27

The Roman Palazzo as Described by
   Landscape Painters and Travelers   »   35

The Palazzi of the Third Rome   »   41

*Roman Coats of Arms: A Note on
   Heraldry*   »   46

Villas and Palazzi of Rome   51

Casa dei Cavalieri di Rodi   »   52

Palazzo and di Venezia   »   58

Vatican Palace
   Palazzetto   »   66

The Palazzi on the Campidoglio   »   76

Palazzi Massimo   »   92

Villa Farnesina   » 102

Palazzo Farnese   » 110

Palazzo Mattei di Giove   » 126

Palazzo Sacchetti   » 136

Villa Madama   » 148

Villa Medici   p. 156

Villa Giulia   » 168

Palazzo Altemps   » 174

Palazzo Ruspoli   » 186

Palazzo Spada   » 200

Quirinal Palace   » 214

Palazzo Colonna   » 230

Palazzo Odescalchi   » 242

Palazzo Borghese   » 256

Palazzo Pallavicini Rospigliosi   » 264

Villa Borghese   » 274

Casino dell'Aurora Ludovisi   » 296

Palazzo Barberini   » 304

Palazzo Altieri   » 314

Palazzo Doria Pamphili   » 326

Palazzo Pamphili   » 338

Palazzo di Monte Giordano   » 350

Palazzo Corsini   » 358

Palazzo Chigi   » 372

Villa of the Knights of Malta   » 384

Index of Names and Places   » 391

Photographic Credits   » 398

CARLO CRESTI

THE ARCHITECTURE OF ROMAN PALAZZI: SPLENDOR AND PRIDE

The *Domus Aurea* and the Farnese *Dado:* The Custom of "Thinking Big"

In his *De vita Caesarum (Lives of the Caesars)*, written in the second century after Christ, the historian Gaius Suetonius recounts how Nero, at the opening of his *Domus Aurea* (Golden House), exclaimed: "At last I will begin to live like a man!"

Nero's house, which covered nearly one hundred hectares, occupied the Oppian and Esquiline hills and reached the Palatine and the Caelian, resembling a small town. Composed of numerous buildings, pavilions, panoramic terraces, gardens with fountains and nymphaeums, baths, gymnasiums, and even a lake, it was an "adequate" home for an emperor who was, to say the least, a megalomaniac. Nero "knew no restrictions on his liberality and expenditure" and was notorious for "his petulance, his lechery, his love of luxury, his cruelty, and his greed."

Suetonius also took on the task of describing for posterity the considerable dimensions of the golden residence. "To have an idea of its size and its magnificence, it suffices to recall the following details: there was a vestibule in which a colossus was erected in his [Nero's] likeness, one hundred

Domus Aurea (Golden House), The great octagonal room.

and twenty feet high. So vast was this vestibule that in its interior it had arcades with triple rows of columns for a length of one thousand paces, and a pond that looked like a sea, surrounded by buildings formed like cities.

Furthermore, inside there was countryside rich with fields, vineyards, pastures, and woods, with a great number of wild and domestic animals of all species. In the rest of the building, everything was coated with gold and embellished with gems and mother of pearl. The ceilings of the banqueting halls were of moveable, perforated ivory so that flowers and perfumes could be sprinkled over the guests. The greatest of these halls was round and turned continuously all day long on its own axis, like the world. In the bathrooms ran sea water and water from Albula...."

Long afterward, during the course of the eighteenth century, Charles de Brosses, confiding impressions of his stay in Rome in his *Lettres familières sur l'Italie* (Informal letters on Italy), wrote that one of the most grand patrician residences of the Roman sixteenth century, the "famous Palazzo Farnese," commissioned by Cardinal Alessandro who became Pope Paul III, showed "in its external architecture more majesty, grandeur, and solidity than grace or ornament. And yet it is the work of the most famous architects, including Michelangelo, who made the cornice; it is true that this is also the most beautiful part.... The square courtyard is decorated by several levels of arcades and columns and by colossal statues."

In de Brosses's opinion, a building without columns could not be called "perfectly beautiful," and he declared himself indignant that "those idiots of Farnese," in order to build this palazzo, had destroyed, as was then supposed, "part of the Colosseum—which for them represented a convenient quarry, near at hand and a cheap source of stone."

Nevertheless, he could not help eulogizing over the gallery painted by the Carracci. "Frescoed on the ceiling and on the walls, in sections of uneven size, are the stories of Ovid's *Metamorphoses*. Some have been done in green chiaroscuro to give

G. Vasi dis. sc.

1. Chiesa di S. Brigida, 2. Chiesa di S. Maria del Orazione detta la Morte, 3. Arco, che passa su la Strada Giulia, 4. Palazzo della Religione Teutonica, 5. Palazzo Mandosi. Palazzo Farnese

Palazzo Farnese in an eighteenth-century etching by Giuseppe Vasi.

a greater effect of variety, but almost all are in color. Most of this is the work of Annibale Carracci, with the collaboration of Ludovico and Agostino. Among large-scale works, this gallery is a masterpiece. Taking all of it into account, it is to be considered equal with the great works of Raphael."A leap through the centuries through the literary memoirs of two witnesses to their respective periods and the proposed connection between the ancient palace of an Emperor and the Renaissance palazzo of a member of the Farnese family who was first a cardinal, then pope may at first seem perplexing, since the two buildings do not seem comparable.

However, between these two extremes, Nero's *Domus Aurea* and the Farnese palazzo, that is, between these two types of dwelling apparently so distant and different, links do exist. Both were conceived as residences, both were constructed as status symbols. Between them occurred the events of the most important part of Rome's history and the vanity and hedonism of both owners, though in different periods, are reflected in the architectural character of the buildings. To make reference to these two extremes, pointing out what is readily identifiable in both, therefore, is an immediate and fruitful way to enter into the history and significance of the palazzi of Rome. It is not by chance that the vicissitudes of construction of these residences lead to two absolute protagonists, in good and evil, symbolic of the history of Rome: the emperor with limitless power and the powerful cardinal who became pope.

Two other types of individuals, constants in human history, also recur in the history of the Eternal City: the secretary, the bureaucrat, the "palace insider;" such as Suetonius, who writes the biographies of the worthy or less-than-worthy rulers be they successors to the throne of an earthly monarch or heirs to St. Peter; and the traveler, either the religious or the lay pilgrim, dedicated to the Grand Tour (de Brosses), who makes contact with urban reality, notes the beauty or ugliness of the buildings and, the good and bad aspects of the social life, and discovers new knowledge and new interpretations of that reality.

Analysis of the above-mentioned residential typologies, expressions of the same persistent ideology of power, reveals the similarities and continuity of programmatic method and achievable practice. Both these great palazzi display majestic proportions outside and impressive size and grandiose height inside; both utilize decoration in order to provide the illusion of tremendous space to interiors that were already enormous and in order to make even more precious and enliven with symbols the prestigious reception rooms intended for the self-promotion of a *dominus et deus* (lord and god), be he emperor or pope (or about to be elected such, as with Cardinal Alessandro Farnese).

These affinities can be seen also in the logic, or strategies and scale, of the urban renewal involved in the construction of the two residences, both of which involved vast urban areas. To build his *Domus Aurea*, Nero expropriated land on the Oppian Hill and in the valley at the foot of the

Palatine, Esquiline, and Caelian Hills. To construct his residence, Alessandro Farnese successively bought up great portions of the Regola district and tore down buildings in order to achieve the broad empty space of the piazza in front of his palazzo. He even dreamed of giving life to an entire Farnese quarter: he built a bridge over Via Giulia behind the palazzo and dreamed of a crossing to link the two banks of the Tiber, which would thus have connected the palazzo with the much-desired Villa Chigi, bought later (in 1580) by members of the Farnese family and appropriately rebaptized La Farnesina (Little Farnese), in response to the massiveness of the other family home.

compact block and having a central courtyard with superimposed architectural orders.

Yet another coincidence can be noted: in Nero's Golden House, dignitary and humble subject alike would encounter the colossal bronze image of the emperor, a manifest symbol of the latter's self-idolatry, while in the Farnese mansion-palace, art lovers could admire, as signs of an ostentatious zeal for collecting, the gigantic marble *Farnese Hercules,* leaning on his club, and the sculpted pyramidal group of the *Farnese Bull*, representing the vengeance of Zethus and Amphion on Dirce, queen of Thebes. The correlations identified in these two examples, chosen as extreme points for an examination of the particular qualities of Roman

Detail of the entrance vestibule-gallery in Palazzo Farnese.

Other aspects too seem in some way to link, through their innovative value, the initiatives taken by emperor and future pope. Under Nero, thanks to the talents of his architects Severus and Celerus, a decisive change took place in Roman residential architecture, in the development, articulation, deep penetration, and structural complexity of the forms built around the spaces. An example is the trapezoidal vestibule facing the valley and the cross-shaped rooms arranged like rays around the octagonal room in the *Domus Aurea*. Under Alessandro Farnese, the work of Antonio da Sangallo the Younger led to the creation of the sixteenth-century classic Roman palazzo, built as a

palazzi, enable us to state that conceiving and "thinking big" in architecture was common to emperors and popes alike, and is thus a distinctive, constant characteristic of architecture in Rome.

In this sense, it is enough to recall the *palatium* designed by the architect Rabirius that Diocletian had built on the Palatine, the mausoleum of Augustus, the Colosseum (raised on the site of the lake of the *Domus Aurea*), the many baths, the Mausoleum of Hadrian (later transformed into Castel Sant'Angelo), and, centuries later, the basilica raised over the tomb of the apostle Peter and surmounted by the immense covering of Michelangelo's dome.

Palazzo, Street, and Piazza

Signs of the intentions of Roman greatness are evident in the streets and piazzas that are directly related to the public and private palazzi established on those streets and piazzas. They were widened, straightened, or newly created in conjunction with the rising palazzo and as a function of the size and role of the patrician edifices that were inserted into these external spaces.

The piazza in front of Palazzo Farnese took shape while the palazzo was being built, and steps were taken to furnish the public way by placing there two granite basins previously before Palazzo San Marco in Piazza Venezia. According to a print of 1549, the layout of the urban area around the rising Farnese *Dado* (cube, or die-shape) provided both for the paving of the piazza (which was disregarded) in squares that would have corresponded to sections of the mansion's façade (according to James Ackerman) and for the widening of Vicolo dei Baullari (realized in 1548) in order to improve access to Campo dei Fiori. At the same time, those who lived there obtained an increased line of vision and enhancement of the panoramic effect that focused on the central part of the façade of the Farnese palace, with a view to ensuring that "by the direction of the main door that opened into Campo di Fiori one could see at a glance the courtyard, the fountain, Via Giulia, and the bridge and the beauty of the other garden, up to the other door that exited into Via del Trastevere," recalling, as Vasari wrote in 1568, that Michelangelo had proposed "that in that direction a bridge should be made that would cross the Tiber so that it would be possible to go from that palazzo to another garden and mansion of theirs in Trastevere [Villa Farnesina]."

Another episode, perhaps the best known and most significant confirmation of the consistent partnership between palazzo and piazza when both were in the process of being built, is Michelangelo's reorganization of the Campidoglio (Capitoline Hill). Pope Paul III and the Conservatori of the Roman Commune decided in 1537 to install the equestrian statue of Marcus Aurelius in the center of the flat area in front of the Palazzo del Senatorio. They assigned to the latter, with its tower and its two-ramp entry staircase, the function of picturesque backdrop to the urban stage, which was designed as a trapezoidal space, open to the sky (with a side balustrade decorated with marble trophies and statues of the Dioscuri) and facing the city below. This space was to contain, and be directed through, two horizontal lateral structures, whose differing arrangement was due to the oblique position of

the fifteenth-century Palazzo dei Conservatori, which formed an acute angle with the Palazzo del Senatorio.

It was just these preconditions, the presence of the equestrian statue and the planned long access ramp to the secular Capitoline acropolis, giving undeniable emphasis to the longitudinal axis of the piazza, which suggested the design of the accentuated lateral elevations. It could also be said that they determined the reconstruction of the earlier façade of the Palazzo dei Conservatori and the construction of the façade of the new building opposite. This is symmetrical, a mirror image, following the strong texture of two trabeated superimposed levels: a portico on the

View of Piazza del Campidoglio in an eighteenth-century etching by Giuseppe Vasi. Below, the Piazza with one of the Dioscuri, and, in the background, the Palazzo Nuovo, symmetrical with and mirroring the Palazzo dei Conservatori.

lower floor and a series of windows on the upper, unified by pilasters of a colossal order.

There are many more examples of palazzi designed to fit the formal arrangement of the surrounding urban space. When Gregory XIII, in 1583, gave orders to start rebuilding and extending the villas of Cardinals Carafa and Este in order to create his summer residence on the height of Monte Cavallo (the Quirinal), at the same time as the construction "with a beautiful loggia," as recounted by Baglione, "portico, and extraordinary spiral staircase, a work worthy of the Pontifical Palace, and designed by Ottavio Mascherini …", the broad way at the crossing with Via Pia also began to take the shape of a piazza.

Similarly in 1586, while construction intensified at the corner of Via Pia and decoration reached that street, Sixtus V entrusted to Domenico Fontana the task of designing the piazza as a meeting point of the three arterial roads and as a space to accommodate groups of pilgrims while they waited for the papal blessing. Since the proposed piazza needed to be compatible with the other buildings on it, the pope ordered the removal of the colossal Dioscuri and their horses to the near end of Via Pia, thus making them become the terminus of the long straight street that led to Porta Pia.

Another conspicuous example, notable for its sensational formal result, is the relationship between Palazzo Poli and Piazza di Trevi, onto which it faces. Extended by incorporating several adjacent buildings which were bought by Innocent

Veduta della vasta Fontana di Trevi anticamente detta l'Acqua Vergine.
Architettura di Nicola Salvi.

View of the Trevi Fountain in an etching by Giovan Battista Piranesi.

XII, the original property of the dukes of Poli arrived at an uncompleted fountain which, like the present one, was placed on the north side of Piazza di Trevi. Pope Clement XII in 1731 restarted the suspended work on the fountain and blocked the area with a grandiose show of water, ordering that the new fountain (begun following a design by Nicola Salvi in 1732) should occupy the entire external wall of the Poli palazzo. The Poli, needless to say, protested against the pontiff's arbitrary decision, but in the end, instead of erecting the usual kind of frontal edifice, they benefited from one of the most tumultuous of Roman façades, a triumphant, theatrical conflation of architecture and sculpture, placed on artificial rock, crossed by gushing showers of water and centered in a spectacular niche from which emerge Neptune's pair of winged horses led by tritons.

The connections between the walls of the Roman palazzi and the streets and piazzas imply other forms of contiguity as well, other types of contact and integration which are perhaps less obvious but are equally distinctive and expressive of experimentation through reciprocal exchanges and achievements. A number of questions can be asked. In what ways and through what channels did the interior of the palazzo communicate with the exterior? How, and with what features, did owners prefer to express their individuality, translated into bricks and mortar, to the public eye? Which aspect did they choose to keep private? How does the palazzo connect to the ground and how does it join the paved level of the street or piazza? How does it

Detail of the Trevi Fountain against the façade of Palazzo Poli.

15

rise from ground level? Which and how many formal elements are employed, and which and how many changes were made to the members at each successive level?

Almost all the palazzi of any importance, because of their noble (or less than noble) family crests or because of their size, have in their interior a street or a private piazza. The street might be covered by the entrance gates, the space enclosed and boxed in by the courtyard. It is only this covered way on the ground floor, or the vestibule as a branch of lateral and private continuation of the street or public square, that is the element of contact (or junction, or passage) between exterior and interior. The vestibule is the place of transition and mediation, placed between the entry into and exit from the palazzo. Within this limited area, the changes of scene are graduated between the macrocosm of the city and the microcosm of the palazzo. Thus, even if only momentarily, the contrast between outside and inside is diluted, the difference of sound and light, and even variations of mood attenuated. The longer the vestibule, the longer and slower is the time and act of entry, and the greater the sensation of having access to something crucially important.

Proof of this is the sequence—the portico on the street, the corridor-gallery of the entrance, and the open portico of the inner courtyard (or rather, of the alternating light-shade-light)—which leads into Palazzo Massimo alle Colonne. The interior-exterior space of the portico, curving and provided with benches, and characterized by the dissimilarity of the columnar interaxials, follows the direction of the street, based on the foundations of Domitian's Odeon. The portico leads to a corridor with a vaulted ceiling which in turn leads into the half-open space of the portico facing the courtyard. In other words, three successive filters of differentiated space and three diversified intensities of light lead into the heart of the palazzo—and, inversely, from the inner courtyard toward the street.

The vestibule-gallery of Palazzo Farnese, with its three aisles (including the half-covered one with its coffered barrel vault), marked by six columns on each side and six niches hollowed out of the surrounding walls, is the confirmation of the above-mentioned typology of penetration from external space (piazza) to the central internal court and vice versa this penetration. Here too the architecture takes advantage of the calculated effect of the succession of modulated spaces and passages through bright light on the one hand and shaded porticoes on the other.

Additional examples of similar linking between outside and inside can been seen in the wide and deep porticoed atriums of the seventeenth-century central section of Palazzo Barberini (with five aisles) and in the eighteenth-century Palazzo Corsini (with three aisles), as well as in the more modest and narrow single entry hall which, in the sixteenth-century Palazzo Gandi-Niccolini in Via del Banco di Santo Spirito and in the Palazzo Mattei di Giove, of the same period, links the hectic bustle of the street and the peaceful tranquillity of the private courtyard.

The unifying channels of contact and communication between the outside and the inside of the palazzo are also seen in the inviting colonnaded portals, which support a loggia and protrude from the line of the façade, invading the external space, and in the large windows, with or without balconies, that can be thrown open and are located preferably in the center of the front elevation in order to project the interior of the building toward the attractions of its surroundings. Examples of this can be seen in the fifteenth-century Palazzo Venezia and in the eighteenth-century Palazzo di San Luigi dei Francesi, as well as in the twin buildings on the Campidoglio. The formal theme of the colonnaded portal with a loggia over it is visible as a secular prothyrum on the sixteenth-century façades of Villa Giulia, Palazzo Farnese, and Palazzo Borghese. It was the focal point on the main façade of the Quirinal Palace and constitutes the primary vertical accent on the façades of the seventeenth-century palazzi of Propaganda Fide, Doria Pamphili, Altieri, and Chigi Odescalchi.

The communion between adjacent open and covered space is facilitated also by the porticoes located on the ground floor and by the roof-terraces, a synthesis of little towers, loggias, and belvederes that dominates the urban panorama.

Opposite:
Two-order loggia in the courtyard of Palazzo Mattei di Giove.
Below, antechamber on the first floor of the eighteenth-century Palazzo Corsini.

Detail of the central portal of Palazzo Borghese on Piazza Borghese.
Below, façade of Villa Medici with, in the distance, Michelangelo's dome at St. Peter.

Pius IV's Casina in the Vatican gardens, built to the design of Pirro Ligorio.

Remarkable examples of such terraces rise above the roofs like crowns on the Villa Medici and on Palazzi Altemps, Vecchiarelli, Ruspoli, Falconieri, and Rospigliosi-Pallavicini. Borromini even designed three for Palazzo Pamphili on Piazza Navona. Vasi and Falda, depict in their etchings the roof-terraces of Palazzi Borghese, Mattei di Giove, and Doria Pamphili.

With the exception of the mirror-image Capitoline palazzi (originally intended for administrative functions), whose porticoes belong to the buildings themselves as well as to the piazza onto which they face, the other palazzi in which porticoed spaces appear on the ground floor are more likely to be suburban residences (the Farnesina, Villa Medici, and Villa Borghese, Pius IV's Casina in the Vatican) or homes more distant from the city, surrounded by secluded gardens or protective walls, and thus not closely associated with the public road system of the period.

Less effective, and often unresolved, however, are the links between the palazzo and the ground on which it stands. An analysis of the way in which the walls above ground make explicit their continuity with the foundations beneath, or of the way in which the forms and architectural devices express the connection of the building to the ground, reveals that the solutions are not always convincing.

In Palazzo Venezia, for example, the perimeter walls emerge from the ground without any indication of what lies beneath. The sloping wall of Villa Medici facing the city is certainly more effective in announcing its function of support and link with the ground. However, for the Palazzi Acetti, Chiovenda, and Caffarelli Vidoni, which were built in the first half of the sixteenth century, it would seem that Serlio's belief that architectural orders should be considered as "*opera di mano*" (literally, work of the hand, that is, artificial) and the ashlar construction as "*opera di natura*" (work of nature) had been borne in mind. Thus revetment of rusticated ashlar blocks on basement fascias should make the rising of the edifice from street level seem "naturalistic." In truth, however, in Palazzo Caffarelli (begun in 1615 on Lorenzetto's design) it is rather the ledges of the knee-high windows (extra-long) that give the impression of being rooted in the ground. On Palazzo Spada, too, ashlar is employed for its attachment to the ground, despite the fact that the flattening of the surface makes the "rustication" of the basement minimal and therefore practically eliminates the naturalistic metaphor.

For the purposes of linking the buildings to the ground, the faced ashlar that dresses the façades of the fifteenth-century Palazzo della Cancelleria and the sixteenth-century Palazzo Massimo alle Colonne is quite ineffective, so much so that in the Cancelleria recourse has had to be made to three superimposed and slightly protruding fillets (which, however, are not able to take on the relief of a cymatium), to indicate the greater width of the foundations the only entity emerging from the base of the perimeter wall. In the second palazzo, its anchoring to the ground seems to have been entrusted to the central columns and the pilasters (the "*opere di mano*"), which in reality rise from an apparently continuous foundation that appears barely above ground level and is thus of no influence as a connecting element.

Equally inadequate, considering the size of the buildings, is the solution of the transitional passage between the horizontal plane of the street and the vertical surfaces of the palazzo in the form of a

Detail of the decoration on the inner façade of Palazzo Spada.

Detail of the façade of Palazzo Doria Pamphili on Via del Corso.

modest, rather low base on which rest the sills of the knee-high windows. Such is the case in Palazzi Borghese, Caetani, Chigi Odescalchi, and Corsini. The walled benches at the foot of the sixteenth-century Palazzi Farnese and Ricci, acting as extensions and "invasions" of their respective buildings into public space, provide, however, supplementary functional motivation in the form of a continuous pedestal, placed at the base of the façades, which achieves an effective connection between these and the paving stones of the piazza onto which the palazzi face. Finally, in Palazzo dei Conservatori, the high and robust plinths of the colossal-order pilasters give credibility to the linking of the building to the ground. This is emphasized by the clear strip of paving that follows the contour of the whole façade and seems to widen the support area.

Grotesque mask on the portal of the house of Federico Zuccari in Via Gregoriana.

Leaving aside the formal solutions (some more convincing, some less so) for the foundation facings, Roman palazzi, in particular those of the sixteenth century, are mainly characterized by external features that are undoubtedly austere and heavy because their prototypes were derived from Florentine and Tuscan models which increased enormously in size, however, once they came into contact with the Roman way of doing things.

Normally the façades of these buildings, and those of a certain number of seventeenth-century palazzi, have no superimposed architectural orders. Instead they are divided horizontally by simple string-course cornices, with processions of windows (trabeated or adorned with gables) placed symmetrically to the sides of the central vertical axis made up of the portal-loggia sequence. The varieties of these unadorned façades, concluding at the top in a projecting cornice and at the corners in the reinforcement of a stone quoin revetment, are usually characterized by the length of the façades and the number of floors, and thus the numbers of windows in a row for each floor. The sixteenth-century Lateran Palace for example displays these features of exterior monotony, as well as the residences of the same period belonging to the Caetani, Sacchetti, Borghese, and Maffei, the eighteenth-century Palazzo Corsini, and the seventeenth-century San Callisto. Other related structures, dating from the seventeenth century, are Palazzi Mattei di Giove, Giustiniani, Carpegna, Altieri, Pallavicini Rospigliosi, and Chigi, this last certainly as colorless as the many governing ministers who have lived there.

Not particularly noteworthy for imagination are Palazzetto Spada in Via Capodiferro and Palazzi Ossoli (1520–1527), Salviati alla Lungara (Giovanni Lippi, called Nanni di Baccio Bigio, c. 1560), Cesi (Martino Longhi the Elder, 1569–1576), Mancini (Carlo Rainaldi, 1662), Chigi Odescalchi (Bernini, 1665), and Cenci Bolognetti (Fuga, 1735), whose front elevations are marked at regular intervals by pilasters.

Only a few Roman palazzi (for example, the fifteenth-century Cancelleria, Palazzi Giraud Torlonia and Caffarelli Vidoni, and the seventeenth-century central segments of Palazzo Barberini and Palazzo Doria Pamphili, which overlooks the Piazza del Collegio Romano) have front elevations that are structured through the superimposition of architectural orders. Since this is not always done in the canonical fashion, it must be concluded that the two Borrominian façades of the Convento dei Filippini (1637–1650) and Palazzo di Propaganda Fide (1654–1664) are admirable exceptions. These are resolved in purely architectonic terms through spatial combinations made dynamic by inflections and eversions (and not with summaries of orders and decorative episodes), capable—with their vibrant "profundity" of shape—of incorporating external space while conforming to the requirements placed upon them by internal space.

Despite the warning by Leon Battista Alberti that "the adornments of city houses must be much more somber and serious than those for suburban villas," the façades were nevertheless decorated in a lively manner, with bas-reliefs and statues in niches. This is so for the sixteenth-century fronts of Palazzi Spada and Crivelli, both decorated by Giulio Mazzoni, and for the Casina of Pius IV in the Vatican gardens (Pirro Ligorio, 1558–1563), Villa Medici (the part facing the garden, which according to Henry James looked like "an enormous Rococo clock, all encrusted with figures, arabesques, and tables"), Villa Borghese (before its desecration in 1807), and the Casino del Belrespiro in the park of Villa Doria Pamphili (Alessandro Algardi, 1644–1652).

To a more cheerful, even ironic, genre belong the masks constituting the entrance and windows of the palazzo that Federico Zuccari built for himself in 1593 and the caryatids surrounding the windows on the ground floor of the eighteenth-century Palazzetto Centini.

A successful ornamental composition, which formally and pleasingly shapes the varied window gables of the *piano nobile* and other structures, can be seen in the façade of Palazzo Doria Pamphili overlooking Via del Corso. Built by Gabriele Valvassori, starting in 1731, this façade was

The architectonic and decorative ensemble designed by Giambattista Piranesi for the Knights of Malta and executed in 1765 is unique. The complex includes the entrance façade to the garden of the Villa of the Knights of Malta and the commemorative stelae flanked by obelisks placed on the enclosure wall of the piazza in front of it, almost like a piazza in front of a church. In this case, however, the ornamental themes that decorate the façade and the stelae are taken from images belonging to the Roman archaeological inventory; these have been creatively reinterpreted, reinvented, and reassembled.

To this decorative category also belong the painted façades which were fashionable in sixteenth-century Rome. Among the few that have survived must be counted Palazzo Massimo (also called *istoriato* [frescoed]), frescoed in grisaille in 1523 by pupils of Daniele da Volterra, as well as Palazzo Ricci, frescoed in 1525 by Polidoro di

described by Valesio as "ostentatious and unpleasing architecture." The classicist de Brosses called it "deplorable … of a taste they thought was gallant, but in fact is nothing other than Gothic, if not more barbaric still." "More serious," however, are the figure of Fame supporting the family crest (Benaglia, 1734) and the statues (Maini, 1739) seated on the tympana of the entrances of Palazzo della Consulta (erected after a design by Fuga between 1732 and 1736).

Caravaggio and Maturino di Firenze. Painted figures too, or rather the use of more economical decoration, on the outside of buildings intended for habitation, was a way of declaring the social prestige of patrons, a way of convincing the humble citizen of the economic and political power of the owners. Not by chance, when speaking of Roman palazzi, did Hippolyte Taine declare that "the animal is well known by its shell."

View of the entrance to the Villa of the Knights of Malta on the Aventine Hill by Giovan Battista Piranesi.

Courtyards and Gardens

Despite the wish for ostentation, one part of the palazzo was kept hidden and reserved. This was the inner courtyard, which was usually forbidden to the "indiscreet" curiosity of the mere citizen. This might seem to be in direct contrast with the desire of the powerful to show their authority were it not for the fact that, over and beyond the requirements of service and the need for ample margins around their privacy, it was part of that same authority to impose graduality in their ostentation, in other words, to regulate the quality and the openness of the palazzo as a function of the social status of the privileged guest, no matter what the reason for, or how pleasant, the visit. The courtyard figures as a counter-façade of the building, the secret face, the other side of the coin, with the advantage of even offering surprises. What was not considered appropriate to show in public for reasons of social sensitivity or political convenience could be shown in the contained space of the courtyard. In other words, the habitual somberness and severity of the external façade acted as a foil to the cordiality of the façade of the enclosed court.

This explains why the architecture of the courtyard is almost always more vibrant than that of the façade facing the city. The tedious repetition of two-dimensional windows overlooking the confines of streets and piazzas is transformed inside the courtyard with the three-dimensionality of the colonnades, the succession and depth of arcaded dynamics, the shaping of structures and the

Colonnade of the courtyard of Palazzo dei Conservatori on the Campidoglio.

Detail of the loggias in the courtyard of the Cancelleria.

play of chiaroscuro. The heavy, defensive compactness of the external walls was transformed in the courtyard into the contrasting lightness of superimposed loggias.

Amid numerous examples, a start can be made with the square central courtyard of Palazzo Farnese. This has three architectural orders, one above the other, and five arcades on each side, of imposing dimensions and plasticity (in Stendhal's words, they "ventilate the Colosseum"). In contrast, one can

move on to the subtle effect of the two elegant orders of arcades (five on the short side and eight on the longer) which support the airy top floors of the rectangular courtyard of the Cancelleria.

Contact may also be made with legend through the surreal presence of the gigantic marble head (of Constantine), two colossal feet, and an enormous hand with forefinger raised (surviving fragment of overgrown Imperial statuary), which keep company with other archaeological remains in the courtyard of the Capitoline Palazzo dei Conservatori, and, in the central arch of the framing travertine colonnade, the image of the goddess Roma.

Moving on one can enter through the lively wings of the courtyard of Palazzo Spada, filled with statues in niches and relief friezes and festoons, and discover on the side without the portico the astonishing Borrominian perspective device of the columned gallery, which seems to be long and regal but in reality is no more than nine meters long.

Still with this courtyard-museum, crowded with guests of marble, *cippi*, and other typically Roman fragments, it is difficult to decide which is the more picturesque: the rhythm of the double loggia with its two architectural orders that surrounds the first small courtyard of Palazzo Massimo alle Colonne, or the equally rich courtyard where the Mattei di Giove family packed in their collection of marble busts and various ornaments in the open air between a double arcaded loggia and a terrace opposite placed on two blind arches and a central open supporting arch.

oversized windows, one above the other, corresponding to the landings of the staircase.

Finally, the remarkable courtyards of Villa Giulia and of the *casina* of Pius IV must be drawn to the visitor's attention. Neither of these was carved out between four high screen walls. Rather they were inserted into articulated complexes between gardens and surrounded by side walls lower than those of the main fabric of the building.

Perhaps best of all is the great porticoed courtyard, cadenced by arches on paired columns, at Palazzo Borghese, which is further embellished by the panoramic sensation of the double loggia linking the two wings of the building and giving onto the garden. Deserving particular mention is the courtyard of the Palazzo della Consulta (Fuga, 1732–1737), noteworthy not only for the form of a cube inserted into the trapezoidal volume of the building, but also for the originality of one of its elevations, which has imprinted on its external surface the projection of the diagonal lines of the main double-flight staircase inside. These lines converge on the vertical axis made up of two

In Villa Giulia, the courtyard has one side that coincides with the porticoed hemicycle, which, branching off from the two-storey *palazzina*, faces and encompasses the posterior space and continues in the shape of a rectangle to a transitional loggia. From here, a divided semi-circular stairway leads to a lower level, to the small nymphaeum, and frames the "secret fountain" of the Acqua Vergine. Instead of the usual box open to the sky, this courtyard resembles a piazza, but with the character and significance of a private place, composed of a continuum of architectural episodes that are not oppressive and are arranged on different levels.

Spectacular double loggia in the courtyard of Palazzo Borghese.

Even the elliptical basin excavated in the grove in the Vatican gardens and completed (between 1558 and 1563) at the foot of the Casina of Pius IV suggests an elegant and small private piazza, furnished with a central fountain surrounded by a low parapet with consoles (like seats to watch performances). Access to the fountain and "piazza" was gained via two identical vestibules placed at the far ends of the main axis, symmetrical to the ornately decorated façade of the Casina (plasterwork by Rocco da Montefiascone, Paolo Pianetti, and Girolamo da Como). On the other side

The Farnese gardens in a seventeenth-century etching by Giovan Battista Falda.

View of the garden and rear of Palazzo Corsini on the Via della Lungara. In the middle, beyond the Tiber, can be glimpsed the Dado *of Palazzo Farnese. Detail of mosaic from the Gilbert Collection, Los Angeles.*

of the minor axis, a loggia, equally decorated, opens onto the "piazza" and overlooks a fishpond behind and below it.

If the courtyard was seen as a private place, the garden of the city mansion was imagined as a place even more intimate and secret, where communion between nature and artifice could be experienced with the aim of creating rest and pleasure for the benefit of a few selected high-ranking guests. The garden, or rather the sixteenth-century vineyard, even if it was promoted by a cardinal, thus became

the pattern of a very earthly paradise, in the epicurean sense.

The concept of garden must be understood as a projection of an idealized nature which could be translated in terms of culture into the shape of a constructed space with terraces, flights of steps, nymphaeums, exedras, fountains, arbors, and ever green walls that acted as an extension of the palazzo's architecture.

The Farnese gardens (Orti Farnesiani) on the Palatine Hill (planned by Alessandro Farnese, nephew of Paul III, and realized by Vignola, 1565–1573) are the first clamorous example of the rebirth of the taste for a garden as a "caprice," "a place of delight." This type of garden became possible thanks to the restoration and reinforcement work decided upon by Pius V, Sixtus V, and Paul V, respectively, on the acqueducts of the Acqua Vergine (1570), the Acqua Felice, and the Acqua Paola (1609). These restorations not only made it possible to irrigate cultivated land but also permitted the introduction of running water (a sound peculiar to the Rome of the time) into public fountains in streets and piazzas, as well as into private fountains in courtyards and gardens.

In gardens, the fountain, as an expression of formal acrobatics between architecture and sculpture, "the fount of life," corroborating the sentiment of Eros, with the water's copious and multiple ways of being and appearing in the form of a warning, an animation of nature, and a symbol of fertility, became the central point or the bedrock of axiality, symmetry, a green weft of boxwood or laurel, an allusion to urban geometry. It was there, in addition to statues and scattered archaeological remains, to form points of recognition, or meeting, or direction, in a labyrinthine organism as a function of a play for vanity; it was useful for contemplation, for the carrying out of pagan-type rites of temporary idleness, a complement to the business transactions that were preferably conducted within the palazzo.

To have an idea of the architecture of the Farnese gardens, which were destroyed in 1883, the only recourse is to the *vedute* (view paintings and etchings) of Falda, Percier, Fontaine, and Letarouilly, or to the laconic note made by Goethe in 1787: "thanks to … the flower beds, the spaces between the ruins and the imperial palaces have been made fertile and gracious."

To find a true example of a sixteenth-century garden, the Villa Medici is the place to visit. The remaining grid pattern of the Italianate flower beds around the obelisk, and the grove where the so-called mausoleum stood, ringed by cypresses, are now only faded memories compared to the sensations experienced by Charles de Brosses during his stay in Rome in 1739–1740. It was described between 1745 and 1755 as "a gracious garden, an obelisk that was once in Flora's Circus, some pleasant fountains, especially the one where there is a beautiful lion, an artificial mountain in the style of a pyramid, covered with well-placed trees, and a small castle at the top."

The remains of the Villa Medici gardens today are equally far from the original when compared to what the marquis de Sade had to say during the course of his travels in Italy in 1775–1776: "On a small elevation there is another [garden] which is usually kept closed. Its narrow pathways, covered and always green … form a walk that is solitary and extremely pleasant. On the highest part a little walkway has been carved out which is all curves and leads right up to the top, where there is a small pavilion open on all sides, from which the most vast and attractive panorama of Rome can be enjoyed. This little place has been given the name of Parnassus. In truth, those who visit it can feel only some of the emotions that once animated the home of the Muses, but desired as they may be, they cannot be found, and one ends by coming down again, complaining about having been deceived." After telling us that Villa Medici "enjoys the best air in Rome" and that the garden was open to the public, this irrepressible libertine added that "since it is also very isolated, it usually serves as a

Fountain in front of the palazzina of the Coffee House in the gardens of the Quirinal Palace.

meeting place for new lovers. There, understandings are knotted and loosened I cannot say whether it occurs sometimes that they are brought to consummation; what is certain is that one could do so, I believe, in perfect privacy."

A place for meetings of a very different type, probably, were the gardens of the Quirinal Palace, originally part of the gardens of Cardinal Ippolito d'Este. Thanks to Pope Clement VIII and to work from 1595, this garden, upon completion of its organ fountain, nymphaeums, lodges, well-positioned statues, with its arrangement of walkways, paths, and flower beds, demanded admiration from all its visitors, becoming an essential part of the papal residence. This was noted by Baglione, who in 1642 wrote: "The garden was embellished and several fountains made, among which the most noble was that of the large niche under the courtyard with no different inventions, decorated with pouncing and mosaic, and an organ which works from force of the water and makes sounds in different registers, a delight worthy of the greatest pontiffs."

That the garden continued to stimulate the imagination and admiration of visitors is shown by de Brosses: "The gardens are large and very beautiful…. There are many sparkling fountains and, in a room of mosaic, a Mount Parnassus where the nine sisters and their leader Apollo, with lyre in hand, give on request a little concert by means of the water." The marquis de Sade wrote "the gardens of this palazzo are very pleasant indeed, but sober, and aim rather at a simple beauty, avoiding empty luxury. Waters and water organs can be seen there." Herman Melville summarized: "The gardens—a paradise without joy … fantasies and whims of limitless wealth … like stone that is sculpted until it takes the shape of a leaf and leaves that are brought to take on the forms of sculpture–walls–niches–arches–glazed objects–columns, plinths, rooms (sculpted in the foliage)–arcades–cloisters of leaves–the water organ–Vulcan's workshop–the fountains."

In 1580 Montaigne marveled that it had been possible to create "gardens and places of delight of singular beauty" despite the hilly topography of Rome. He was amazed that "art can so ably take advantage of a place that is all humps and hills and unevenness." In the seventeenth century, this ability continued to prove true, with leaps of creative quality in the gardens of Palazzo Colonna, spread over the slopes of the Quirinal, and those of Villa Doria Pamphili, outside Porta San Pancrazio, which de Brosses described as "the most beautiful in Rome" with "a large and pleasant, very varied garden, well stocked with plants; beautiful paths, beautiful flower beds, beautiful pall-mall (the forerunner of today's game of cricket), an abundance of graceful fountains." Émile Zola too admired this garden with its "planned flower bed in which the colored plants form arabesques." Halfway through the eighteenth century, Giuseppe

Vasi wrote about the Colonna garden, connected to the palazzo by four bridges, or elevated walkways, on Via della Pillotta; it is, he says, "decorated with statues, fountains, paths, citrus trees, and flowers of all kinds." In 1872 Henry James recounted: "It is a precious and antique place that rises with terraces full of moss and trees, steps and winding paths, from the back of the palazzo up to the top of the Quirinal. It is garden art in its highest form."

One year later James explained, with felicitous conciseness, the intimate relationship between the eighteenth-century Villa Albani outside Porta Salaria and its gardens: "More than formal, it is … too similar to a garden in which tea is served; nevertheless, it has magnificent flights of steps and the splendid geometrical lines of an immense square hedge, intersected with high pedestals on which small antique busts are placed." Melville was also particularly effective: "terraced gardens, two hundred years old" at Palazzo Rospigliosi, "the steps leading to the garden dug out of the cave–moss-covered balustrades–the lemon path faced with tiles–the basin with fish, the fountains, violets wet with dew–the Lodge–bas-reliefs–dawn–sails on high like clouds dried by the sun."

The garden-park of Villa Borghese which, according to de Brosses, had "long paths, little squares, woods, parks, aviaries, and happy birds," has always been appreciated, especially for its large imaginative aviary built to the design of Girolamo Rainaldi (1616–1619). In the inside garden-museum, however, at Palazzo Borghese, what were remarkable were the nymphaeums (Giovanni Paolo Schor and Carlo Rainaldi, 1672–1673), placed against the high enclosure wall, and the many statues arranged as decoration to the flower beds.

When one looks at the great garden façades decorated with caryatids and the niches of three nymphaeums crowded with sculptures, and enjoys the agitated gesticulations of exuberant Baroque statuary in the space of this garden-courtyard, which D'Annunzio might have termed "sonorous as a nave," it seems as if one can hear the words that this imaginative poet dedicated to a different but equally Roman-style fountain: "The marble mole—a magnificent composition of Neptune's horses, tritons, dolphins, and shells in triple rows—rose before us covered in grayish encrustation and lichens…. The conches of the tritons blew, the dolphins gurgled. From the top, a jet of water erupted sibilantly, shining and fast as a rapier-thrust into the blue … It was like a powerful roar of laughter, a burst of applause, a heavy shower of rain. All the mouths gave voice to their jets of water which curved in arcs to fill the conches below…. As the instantaneous plays of water multiplied because of the diversity of the sculptures, so, at the same time, the uninterrupted sounds grew, making music that was ever deeper in the great echo of the walls" Le Vergini delle Rocce (The Virgins of the Rocks) 1895.

Sumptuous Interiors: Decoration, Furnishing, and Picture Galleries

Having pointed out the external features that typified the Roman palazzo from the sixteenth to the eighteenth century—the grandeur of its size as a concomitant to the gravity and severity of the form, and the sometimes banal serial nature of the constituent parts (portals, loggias, windows, cornices), and the considerable "moralistic" severity of the façades—it is essential to enter the rooms and salons and note their space, volumetric scope, and decorative splendor. In this way, it will be possible, in the unity of the complex architectonic shell, to understand and evaluate the expedient duplicity that provoked this "split personality," and thus the typical image of the palazzo itself.

If courtyards had the function of expanding the formality and status of a reception area, then the change of formal register, the increased pace of ambition, the fervor for monuments, and the emphasis on luxury were even more evident in the flights of stairs that led to the upper floors of the palazzo. From the beginning, the breadth and luminosity of the stairway, the unfolding of the stairs, the furnishings of the landings (with antique statues, niches, cornices, and bas-reliefs in stucco) are all signs of the introductory *crescendo* that is commensurate with the magnificence of the rooms reserved for living, reception, or entertainment. These, located on the main "noble" floor, the *piano nobile,* constitute the most intimate and meaningful part of the palazzo, the part that reveals the real and many aspects of the owner's identity.

The commitment dedicated both to project and realization in order to obtain the quality of such introductory *crescendi* can be seen the rich examples that range from the elliptical staircase of the Quirinal Palace, devised by Mascherino and supported by coupled columns (1583–1585), to the same oval types of the Borromini stairway in Palazzo Barberini and the one in Palazzo Borghese, and the more conventional grand staircase in Palazzo Ruspoli (Martino Longhi the Younger, 1640), considered for more than two centuries to be one of the four marvels of Roman civic architecture. Such examples include the paneled splayed arch at the entrance to the staircase in Palazzo Mattei di Giove (Carlo Maderno, Donato Maggi), as well as Borromini's triumphal portal that opens onto the helicoidal flight of Palazzo Carpegna and Bernini's entry arch, almost Serlian, to the right-angled Scala Regia (Royal Staircase, 1665) in the Vatican Palace.

Having reached the *piano nobile*, the very heart of the palazzo, one is attracted to and absorbed by the flowing suite of rooms and salons that, following one after the other in a striking perspective continuum, form the prestigious apartments, among which is usually a *galleria* (gallery), richly decorated with mirrors, pictorial decoration, and other works of art.

In the city of the popes, these sequences of rooms reflect, in most cases, the wealth and power of noble families whose pedigrees boast cardinals and pontiffs. They reflect, therefore, the lifestyle, both curial and sumptuous, of princes of the Church, surrounded by the admiration and veneration of the plotting family courts which proliferated in the hope of benefits from nepotism. Thinking back over his own Roman experiences, de Brosses wrote in the middle of the eighteenth century: "It is still an excellent profession, that of being nephews to the pope, without speaking of the title of prince that these maintain, just as they keep the great dignity and great benefits … One pontificate is enough to enrich a family." And the lifestyle of such an enriched family brought with it the display of a patrimony valued, above all, by concrete evidence.

Such display was manifest in walls laden with paintings by famous artists, frescoed with allegories, or covered with tapestries or *quadrature*; or else in heavily decorated wooden ceilings or majestic vaults representing heavens open to tumultuous flights of angels and figures celebrating the glory of the noble family.

In a mixture of the sacred and the profane, the display ended by reserving, in the continuum of rooms and salons, a special place for the indispensable highly ornate chapel for religious ceremonies, as well as a place of honor (in homage to the cult of personality) for portraits, both painted and sculpted, of the most illustrious members of the family, executed by the most celebrated artists of the moment. For example, Palazzo Doria Pamphili has a portrait of the Pamphili pope, Innocent X, by Velásquez, as well as marble busts of Innocent X and of Olimpia Pamphili Maidalchini, sculpted respectively by Lorenzo Bernini and Alessandro Algardi. Similarly, the bust of Cardinal Scipione Borghese by Bernini was in the *galleria* of Palazzo Borghese (up to 1891), and the portrait of Cardinal Bernardino Spada by Guido Reni hung in the *galleria* of Palazzo Spada.

The purpose of walls decorated with mythological tales and *trompe-l'œil* scenes was already well known and used widely in the fifteenth century, as shown by the painted pilasters that frame views of trees and landscapes in the loggia of the *palazzetto* of the Knights of Rhodes (1466–1470). The Sala della Piattaia in Palazzo Riario Altemps contains a *trompe-l'œil* depiction of tableware against a background of flowered drapes, a Corinthian column, and a wall faced with marble ashlar (1477–1491). Similarly, in Palazzo di Venezia the frieze with the *Labors of Hercules* (by Girolamo da Cremona) in the Sala dei

Elliptical staircase built to Mascherino's design in the Quirinal Palace.

Similarly, the salon of the *Fasti Farnesiani*, frescoed by Francesco Salviati and Taddeo Zuccari (1554) in Palazzo Farnese, illustrated the deeds of Alexander (founder of the dynasty of the dukes of Castro) and Ranuccio the Elder (military defender of the Church on whom Eugenius IV conferred the Golden Rose). The purpose of these frescoes was to provide references that could inspire successive proprietors of the house in further undertakings of their own.

The themes of the pictorial decorations showing the merits of Pope Clement I were also allegorical, executed by Giovanni and Cherubino Alberti (1595) in the Sala Clementina on the second floor of the Sistine Palace in the Vatican. Still inside the Vatican Palace, in the Sala di Costantino (Hall of Constantine), on the instructions of Leo X, the followers of Raphael highlighted episodes of earthly apotheosis which intended to show the power of Pope Silvester I and thus pontifical superiority over Constantine and his imperial power (1520–1523). In the nearby Sala Regia, where "Christian emperors and kings" publicly swore obedience to the Roman pontiff, the historical events represented on the walls (for example, the *Submission of Frederick Barbarossa to Alexander III* and *Christian Victory at the Battle of Lepanto)* also exalted papal authority and inculcated in guests a strong sense of deference.

Entering the Sala dei Mappamondi in Palazzo Sacchetti, too, guests must certainly have undergone a sense of subjection and suggestion from the walls, which were heavily decorated by Francesco Salviati (1553–1554). This painted decoration narrated events from the life of King David, but its striking effect was due less to the implied allegory than to the completely illusionistic and strongly antiquarian effect. The simulated painted architecture appears to be a base of caryatid consoles supporting Ionian columns, on which are hung cornices, standards, festoons, and tapestries (fully opened compared to those painted in the Hall of Constantine in the Vatican and in the Hall of the *Fasti* in Palazzo Farnese).

Other complex simulated painted architecture occurs in the Sala delle Prospettive (Hall of Views) on the main floor of the Farnesina and in the Sala dei Cento Giorni (Hall of One Hundred Days) in the Cancelleria. While these depictions are not yet in the artificial terms of a sophisticated *quadratura*, nevertheless Baldassarre Peruzzi's mastery created in the Farnesina two simulated colonnaded loggias over Roman landscapes (1511–1514), while Vasari's in the Cancelleria (1546) produced frescoes representing scenographic views with niches, split gables, and concave staircases in perspective. One of these marvelous views includes a mock colonnade supported by powerful spiral columns—a pictorial anticipation of the dynamic spaces of the Baroque.

Still in the Farnesina, the room with Raphael's *Galatea* (1511–1514) and the *Loggia of Cupid and*

Paramenti (Tapestry Hall) and, in the next room, the Sala del Mappamondo (Hall of the Mappamundi) in the Barbo apartment display illusionistic architecture with Corinthian columns on high plinths, the trabeation decorated with phytomorphous scrolls, winged sphinxes, and medallions (1488–1490).

To this marked development in the use of wall decoration was added in the course of the sixteenth century an emphasis on the symbolic content of the decoration itself. The stories of ancient Rome depicting Hannibal and, later, the Horatii and Curatii in the Palazzo dei Conservatori (1507–1509) was nothing other than a memento or an urge to reawaken the will and the strength that had inspired the city's past glories. So it was too that stories of Alexander the Great by Perin del Vaga (1545) in the Sala Paolina, or Sala Regia, in Castel Sant'Angelo, were more or less explicit allegorical pretexts intended to exalt the virtues of the patron, Paul III.

Psyche (1517–1518) appear as splendid previews of what would become the decorated *gallerie* inside the Roman palazzi of the seventeenth and eighteenth centuries. This association of the Farnesina wall decorations with those of the *gallerie* of the great palazzi might seem to be somewhat imprudent since the suburban villa and the city palazzo were different types. In effect, however, both types come together in a constant, the unmistakable common denominator of Roman architecture in its widest sense. It is possible to recognize a desire to echo the surrounding garden not only in the many products of nature (flowers, fruit, cereals, and legumes from the New World and the Old) that decorate the festoons framing the vault pendentives in the *Loggia of Cupid and Psyche* (Giovanni da Udine, 1517), but also in the painted pergola, possibly by Prospero Fontana, on the vault of the semi-circular portico in Villa Giulia. In both villas the decorative motifs certainly refer to the relationship with the surrounding gardens and are more inclined toward the distinctive features of villa life.

In the same way, scenes more suitable to a bedroom setting were frescoed there, such as the *Marriage of Alexander and Roxane*, with the figure of the Persian princess gracefully seated on the royal nuptial bed, painted by Sodoma (1516–1517) in what was the bedroom of Agostino Chigi, the first owner of the Farnesina.

Many of the above-mentioned, splendidly decorated "jewel boxes" have their lid—or rather their ceiling—as rich as the wealth of ornamentation on the walls. Often however, the ceilings are not in formal agreement with the figural decoration on the walls. This disjunction frequently occurs where the ceiling is flat and made of wood; these masterpieces are almost always gilded, with square, rectangular, and curvilinear matrixes that make up complicated labyrinths, suspended on high, with sections carved and enriched with rosettes, spirals of foliage, heraldic devices, and disturbing mythological creatures (like the one on the ceiling in the salon-*galleria* in Palazzo Sacchetti). The modular repetitions of square coffering (the Sala del Mappamondo in Palazzo Venezia and the Sala delle Prospettive in the Farnesina) and of octagonal coffering (the Sala dei Semidei [Hall of the Demigods] in Palazzo dei Conservatori), or the variety of the enmeshing of linear and curvilinear lacunars (as in the Sala Regia in the Quirinal Palace), contribute to effects of undoubted formal redundancy, as well as to the exuberance of the rooms' appearance. As a result, these ceilings seem to be isolated surfaces, unrelated to the pictorial fabric that covers the walls, and even weighing on the box-like space that the pictorial decoration attempts deceptively to broaden. In their totality, the rooms, salons, and galleries appear organic; there is a perception of an enveloping continuity where the pictorial decoration invades the vaulted, carenated ceiling—

which also constitutes the curving link between the opposing walls.

The desire to live in a less static space, and with the illusion of greater transparency, together with the concomitant revival of the antique and Roman "grotesque" decoration (for example, the Loggia of Raphael in the Vatican Palace, 1517–1519, and Villa Madama, 1525), inspired experimentation with pictorial ornamentation on curving surfaces. The results, which caused a stir, can first of all be assessed on the vault of the *galleria* on the *piano nobile* of Palazzo Ruspoli, frescoed by Jacopo Zucchi and depicting the *Genealogies of the Gods*. Its iconographic conception and allegorical references allowed the artist's creativity to free itself to create imaginative compositions that wholly cover the walls.

Following this episode is the visual poem of pagan celebrations of love in the *Triumph of Bacchus*, painted by Annibale and Agostino Carracci (1597–1600) in the *galleria* on the first

Series of rooms on the piano nobile *of Palazzo Pallavicini Rospigliosi.*

floor of Palazzo Farnese. Here the luminous colors, in an open display of sensual male and female nudes within a landscape framework open to the skies, are amalgamated with the simulated reliefs, simulated statues, and simulated architectural features to contribute to the composition of a complex decorative ensemble, presaging the forthcoming hyperbole of Baroque ornamentation. Here the contorted and agitated gestures of the participants are the harbingers of the dynamism that only a little later would create a whirlwind acceleration on the airy trajectories of bodies engaged in virtual "triumphs" and "glorification."

Significant works in the period before the culminating fresco of Pietro da Cortona which

the celebration of the virtues of the Barberini pope Urban VIII and the glorification of his family, frescoed on the enormous vault of the salon in Palazzo Barberini (1633-1639), marks the highest point of decoration intended—not in the sense of "charming" appendix, but as a means, even if overdone—to upset the closed forms, to go beyond the boundaries of the walled shell, to unleash the fear of infinity inherent in the dynamic concept of space that was typical of Baroque. The glory of the Barberini family, more than suggesting moral values, was a pretext to imagine, with boundless fantasy, the exaltation of a titanic humanity moving toward targets of light: it was a pretext to paint the surge of agile bodies which in a thrusting upward

marked the apotheosis of the Barberini family and of Baroque painting include the *Aurora* painted by Guido Reni (1613–1614) as a decoration of the ceiling of the Casino Pallavicini Rospigliosi, *Gods Gathered around Jupiter*, painted by Giovanni Lanfranco (1624–1625) and commissioned by Cardinal Scipione Borghese, the representation of the airy meeting (held up by pairs of grisaille telamons) on the vault of the loggia of the *piano nobile* of the Villa Borghese, and the frescoes by Pietro da Cortona (before 1625) on the vault of the *galleria* of Palazzo Mattei di Giove, illustrating the history of Solomon, with the narrative scenes accompanied by festoons of fruit, executed by Pietro Paolo Bonzi, which underline the articulated structure of the vault.

The vast composition by Pietro da Cortona, representing the *Triumph of Divine Providence*, or

escalation pass over the threshold of the vault to be immersed in the immensity of a sky set on turgid clouds. The virtues and large angels that assist the flight of the family crest with the Barberini bees, the papal tiara, and the supreme intertwined keys are only a few among the many components of the crowded scene of the convulsed choral and mainly pagan triumph that takes place in all-embracing gilded splendor.

It was from this extraordinary model by Pietro da Cortona that later decorations descended, which, as a pictorial language of family vanity, opened wide the ceilings of other principal salons and galleries, or, in other words, those domestic "show" places where the rites of profane "sacredness" were carried out.

The type of decoration that simulated, on a vaulted ceiling, the foreshortened view of figures in

the open air was taken up again by Pietro da Cortona in scenes from the *Aeneid*, executed as frescoes (1641–1654) on the barrel vault of the *galleria* of Palazzo Pamphili on Piazza Navona, and continued with the representation of the *Chariot of the Sun* by Fabrizio Chiari (1675) in the central octagon of the ceiling of the Sala degli Specchi (Hall of Mirrors) in Palazzo Altieri. It was used in the furious *Battle of Lepanto* frescoed by Giovanni Coli and Filippo Gherardi (1675–1678) on the vault of the great salon of Palazzo Colonna, and again in the cold *Parnassus*, which was painted by Raphael Mengs (1761) and seems to float in the vault of the *galleria* of Villa Albani, and it was rekindled with luminous golden colors and animation—even if mannered—in the *Labors of Hercules* frescoed by Aureliano Milani (1767–1769) on the vault of the Galleria degli Specchi in Palazzo Doria Pamphili.

It was in association with this type of decoration that the genre of *quadraturismo* was developed, that is, of perspective painting of simulated architecture which acted not only as a frame to the frescoed stories, but attempted through the illusionistic representation of descending levels, semi-circular exedras, loggias open to the skies, and infinite landscapes, to multiply the real volume of the rooms and salons, immersing it in an atmospheric, colored, and luminous space.

Particularly suggestive are the ceilings with perspectives seen from below (*di sotto in su*). Such spectacular *quadrature*, frescoed by a specialist like Agostino Tassi, modifies the curve of the ceiling of the Casino delle Muse at Palazzo Pallavicini (1611–1612) through the acrobatic representation of an airy loggia with paired columns and arches, as well as that of the Sala di Rinaldo e Armida (Hall of Rinaldo and Armida; 1621–1623) in Palazzo Costaguti, through painted spiral columns that support a trabeation with a balustrade over it, both projected onto preponderant backgrounds of sky. Again in Palazzo Costaguti, in the Sala di Apollo, the *Chariot of the Sun* by Domenichino is in the center of four segments of cornice that rest on angular columns and pilasters, and in Palazzo Lancellotti ai Coronari, Tassi again (1617–1623) surrounded an allegorical figure floating in the sky with an almost transparent colonnade crowned with trabeation.

Tassi, yet again, adding the distraction of an arch in ruins, converged even more the *di sotto in su* view of the walls and pilasters that encircled the sky around the chariot of Guercino's *Aurora* (1621) in the Casino Boncompagni Ludovisi, and perfected the architectural theme of the loggia with the addition of spiral columns, which framed the rectangle of sky within which fly *Fame, Honor,* and *Virtue,* also by Guercino.

Architectural backgrounds, drawn in perspective on the walls and framing country views of archaeological ruins, representations of contemporary Rome (like those painted by Gian

Paolo Pannini inside the Coffeehouse in the Quirinal gardens), exotic subjects (like those in the Sala Egizia (Egyptian Hall) in Palazzo Massimo alle Colonne and Villa Borghese), or "histories" impaginated with neo-Pompeian taste (as in the hall of Palazzo di Monte Giordano (or Taverna), frescoed by Liborio Coccetti, 1809–1816), form part, rather, of the seventeenth- and eighteenth-century taste for furnishings that made wide use of the pleasing illusionistic effect of *trompe-l'œil*, using it to replace the tapestries of the past.

A decorative cycle worthy of note for its undoubted originality and particular value is that by the Nazarenes which covers all the ceilings and walls of the three rooms in the Casino Giustiniani-Massimo which are dedicated to the three great Italian poets. The themes, taken from Dante's *Divine Comedy*, Ariosto's *Orlando furioso*, and Tasso's *Gerusalemme liberata*, were frescoed (1817–1827) with religious candor and rigorous purism by the painters Julius Schnorr, Joseph Anton Koch, Philipp Veit, Friedrich Overbeck, and Joseph Führich.

Since in many cases the original furniture has been lost, this discussion of furnishings must necessarily be limited to the surviving unified complexes represented by the sumptuous *gallerie* with their gilded plasterwork and mirrors. These rooms always have classical statues and are also adorned with other antiques and console tables (veritable explosions of curves carved into the wood), as in the Palazzi Ruspoli, Colonna, and Doria Pamphili, and Villa Borghese.

Worthy of attention, too, are the gigantic fireplaces which can still be seen in the salons of Palazzi Farnese and Massimo alle Colonne, and Villa Albani, as well as the mosaics of ancient Rome that have become precious archaeological carpets in the Sala degli Ambasciatori at the Quirinal and in the entrance hall of Villa Borghese.

The private chapels in these patrician palazzi could all be examined one after another, endowed as they are with gilded altars and kneelers, candelabra and other items necessary for religious observation, and decorated with paintings and stucco figures. Examples include the chapel

*Opposite, above:
Frescoes by Giorgio Vasari in the Sala dei Cento Giorni (Hall of One Hundred Days) in the Cancelleria.
Below, eighteenth-century fresco showing the story of Marcus Furius Camillus painted by Mariano de' Rossi di Sciacca on the vaulted ceiling of the entrance salon in Villa Borghese.*

The splendid furnishings of the Salone degli Imperatori (Hall of the Emperors) in Villa Borghese.

decorated by Francesco Salviati (c. 1500) in the Cancelleria, that on the first floor of Palazzo Barberini with the *Crucifixion* over the altar and painted lunettes by Pietro da Cortona (1631–1632), the chapel designed and executed by Carlo Fontana (1689–1691) in Palazzo Doria Pamphili; and, above all, the Chapel of the Annunciation in the Quirinal, decorated by Guido Reni and Giovanni Lanfranco, and those in Palazzo Altemps and Palazzo Borghese.

In order to evoke period furnishings, recourse has to be made to the evidence provided by small rooms, usually enriched by stucco wall decoration and frescoes, as in the case of the small *stufa* (bathroom) of Clemente VII in Castel Sant'Angelo, decorated with grotesques by Giovanni da Udine, and the *camerino* (study) of Cardinal Odoardo in Palazzo Farnese, with its barrel-vaulted ceiling, lunettes, and round and oval medallions, frescoed by Annibale Carracci (1596) with myths of Hercules. Their symbolic significance—as identified by Bellori—is centered on the theme of the dilemma or, rather, the choice—between lasting virtue and ephemeral pleasure.

Similarly worthy of examination is the mini-gallery in Palazzo Spada, lined with stucco figures in high relief which support the frames of the painted panels on the walls and the vaulted ceiling, as well as the so-called *saloncino d'oro* (golden drawing room) on the second floor of Palazzo Chigi, designed by the architect Giovanni Stern (1765–1767) on the occasion of the marriage of Prince Sigismondo Chigi and Maria Flaminia Odescalchi. The *saloncino* is decorated with

figures, some in low relief and some fully in the round, with festoons of fruit and leaves, trophies and candelabra, and pilasters of simulated marble, and with gilded bronze foliage that frames the great mirrors and forms the arms of the candelabra. The painted ceiling has *trompe-l'œil* hexagonal coffers and the floor a meander design that reproduces the geometric motifs of the ceiling.

In the apartments on the *piani nobili* of palazzi, there are rooms that are apparently less "precious" because their walls are only plastered or lined with cloth wall-covering. These undecorated walls, however, constitute vertical planes ready to receive valuable picture collections together with displays of antique statuary. These collections of works of art resulted from the collecting fervor that was one of the preferred pastimes of the great Roman patrician families. All the decoration of these rooms, as de Brosses wrote, "consists of pictures that cover the four walls from top to bottom, with such profusion and at such scarce intervals that, in truth, the eye is more often wearied than pleased."

From the eighteenth century onward, these private collections were duly noted and described in contemporary guidebooks. They could be visited for the consideration of a substantial tip, which would be explicitly requested.

Gilded cupboard, part of the furnishings of a room in the Quirinal Palace.

The Roman Palazzo as Described by Landscape Painters and Travelers

It is the art collections, those "priceless rareties" contained within the noble mansions, that constituted the "greatest value" of the palazzi themselves and attracted the curiosity and attention of the traveler who, generally, remained indifferent architecture the task of reciting the encomium of the papal society of that era. They are also the protagonists who furnish the images provided with greater topographical detail and the directors who place on show the role of architecture in the new palazzi and the relationship these have with the anonymous surrounding buildings, and the scenographers who exalt urban theatricality, accentuating the oblique angles of the façades— "stage curtains," exaggerating the length and breadth of the streets and piazzas.

Landscape painters tended to invent reality anew—or rather, they represented the Rome of the

to the architecture, especially the external features, of the building. Much of the travel literature of the eighteenth century emphasizes the quantity and quality of the collections of paintings (on religious and secular subjects), statues, and antique inscriptions, and is frequently uncomplimentary on the architectural features of the palazzi of the great families.

It is difficult to decide whether the impressions of the travelers are more sincere or whether the graphic descriptions of contemporary landscape painters are too much of an apologia. Certainly, many travelers who made the Grand Tour to the Eternal City had seen the *vedute* of Rome and the surrounding countryside, etchings of landscapes brought home by other travelers as illustrations of their travels, as nostalgia for Romanism, as souvenirs, and as fragments of the spectacle of the ancient and modern Rome which offered itself to the foreigner with the apathetic, good-tempered, complacent awareness that sublime ruins of past beauty still constituted its splendor, and that its Baroque face-lift had once more made it triumphant and beautiful.

The painters of landscapes, with their visionary, capricious, heroic, or pictorial representations, are the exegetes of this spectacle, giving to modern

popes by expanding its dimensions (as did Giuseppe Vasi, defined as "a modest portrait painter of buildings") in order to attribute to seventeenth- and eighteenth-century urban fabric an attempt to resuscitate the monumental magnificence of imperial Rome. It is not by chance that Giovanni Battista Falda, in 1665, gave his collection of *vedute* the title *Nuovo teatro delle fabbriche et edifici in prospettiva di Roma moderna (New Theater of the Fabric and Buildings in the Perspective of Modern Rome)* and that Alessandro Specchi drew up his *Primo libro del nuovo teatro dei palazzi in prospettiva di Roma moderna (First Book of the New Theater of the Palazzi in the Perspective of Modern Rome)*. Nor is it accidental that in the ruins portrayed by Piranesi in his *Varie vedute di Roma antica e moderna (Various Views of Ancient and Modern Rome)*, there is no melancholy, but rather pride and the still preponderant gigantism of past grandeur.

The travelers for their part were mostly lay people who wished to deepen their own cultural knowledge and not bigoted pilgrims piously seeking plenary indulgences; they were intellectuals interested in "physical" Romanism rather than "spiritual." They visited the

View of the bridge over the Tiber at Castel Sant'Angelo by Antonio Tempesta and Matteo Brill, a fresco in the loggia of the "second arm" built for Gregory XIII in the Vatican Palace.

innumerable churches (the instruments of Christian apologia) but were not involved in the persuasive arts of religious Rome. They therefore had a greater inclination to look at civic architecture, or rather, the new private palazzi that contributed to the embellishment of the city. And yet, with only a few exceptions, the exteriors of modern Roman palazzi did not give rise to admiration at all and did not fascinate travelers.

Already in 1581, Michel de Montaigne, despite being able to choose among representative palazzi of the fifteenth century (Palazzi Venezia, Giraud, Altemps, and the Cancelleria) and the sixteenth century (the Ville of Agostino Chigi, Madama, Medici, Pope Julius, and Palazzi Caffarelli Vidoni, Massimo alle Colonne, Sacchetti, Spada, and Ricci, and the lodge of Pius IV), and those incomplete or only just started (Palazzi Caetani, Farnese, Borghese, and Chigi), did not dedicate a single word to the architectonic morphologies of these buildings. Instead, he simply limited himself to writing that "the palazzi have interminable series of rooms, one after the other; to arrive at the principal room, you have to go through three or four others. In certain places … the sideboards are not where repasts are eaten, but in another room preceding it, where they go and take the drinks when they are requested. It is there that the silver plate is on display."

Montesquieu, passing through Rome in 1729, while expressing his own judgment in brief notes, shows that he knew how to look at and understand architecture when he affirmed that Palazzo Farnese "is so compact that it seems to have been shaped by a mold; it is a cube," and that Borromini "generally built the avant-corps convex and then the back part concave." However, he reserved his main interest for painting and sculpture, noting that in Palazzo Borghese "there is a huge collection of every kind of picture by the best artists, above all Titian," that in Villa Mattei "there are excellent statues: an *Apollo Flaying Marsyas*, a head of Cicero, a beautiful *Antinous*, and a great number of other precious statues," that Palazzo Giustiniani "is full of statues and paintings by the best artists. There is a gallery full of statues, especially the beautiful statue of Pallas that … they say is priceless. There are many pictures by Caravaggio and all the other greatest artists."

At the Farnesina he admired the *Loggia of Cupid and Psyche*, writing that "of all these numerous figures, there is not one that resembles another. All the faces are different, as is not the case, however, in the galleries painted by Pietro da Cortona." Of the *Galatea* he noted that, like other works by Raphael, "at the beginning [it] is not striking, because it imitates nature so well that it can be mistaken for nature itself." In the Vatican he was moved to see the *logge* of Raphael, "a divine and stupendous work." The *School of Athens* he termed "truly marvelous." *Apollo, Laocoön*, and *Antinous* were in his view "the three famous statues"; and of the Sistine Chapel he wrote that "it gives a complete impression of the genius of Michelangelo."

It is less clear, however, what Charles de Brosses liked. Initially he wrote that "the most beautiful part of Rome … is the fountains…. The number of these fountains to be found at every step, and the actual rivers that these create, are still more pleasing and surprising than the buildings, even if these in general are magnificent, especially the ancient ones. The little that is left of these latter, while deformed, is nevertheless quite superior to the modern buildings, because of their simplicity and grandeur, in the same way as the Roman Republic was superior to the Pontifical State."

On a second occasion, he proposed to give the first prize for civic buildings to Palazzo Barberini because he declared "it is more beautiful than the Vatican for the regularity of its proportions; by extension, it is equal to Monte Cavallo, Palazzo Farnese, and Palazzo Altieri, not inferior to these, nor to Palazzi Borghese, Giustiniani, Chigi, Colonna, or Pamphili, nor to all the others for furniture and collections of paintings and ancient and modern sculptures. Over and beyond all this, it has an external aspect that is more beautiful than all the others." He adds that in the interior salons there is "a way to satisfy fully the concupiscence of your eyes," especially with "the marvelous ceiling by Pietro da Cortona representing the triumph of Urban III."

On a third occasion, partially contradicting what he had said earlier, he affirmed, referring to Palazzo Altieri, that "there is no other in Rome that I prefer." He justified his prediliction by sustaining that "the external façade, which gives onto two streets, is immense, regular, and magnificent, the luminous, well-arranged rooms richly furnished and full of an excellent collection of paintings."

In de Brosses's opinion, Palazzo Borghese is "certainly among Rome's most beautiful buildings. It is situated on a small square piazza, with the entrance façade giving onto it, but the longer and more beautiful façade on the side. The building is a sort of irregular pentagon, almost the shape of a *harpsichord*. The first courtyard is square, enclosed by four structures at different levels, around which, in the interior, open two porticoes, colonnades, or loggias…. The second portico is closed by a balustrade between the columns and forms a tribune or corridor that goes all the way around, linking all the apartments…. This way of building with two or three colonnades, one on top of the other, is really magnificent; and it is in this way that most of the great palazzi here are built." Despite the unaccustomed length of his description of the architecture, de Brosses thinks that "the most remarkable thing about Palazzo Borghese is the endless number of pictures."

According to de Brosses, the Cancelleria "is sad, as sad on the outside as it is on the inside," Palazzo Spada has "an architecture that tends

toward a rustic style," Palazzo Farnese is a "great square building, solid and majestic in the Florentine manner," Palazzo Caetani "has a very extended and noble façade but is rustic and thus of no great taste," though in compensation "it has a truly grandiose, enormous stairway and some antique statues …." Palazzo Colonna, too, "compensates for the sparse appearance of the exterior with the magnificent staircase that is found inside, with its rich furniture, the orange garden, and above all, the superb gallery, perhaps more beautiful than that of Versailles, and full of delicious pictures." Palazzo Chigi "is a vast and beautiful building, rich with statues and pictures, furniture, books, and manuscripts." Villa Pamphili has "its façade … all covered with antique bas-reliefs arranged by Algardi in a very pleasing order," while Villa Borghese, apart from being "encrusted with bas-reliefs," has "a full gallery … of incomparable statues," among which are some done by Bernini, whose "mannered style is far f rom the pride, good taste, and noble simplicity of the ancients."

Although it is possible to recognize the general nature of de Brosses's comments, which were made with such superficiality—and avoiding entering into a discussion regarding the merits of the statement about Bernini—it is not possible to remain silent about the mistaken architectural analysis contained in his judgment of Palazzo di Montecitorio., This palazzo possesses "one of the most beautiful and broad façades that could ever be encountered," but according to de Brosses, it has the defect that "the two parts of the façade that continue the avant-corps of the building, instead of being parallel to this, are diagonal and lead away obliquely, with an angle of several degrees, a refinement of no visual effect."

Characterized by facile enthusiasm rather than greater competence are the opinions of Goethe (in Rome in 1740) when he referred to Villa Borghese as the "most delicious and remarkable place in the whole of Italy" and a construction "of a taste and magnificence without equal," and to the palazzo of Duke Mattei as "worthy of being considered" because "it is full of antique things, statues and busts." The palazzo of Prince Colonna is worthy of note for its "magnificent great hall," where there are "many painted mirrors that seem to be real. Large marble tables. Thirty-two candlesticks in crystal. Thirty marble statues. A hundred pictures by different artists. A cupboard in ivory with bas-reliefs. Another in ebony. Another, even more precious, studded with fine stones, of great value, amounting to more than ten thousand scudi. Thirty other pictures by good master painters. And a cabinet of small portraits. The ceiling of this hall is wonderfully frescoed."

Edward Gibbon too, who stayed in Rome in 1764, did not show generosity in his appreciation of the city's palazzi. He passed over Villa Albani as "gaudy and ostentatious" and considered Villa Borghese "insignficant" and "covered with antique bas-reliefs," while he considered "astonishing" the wealth of bas-reliefs, statues, and urns inside the villa itself. About the *Aurora* by Guercino in the Casino Boncompagni Ludovisi, he judged that "the idea of morning breaking night through a broken bow" was infelicitous and he wrote that he did not understand clearly "whether the architecture formed part of the fresco or of the room."

Charles Duclos, on the other hand, was loudly of the opinion that "there is nothing, in any state, that can be considered equal to the magnificent fountains that can be seen in Rome in the piazzas and at the crossroads, combined with the abundance of waters that never stop flowing, a magnificence yet more pleasurable inasmuch as this is also a public utility."

The marquis de Sade, passing through Rome, defined as "architecturally very attractive" the Capitoline palazzi built to Michelangelo's design, and "magnificent" the fountains of Piazza Navona, which he considered "one of the most beautiful piazzas in Rome." About Palazzo Borghese he said only that "it is one of the most beautiful in Rome. Its dimensions are gigantic and its form irregular, but not for this is the interior any less beautiful and subtle. The courtyard is beautiful and noble." He dedicates a long list to the "works of the greatest masters" that comprise the collection, which is among the most beautiful "that can be seen in the world."

In the opinion of the "divine marquis," other works worthy of detailed description were the ceiling frescoed by Pietro da Cortona in the salon of Palazzo Barberini, the "collection of rather beautiful pictures" in Palazzo Doria, the "many beautiful works" in Palazzo Giustiniani, the "great number of beautiful pictures" in Palazzo Colonna, and the "pictures of the greatest beauty" in the apartments of the pope at Montecavallo.

About Villa Giulia, the Marquis de Sade recounts that "the external architecture of this house, on the side of the courtyard, could not be more attractive. It forms a semi-circle with a gallery that completes the enclosure of the courtyard." He describes the nymphaeum by Ammannati as "a sort of courtyard, richly decorated with statues and colonnades, at the end of which can be glimpsed two plaster statues representing rivers…. But what seemed very beautiful to me were the four caryatids that supported the platform."

Goethe's Roman objectives (1786–1788) certainly did not seem very original: he visited the Farnesina and judged the *Loggia of Cupid and Psyche* "the most beautiful decoration I know of"; he went to Palazzo Barberini "to see the superb Leonardo da Vinci and the mistress of Raphael that he himself painted"; he included the gallery of Prince Aldobrandini in order to take a look at "an exquisite Leonardo" (actually, *Christ among the Pharisees* by Bernardino Luini) and took in Palazzo Colonna "where the pictures of Poussin, Claude Lorrain, and Salvator Rosa are housed."

After visiting the Sistine Chapel, he saw the *logge* by Raphael, but "my eyes were so dilated and satiated by the great forms by Michelangelo and the stupendous perfection of all the parts that they could not dwell on the virtuosity and the play of arabesques, and the stories of the Bible, no matter how beautiful they may be, as they could not stand comparison." His visit to the Vatican Palace also gave him the opportunity for some acute critical observation: "Raphael never allowed himself to be limited by the space the architect assigned to him; it is a feature of his greatness and the elegance of his genius that he knew how to fill and adorn any space in the most exquisite way. Even the superb pictures of the *Mass at Bolsena*, the *Liberation of Saint Peter*,

and the *Parnassus* would not be as outstanding without the singular limitation of space."

The declaration of Lady Sidney Morgan, who traveled to Italy in 1819–1820, is undoubtedly too categorical: "The palazzi of Rome, more numerous, large, and luxurious than all the others in Italy, are completely devoid of historical interest…. A Roman palazzo, among the more important ones, is an extended and massive building, which impresses more for its size than for the beauty of its architecture."

Stendhal, while not distancing himself in the course of his Roman walks (1827) from the clichés of the cultural tourism of the time, kept some particular comments for the palazzi. About Palazzo

The fountains on Piazza Navona, one of the sights of Rome most appreciated by eighteenth- and nineteenth-century travelers.

Farnese he wrote that it is "the most beautiful of them all…. Like all palazzi in Florentine style, it has something of the fortress … It is really majestic…. Three rows of colonnades decorate the four façades of the courtyard, which is square and very sad." Villa Madama seemed to him "one of the most splendid things that Raphael realized in architecture"; Palazzo Barberini, instead, was "an example of Bernini's bad taste"; the palazzi flanking the Corso "are rich in 'style'"; the two lateral buildings of the Campidoglio lacked strength; Palazzo Sciarra was "good architecture," whereas "the great Palazzo Doria is much more interesting for the superb pictures kept there than for the architecture, which dates back to the seventeenth century, a period of decadence." Stendhal even gives advice on which palazzi to see, with the warning that "the first twelve are those that it is absolutely compulsory to visit. As for the rest, it is enough to go in for a moment when one happens to go past them."

He also provides indications about the things that should receive attention: "The Vatican (ten thousand rooms); the Quirinal; Palazzo Rospigliosi (*Aurora* by Guido Reni); Palazzo Farnese; the Farnesina (*Psyche* by Raphael); Palazzo Borghese; Palazzo Doria Pamphili (magnificent galleries); Palazzo Corsini; Palazzo Chigi (some good pictures); Villa Medici; Palazzo Barberini (portrait of Beatrice Cenci and *La Fornarina, Death of Germanicus* by Poussin)."

The twenty-five palazzi following are "less important": "Altieri: enormous; Braschi: marvelous staircase; Colonna: beautiful gallery; Palazzo dei Conservatori: statue of Caesar; Palazzo della Consulta: nothing noteworthy; Palazzo Costaguti: frescoes by Domenichino and Guercino; Falconieri: some good pictures; Ruspoli: magnificent staircase; Giraud: some Bramante; Giustiniani: many interesting statues; Massimo; Montecitorio; Odescalchi: façade by Bernini; Mattei: good collection of objets d'art; Bonaparte; Pio; Salviati; Venezia; Sciarra on the Corso: lovely collection of pictures; Palazzo dei Senatori on the Campidoglio: the Etruscan wolf; Spada; Stoppani: designed by Raphael; Verospi; Torlonia: full of all the beautiful things collected by this former haberdasher who became the richest man in Rome."

It is not surprising that the medieval enthusiast Ruskin (1841) should describe Palazzo Doria as "a lurid cavern, dim and gloomy, though pleasant if seen from the outside," and Palazzo Farnese as "ancient and desolate." Paul De Musset (brother of the more famous Alfred), conformed to the current attitude (1845) of other travelers, primarily interested in the art collections housed in the noble palazzi. Of Villa Albani, De Musset wrote only that "the loggias, the coffee pavilion, the billiard room, and the gardens made up an immense museum"; Palazzo Doria on the Corso was "one of the biggest and richest in Rome. He took the trouble to underline that the gallery was "immense" and that inside the gallery he had seen the portrait of

Machiavelli by Andrea del Sarto, three pictures by Rubens, two "charming" Madonnas by Sassoferrato, an *Ecce Homo* by Michelangelo, and "the portrait of Giovanni di Napoli" by Leonardo. At Palazzo Barberini, he admired what he called the "Baker *Venus*" by Raphael and, in the same room as the *Fornarina*, he was struck by the portrait of Beatrice Cenci by Guido Reni. (De Musset, like many other travelers, was morbidly attracted to the image of this seventeen-year-old girl accused of murder, sentenced, and executed.) Out of the gallery of Palazzo Borghese, "which houses nearly 1,800 pictures of the first order," he chose to mention just one work: "the portrait of Cesare Borgia, by Raphael." In the picture gallery of Palazzo Corsini he is able to confirm that "the Madonnas of Andrea del Sarto lower their eyes so as not to look at the dark scenes of Gherardo delle Notti."

Even Herman Melville took himself to Palazzo Barberini (1857) "to see the portrait of Beatrice Cenci. An expression of suffering. A look that cries innocence." He visited "the vast gallery" of Palazzo Corsini, where there was "a huge number of works of the first order." After characterizing Palazzo Farnese laconically as "the most beautiful architecture of all the private palazzi," he gives attention to the picture gallery at Palazzo Doria Pamphili as "perhaps the most elegant in all Rome."

Villa Albani, on the other hand, elicited from Hippolyte Taine (1864) the almost bitter reflection that "it is all that remains, the fossilized skeleton of a life that has lasted two centuries, and whose main pleasure consisted of conversation and beautiful performances, and the customs of the salon and the antechamber."

Finally in 1894, Émile Zola, with incisive brevity, marked the "pure Renaissance" of Palazzo Giraud and described the palazzi of Via del Corso as "great square masses, naked and sad from outside, with their reddish yellow plaster. But inside one senses the immensity: must be seen." Palazzo Farnese was "immense, rich and mortal, with its damp and dark courtyard, staircases with their wide shallow steps, the immense corridors, the gigantic galleries and rooms. It makes your bones feel cold." Of Palazzo Sacchetti he wrote: "It is a great square mass that gives onto the street, very high, dark gray, all in bricks covered in a blackened, yellowed patina." And of Villa Medici: "The façade overlooks the garden. Greek bas-reliefs, studiously and deliberately inserted into the façade."

Zola, who was a different sort of traveler, alien to the tradition of the Grand Tour, succumbed neither to the antique nor to picturesque Romanism. Rather, he understood the great speculative construction that was taking place, the building fever which, with the aim of building the Third Rome, Rome as capital of the kingdom, brought with it the destruction of Villa Ludovisi and the urbanization of the Prati di Castello: "a real checkerboard of a city, in its death throes even before it has lived."

Palazzi of the Third Rome

"It was the time in which the operations of destruction and construction on Roman soil seethed most violently," denounced Gabriele d'Annunzio in 1895 (*Le Vergini delle Rocce*), since the cypresses of Villa Ludovisi lay "stretched out on the ground and lined up next to each other, with their roots uncovered, fuming at the paling sky…. And all around on the noble meadows … were white pits of lime, red piles of bricks, the screeching wheels of carts full of stones which alternated with the shouts of the master builders and the raucous cries of the carters, and the brutal work which was to occupy the places which for centuries had been sacred to Beauty and Dreams, grew apace. It seemed as if a barbaric wind blew on Rome and threatened to rip from her the brilliant crown of aristocratic villas to which nothing can be compared in the world of memory and poetry."

In the building sites of the Third Rome, officially opened with the spur of Porta Pia, it seemed as if all the aspirations of the new capital of the young united Italy had to be made to come true, holding their own with the prestigious vestiges of the imperial and papal *urbe*. But above and beyond these intentions, the building yard was above all a mirror of the frenetic and prosaic commercialism of small and large entrepreneurs, of banks that were more or less trustworthy (the scandal of the Banca Romana in 1893 is a case in point), and of members of the clerical nobility who, shielding themselves behind property rights, unscrupulously sold many of the ancient vineyards of the villas to property speculators.

Coexisting with this tumultuous building yard, which gave rise to the disconsolate apprehension of nostalgic writers like Ferdinand Gregorovius ("old Rome is sinking; in twenty years' time another world will be here"), were the materialistic interests of Monsignor Frédéric Xavier de Meróde, a leading figure in the marketing of building sites, who bought and parceled lots in the area of the Esedra, starting to trace out the future Via Nazionale, side-by-side with the ideals of those who theorized on the need for a national style for the architecture of the new buildings intended for the administration of the state, contrasting with those of papal Rome.

On the one hand, the process of construction (which would reach a crisis in 1897) in 1885 brought with it the potential risk of the sale of the park of Villa Borghese as lots (finally bought by the State in 1901), provoked the growth of districts of new buildings which encircled and suffocated the old "silent" nucleus of the city, and triggered age-old vicissitudes regarding bids for the Palazzo di Giustizia, the Palazzo delle Esposizioni, and the Palazzo del Parlamento. On the other hand, given that public building was something important, with respect to size and scale, which would increase the prestige of a specific urban area, as well as of the capital as a whole, discussions took place on what style could be recognized as national.

Camillo Boito wrote in 1880: "Other nations are already approaching the discovery of a style…. For Italy the great difficulty is in the marvelous wealth of its past. However, sooner or later, there must be a certain style of architecture, especially now that Italy has become a nation and has its own capital…. In order that architecture can be a monument to an age and to a people, it must connect intimately with its past: national character comes from historical character, as well as from natural character … Now, since Italian architecture must have a national nature and aspect … it should connect in some way with one or several of the Italian architectures of the past, since at the moment there are none, or, which is the same thing, there are all…. However, to reach the hope of finding, whenever it may be, the new style, the single style, the true style of our native land, there are, first of all in the brains and the hands of the architects … then in the ideas and traditions of our civil society, some not insignificant hitches."

Boito, however, inverted his priorities, or rather, he forgot to say that the hitches were, first of all, due to the behavior of society which conditioned the work of the architects. The society of that period, fruit of a business-like compromise between Piedmontese bureaucrats and Roman and papal nobility, showed no interest in style, though they were interested indeed in the cubic meters of the new *palazzoni* of power, in the big barracks of apartments, in the houses let for rent which were rising in the districts under construction.

The architects' adjustment to this situation, or rather the lack of an authentic ideological model which was not that of celebratory, haughty rhetoric post-Risorgimento and complacent bourgeois pretentiousness, gave rise to facile and always acceptable stylistic exercises in neo-sixteenth-century and neo-classical style, suited to all tastes and aspirations.

Façades created as imitations of sixteenth-century models include those by Gaetano Koch for the Palazzi Calabresi in Via XX Settembre, Lavaggi Pacelli in Corso Vittorio Emanuele (1888), and Boncompagni Ludovisi di Piombino in Via Veneto (1891). Of greater scope in size and scale, and more relaxed in the assembling of the formal elements, were the two semi-circular buildings, also designed by Koch, erected in Piazza Esedra (1886–1890), as monumental, introductory settings to Via Nazionale. The porticoed palazzi that surround Piazza Vittorio Emanuele (designed by Koch and Giulio Podesti in 1882) also bear the stamp of neo-sixteenth-century style, while many others appear to be lazy replicas of styles that are more or less those of Sangallo: Palazzo Sacconi in

Via Firenze by Pietro Carnevale, Palazzo Marignoli on the Corso by Podesti (1874), Palazzo Sforza-Cesarini in Corso Vittorio Emanuele by Pio Piacentini (1886), Palazzo Bràncaccio in Via Merulana by Luca Carimini (1892–1895), and Palazzo Primoli (now the Napoleonic Museum) by Raffaello Ojetti. Of neo-classical taste, however, are the elevations of the destroyed Palazzo Amici in Piazza San Bernardo (1885) and of Palazzo De Parente in Piazza dei Prati di Castello (1867–1890), both by Koch. Dressed with mullioned windows and other neo-fifteenth-century stylistic features is the façade designed by Luigi Rosso (1877) for the Palazzo della Posta

between 1876 and 1888. Evidence for this is the Palazzo delle Esposizioni in Via Nazionale, designed by Pio Piacentini and opened in 1883. Its pretentious external image was considered to be "French style" or, as defined by De Angelis d'Ossat, "the first building in the Third Rome that is tied to Roman tradition." Further evidence is the Palazzo di Giustizia, called locally *il palazzaccio* (the ugly palace), designed with colossal and Piranesi-style awfulness by Guglielmo Claderini of Perugia, and started in 1889 in the Prati di Castello. It was solemnly inaugurated in 1911 and then, according to Alfredo Melani, called by a cabinet minister in the full assembly of parliament (1908),

Allegory of Young Italy Receiving the Gift of Spiritual Endowments *by Aristide Sartorio, a frieze in the chamber of Parliament in Palazzo Montecitorio.*

Centrale (Central Post Office) in Piazza San Silvestro. The elevation of Palazzo Odescalchi overlooking Via del Corso, designed by Raffaello Ojetti (1887), is even wholly armored with ashlar and adorned with mullion windows as an evident academic imitation, with the addition of balconies, of the Florentine Palazzo Medici-Riccardi.

The formal language of Giulio De Angelis is more eclectic, both in the Palazzo "Alle città d'Italia" (now the Rinascente department store) in Via del Corso (1889–1890) and in the complex of Palazzo Sciarra with the cruciform Galleria Minghetti, whose walls were charmingly decorated in 1888 by the Roman Giuseppe Cellini with scenes of middle-class life and figures exalting the virtues of women.

The longed-for national style did not take off even on the occasion of the public contests offered

"a financial disaster, while aesthetic critics could declare it an artistic disaster."

Melani wrote, justly: "Rome has such long arms, she can embrace anything." A symbolic result of this embrace, indulgent and inauspicious, is the monument to Vittorio Emanuele II, or rather, the interminable (1885–1911), oversized mass dreamed up by Giuseppe Sacconi, a tasteless sanctuary of the Third Italy, whose columns "are uncountable like the millions it has swallowed … a clumsy image of an art that knows the excesses of manual labor and does not know the ways of aesthetic probity."

Similar architectural disasters are apparent in the numerous buildings intended to be immense, imposing, important, and above all, "Italian," starting from the headquarters of the Banca d'Italia in Via Nazionale by Gaetano Koch (1892), and proceeding to the Palazzo della Banca Commerciale in Via del Corso by the Milanese Luca Beltrami (1914–1922) and the Istituto Nazionale delle Assicurazioni in Via Sallustiana, built in 1927 by the Florentine Ugo Giovannozzi, whose interior has been refined by the sculpture of Antonio Maraini and the pictures on the walls by Ezio Giovannozzi and Giulio Bargellini, and finally the Palazzo del Poligrafico dello Stato, designed in 1913 by the architect Garibaldi Burba and completed by the engineer Arturo Larderel in 1930.

A few exceptions can be found in the exterior of the contemporary *moderniste* building designed by Ernesto Basile as an extension to Parliament

crowded with buildings whose characteristics are certainly not boring, because they are overloaded with the most varied combinations of decoration (from neo-medievalism to neo-mannerism), and even by the pretentious Palazzo della Civiltà Italiana, the so-called *Colosseo quadrato* (square Colosseum), built for the Universal Exhibition in 1942 which never took place: a concrete epilogue to the metaphysical atmosphere hypothesized in De Chirico's *Piazze d'Italia*.

Protagonists of a titanic battle of façades, however, brandishing the symbols of display and exaggeration, are also the political buildings, the headquarters of the ministries. First among these is

(1906–1926), and in its inside hall decorated with a frieze by Aristide Sartorio (1908–1913) which, with sculpted and symbolic pictures, represents, in a whirling epic of adolescent nudes, draped bodies, and restless horses, the allegory of young Italy aureoled by the solar disk behind it, to whom are offered "spiritual endowments" by the Renaissance: Art, Language, Humanities, Classics, and Courtly Manners.

Architectural episodes that are a little outside the norm are also apparent in the measured formal virility of the Casa Madre dei Mutilati (National Institute for War-Wounded) by Marcello Piacentini (1925–1936) and also in the creative eclecticism of the district designed and realized by Gino Coppedé (1917–1927). This is underlined by the entry arch on Via Tagliamento, decorated by the amusing Fontana delle Rane (fountain of the frogs),

the mastodontic Palazzo del Ministero delle Finanze (Finance Ministry), designed by Raffaele Canevari and built between 1872 and 1877, and the last is the Ministero dell'Aeronautica (Air Ministry), designed by Roberto Marino (1929–1931), while in between one passes along the stages of a route punctuated by the massive Palazzo del Ministero di Grazia e Giustizia (Ministry of Justice), started in 1913 by Pio Piacentini and finished in 1927, the Palazzo del Ministero della Pubblica Istruzione (Ministry of Education) by Cesare Bazzani (1914-1928), and the Palazzo del Ministero della Marina (Navy Office) by Giulio Magni (1928), all related to each other by obvious volumetric hypertrophy and vulgarity.

The "thinking big" of earlier times had been irremediably undermined by the "thinking gross" of later years.

Allegory of Constance Watching while Workers Raise the Building of Civilization by Aristide Sartorio, a frieze in the chamber of Parliament in Palazzo Montecitorio.

Roman Coats of Arms:
A Note on Heraldry

Tombstone of Giuliano Porcari, 1282, in San Giovanni della Pigna.

On the preceding page: Coat of arms of Gregory XIII in the Vatican Palace, Chapel of Redemptoris Mater, detail of the vault.

No other European capital can offer as much as Rome in terms of heraldry. The universality that the city has always enjoyed as the center of the Roman Catholic world has ensured that over the years an extraordinarily wide and varied range of blazons has built up on both its civic and its religious monuments.

An attentive observer, looking along the streets and across the piazzas of the fourteen ancient and eight modern districts into which the historic center of the city has been divided since the Unification of Italy, visiting the immense basilicas and the numerous churches, and entering the courtyards of the majestic palazzi, will inevitably be attracted to the dazzling number of heraldic devices that adorn them. They include subgroups of genuine coats of arms as well as those limited by the surface area of the shield and used for merely ornamental purposes.

Not only is there a large number of heraldic devices, but there is also a multiplicity of family crests, a huge number also from the point of view of the variety of their owners. There are obviously the typically Roman arms of the noble families: Orsini, Colonna, Conti, Savelli, Frangipani, Mattei, Crescenzi, Annibaldi, Pierleoni, Cesarini, Aguillara, Muti, Cavalieri, Cenci, Astalli, Altieri, Massimo, Margani, Mellini, Sanguigni, Alli, Albertoni, Alberini, Santacroce, Palombara, Castellani, Papareschi, Jacovacci, Stefaneschi, Serlupi, Paparoni, Alberteschi, Papazzurri, Capocci, and so on. From this group, one of the oldest is certainly the characteristic triangular mosaic shield of Giuliano Porcari, which dates back to 1282 and is conserved in the church of San Giovanni della Pigna.

There are perhaps even more crests of the families that were "Romanized" through one of their family members acceding to the pontifical throne. Among these are the Boncompagni from Bologna, the Aldobrandini and the Corsini from Florence, the Borghese and the Chigi from Siena, the Rospigliosi from Pistoia, the Odescalchi, originally from Como, the Braschi from Cesena, and so on. Yet others exist through close links with the Roman court: Altemps, Carpegna, Patrizi, Spada, Sacchetti, Salviati, Soderini, Ruspoli, Torlonia, Ricci, Capranica, and many others.

Next to the coats of arms of the Roman families who had always had them or those who acquired them with the passing of the centuries, those of many other ancient Italian families from Piedmont and the Veneto right down to the island of Sicily may be seen especially in churches, confraternities, regional colleges and hospices. Those of families and personages from all over Europe and North and South America are spread throughout the approximately thirty churches of foreign states as well as in their hospices, colleges, cultural institutes, and diplomatic representations. Emperors and ruling houses of almost all the European states and pre-unification Italy have left their heraldic mementoes in the *urbe*, giving witness to the truth of the saying that Rome is seen as the *communis patria* (homeland of all).

Furthermore, in this capital of Roman Catholicism it is natural that the arms of ecclesiastical dignitaries should abound, both as components of the various colleges of the Roman prelacy and as the insignia of the General Fathers of the various Orders and the grand masters and dignitaries of the religious military orders as well as of the bishops and cardinals to whose patronage the city owes the existence of so many artistic monuments, churches, villas, and palazzi.

To give an idea of the variety of the heraldic vestiges existing in Rome and thus of the special interest that this can create, the following observation will suffice. From the moment that the pontifical curia returned to Rome from Avignon on 17 January 1377 at the behest of the French pope Gregory XI (Pierre Roger de Beaufort) until 20 September 1870, fifty-five pontifical sovereigns succeeded to the papal throne. Of these, only the following were of the same family: Callixtus III and Alexander VI, the Borgia popes; the two Piccolomini popes, Pius II and III; the Della Rovere popes, Sixtus IV and Julius II; and the three Medici popes, Leo X, Clement VII, and Leo XI. Bearing in mind that the Borgia popes belonged to two separate lines of the same family and therefore used different heraldic insignia, and that, conversely, Pius IV, while belonging to the Medici family of Lombardy, not Florence, used the Florentine coat of arms, with or without (we do not know) the tacit or explicit agreement of Grand Duke Cosimo, it can be stated that in the course of the approximately five centuries between 1377 and the breaching of Porta Pia in 1870—and without considering the brief period in which Rome was part of the French Empire—the coat of arms of the head of the pontifical state changed at least fifty times. Considering that from the time of King Richard I of England (1189–1199) up to the present, the coat of arms of the English British sovereign has undergone only about ten changes, the difference is immediately obvious.

Moreover, the fifty papal coats of arms just referred to are constituted of heraldic insignia that are certainly not only Roman but come from all over Italy and also other countries, including France, Spain, and Flanders.

A final characteristic distinguishes the heraldic examples existing in Rome: those working on them were very often the greatest artists. The marble coat of arms of Paul III, placed on the main façade of Palazzo Farnese, is the work of Michelangelo; Bernini made the insignia of Pope Urban VIII on the plinths of the spiral columns of his *baldacchino* in St. Peters, those of the Supreme Pontiff on the Fontana della Barcaccia in Piazza di Spagna, those of the Pamphili pope Innocent X on the Fontana dei Fiumi (Fountain of the Four Rivers) in Piazza Navona, and those of Cardinal Corner in Santa Maria della Vittoria, as well as many others.

The imposing compositions with the arms of Pope Clement XII on the pediments of Palazzo della Consulta and the Trevi Fountain are by Fuga and Nicola Salvi respectively. Borromini was responsible for the design of the coat of arms of Pope Urban VIII that adorns the expressive façade of Palazzo Barberini. Martino Longhi devised the Borghese coat of arms for the outside of their palazzo, as well as that of Cardinal Mazarin on the gable, supported by Corinthian columns, of his titular church of Santi Vincenzo e Anastasio in Piazza di Trevi. It was Piranesi who devised the partly heraldic decoration of Piazza dei Cavalieri on the Aventine. The royal coat of arms on the commemorative monument for the last Stuarts is by Canova, sculpted by him at the end of the second decade of the nineteenth century.

Only a few examples have been cited. To complete the picture, reference must be made to the existence of the heraldic works of many other artists, including Bramante, Domenico and Carlo Fontana, Algardi, Maratta, Rainaldi, and Pietro da Cortona. It is to the mastery of the latter that is owed the particular concept, halfway between a coat of arms and free flight, of the bees of Maffeo Barberini in the famous fresco on the vault of the great salon of Palazzo Barberini.

It is not merely by coincidence that Filippo Juvarra, when publishing his *Raccolta di targhe (Collection of Coats of Arms)* in 1722—dedicated to Prince Giuseppe Lotario Conti, duke of Poli and brother of the reigning pope—chose, of the fifty famous coats of arms to be included, forty-eight from Rome.

In what we initially described as the amazing gallery of coats of arms existing in Rome, an interested observer will appreciate the exquisite decorative style and the refined elegance of Roman heraldry which, firmly established in the course of the sixteenth century and flourishing to the end of the eighteenth, left its impression too on the heraldic taste of other regions of Italy and other countries. To Rome came a continuous flow of sovereigns, ambassadors, princes, great personages, high prelates, rich bankers, and men of vast culture, while an equal flow came of simple clerics, friars, small merchants, and pilgrims. Many of these, naturally apart from the Romans, or the Romanized, left a blazonic testimony in the city, entrusting the work, according to their social standing, to small artisans or to a range of artists up to the great and sublime. This is the reason why Rome is so rich in heraldic insignia, ranging from the coats of arms of the Vicars of Christ to those of the simple, small masters of humble trades.

Examples of the latter can be found by the dozen in the blazonic emblems of the members of the guilds: the *ortolani* (market gardeners), *pollaroli* (poultry farmers), *fruttaroli e limonari* (fruiterers and citrus fruiterers), *vermicellari e maccaronari* (pasta-makers), *scarpinelli e ciavattini* (shoemakers and cobblers), *giovani pizzicaroli* (young grocers), and others which are housed in the church of Santa Maria dell'Orto in Trastevere, the place of worship of these guilds and corporations.

Considering the diversity of the geographical origins and the plurality of the heraldic examples in Rome, it is not possible to order these into classes or categories, as they fall into a wide variety of characteristics. To examine these in depth, it would be necessary to enter into the wide subject referred to as national blazonic styles, and within the scope of each of these to examine the narrowest possible themes of the single regional styles. This would require an extremely difficult study which it would be impossible to carry out here. It is sufficient, thus, to reassert that in Rome nothing whatsoever is lacking in this respect. Just one example, the Polish church of San Stanislao in Via delle Botteghe Oscure, is worth mentioning. It is full of heraldic insignia that are so particular to the characteristic representations of the blazon of Poland that it does not respond to the criteria common to the rest of Europe; instead, it is heraldry of *herb*, that is, clans of broad family guilds.

For this reason, it is possible here to make only a few observations about certain characteristics of a number of coats of arms that originated strictly in

Gian Lorenzo Bernini. Coat of arms of Cardinal Federico Corner della Regina, bishop of Albano, in Santa Maria della Vittoria.

The Savelli crest in Santa Maria d'Aracoeli. In the lower part of the shield are the bands indicating, perhaps, a feudal jurisdiction under pontifical right.

In this splendid marble insignia of one of the Altieri princes, the cuneated bordure stands out, typical of the coats of arms of many ancient Roman families.

the city of Rome. Within this group of coats of arms that are very ancient, two distinct groups come to light.

The first group is discernible through the common presence in the shields of bands of silver and gules (red) tincture (Orsini, Damasceni), gold and gules (Savelli, Frangipani, Tebaldeschi), or different tinctures (Margani, Mellini, della Subirra) lowered under a "chief," or the upper third of the shield, always containing different symbolic figures. With the passing of time, the almost systematic habit was formed of having the chief supported by a "fesse," reduced in thickness. There is no doubt that the adoption of this heraldic typology by so many separate houses must have responded to a precise need; it must have had a very precise meaning of its own. In the meantime, we can conclude that the figure present in the chief of the shield (the Orsini rose, for example, or the lions of the Savelli family, or the "speaking" letter M of the Mellini family) had the explicit purpose of recognition.

A plausible interpretation of the bands was given recently by Mario Cignoni. If we exclude the possibility that the ancient, powerful families just mentioned could have originated from a single common stock, or that all of them could have fulfilled the same public role—which would tend to explain the *similarity* of the respective coats of arms—then the presence of these bands would indicate that they were all vassals holding lands belonging to the patrimony of St. Peter, either through direct papal investiture or by acquisition. This was more likely to be so if the bands were impressed on the two colors gold-gules and silver-gules, the colors of Rome and of the Church (although in other cases, the variations could have occurred with the passage of time).

This interpretation responds fully to the purposes of the symbolic significance of legal status, in fulfilment of which European civilization in the twelfth century initiated and eventually canonized this emblematic system known by the name of heraldry.

The second group, more numerous than the first, is characterized by the common presence in the shields of a "cuneated bordure." In this case, too, predominate the two colors gold-gules (Azetta, Crescenzi, Leni, Ruffini) and silver-gules (Anguillara, Bonsignori, Butiji, Ciceroni, della Molara, Jacovacci, Macaroni, Ottavi, Quattracci, della Vetera), even if there are a large number of arms in which the gules cunei of the bordure have been changed to azure: Alberini, Boccacci (gold-azure); Altieri, Bulgamini, Cavalieri, Gabrielli della Regola, Macarozzi de Lioni, Obiccioni, Papazzurri, Velli (silver-azure). As in the bands of the first group, so here: the systematic adoption by so many separate families of a bordure responding to a precise typology must have a significance of its own. There is a strong probability that this indicates the chivalric origins of the families in

question. Its use is typically Roman, as was noted centuries ago by Teodoro Amayden.

More generally, it seems reasonable to say that the heraldry of families originating in Rome shows predominantly the two colors silver and gules (red) (for example, the arms of the Colonna), and that gold and gules refer to the tinctures of the insignia of respectively, the Church and, the city of Rome. The ancient family of Santacroce, for example, bore on a "party shield" (divided vertically into two equal parts) a cross alluding to their aristocratic name, of "patent" form (that is, its arms broadening gradually as they approached the edges of the shield itself) and colored in gules on the field-of-gold half, and in gold on the field-of-gules half.

The family, which is now extinct, bore the insignia described above and used the surname Santacroce Publicola because of the legendary tradition, attested in the registers of Roman families of the mid-thirteenth century, that implied that they descended from the consul Publius Valerius Publicola, himself a personage of doubtful historical reality. It is natural that, particularly in those cases where there was similarity of denomination, myths should flourish and lead some Roman families back to the *gens* of classical Romans.

Typical of this is the tradition concerning the house of Massimo, about which it is of interest to quote an event that took place in February 1797 in Tolentino, near Macerata, during the peace negotiations between the papal state and Directoire France. Napoleon remonstrated ironically with the pontifical plenipotentiary, Francesco (Camillo VII) Massimo: "They say, Sir, that you are descended from Fabius Maximus: that is impossible!" "Effectively, I cannot prove it," peacefully replied the diplomat, who was decorated with the "privilege of the baldachin" and was the head of the marquis line of his family, "but what is certain is that it has been passed down through my family for more than a thousand years!"

Obviously, such traditions cannot stand up to historical criticism that has absolutely none of the indispensable genealogical evidence. Nevertheless, they are suggestive and fascinating.

To return to the question of blazons, however, there is the example of a case where the legend regarding the origin of a lineage has clearly influenced its heraldic insignia. Amayden reports that a remote personage of the Muti family, by name of Bobone, is recorded in a document of 1139, conserved in the archive of the church of Santa Prassede, claiming "a Roman antiquity descending from Priscus Scevola." The Muti placed on their heraldic shield, next to two primitive bundles of arms, the device of a right hand on a burning brazier and they adopted the motto NON VRITVR.

To conclude these brief notes on the features of the blazons of families that have always been Roman, it is relevant to cite an example of the uniting of two separate coats of arms onto a single shield as a consequence of the joining of two families, carried out in a very unusual way, but impeccable from the point of view of heraldic logic.

In the first half of the sixteenth century, Mario di Gabriele Orsini di Mugnano, last-born of Giovanna de' Cavalieri, the last representative of one of the branches of this ancient lineage, renewed the maternal family line by creating the Cavalieri già (formerly) Orsini.

The arms adopted for this new former Orsini line, which would die out with the death of Ulderico di Gaspare in 1814, consisted of the figure of the rampant hare of the Cavalieri. The hare was surrounded, as below, by a cuneated bordure to indicate the ancient rank of *miles,* or *cavaliere* (knight, recalling that in Latin inscriptions the surname Cavalieri is translated as *de Militibus*), lowered under the "chief" with the Orsini rose, referred to above, supported by a small "fesse" bearing an eel, which is also an Orsini symbol. Finally, from this new insignia the bands of the classic Orsini coat of arms disappeared. These had indicated the feudal possessions of this family by pontifical right, as mentioned above, and were replaced by the heraldic symbols of the Cavalieri.

The blazonic choice made by Mario Cavalieri, formerly Orsini, was irreproachable. By inheritance he had renewed the maternal line and had not continued the paternal. As a result, the use of the bands, in the significance we have given them, had lost all legal validity. It was logical, therefore, that he should replace them with the arms of the Cavalieri, while conserving the Orsini rose and eel since, by the male line, he was still an Orsini.

The chapters on palazzi in this volume are preceded by one or two coats of arms belonging to the commissioning personages or families, or otherwise strongly identified with the palazzi themselves.

Crest of Cardinal Marcello Santacroce. The gold and red (or and gules) colors of the shield are used commonly by various families of Roman origin in whose insignia are reflected the colors of the Urbe.

Detail of the Cavalieri, formerly Orsini, tombe in Santa Maria d'Aracoeli. In the lower part can be seen the heraldic insignia that, apart from bearing the hare of the Cavalieri, also has the rose and eel of the Orsini.

CLAUDIO RENDINA

VILLAS AND PALAZZI OF ROME

CAVALIERI DELLA
LINGUA D'ITALIA
(KNIGHTS OF THE
LANGUAGE OF
ITALY)

CASA DEI CAVALIERI DI RODI
(HOUSE OF THE KNIGHTS OF RHODES)

The name "Knights of Rhodes" is that originally given to the Sovereign Military Order of Malta, which in its complete denomination is called "Order of the Knights Hospitallers of St. John of Jerusalem, Rhodes, and Malta." Its origins date back to the religious brotherhood instituted in the Holy Land by the Amalfi monk Gerardo to give hospital care and accommodation to the pilgrims visiting the Holy

Sepulcher, which had been conquered with the First Crusade in 1099. The hospital community, which had its seat in Jerusalem in the vicinity of the church of St. John the Baptist, was recognized officially by Pope Pasquale II in 1113 with the constitution of the Latin Kingdom of Jerusalem; it was thus placed under the protection of the Holy See. However, in order to defend itself from Moslem incursions, the Order was opened to lay brothers and became militarized, passing from monks to knights while keeping its autonomy, independent of the Kingdom of Jerusalem. The community left, however, in 1187 when the city was won back by the Moslems, and moved first to St. John's of Acre, then to Cyprus, and finally in 1308 to Rhodes (hence the name Knights of Rhodes).

Already at the end of the twelfth century, these knights created a sort of "branch office" in Rome in the ruins of the Forum of Augustus, in a small building where they set up their priorate. The aim was to keep a closer link with the pope who—as in all religious orders, would continue to be their superior—and thus maintain their original mystical imprint. The house was enlarged in 1214 to include "in domo Sancti Basili" (the house of St. Basil), consisting of some of the property of the nearby Basilian monks, with their church and monastery. However, the Knights of Rhodes stayed only a few years in this restored seat; it was probably before the end of the century that they moved to the more spacious residence on the Aventine.

The house of the Knights of Rhodes, the ancient name of the Knights of the Sovereign Military Order of Malta, in contrast to the other medieval panoramas Rome offers, faces the archaelogical zone of Trajan's Forum, with the Torre delle Milizie and the former monastery of St. Catherine, seat of the Ordinariato Militare d'Italia.

When Cardinal Marco Barbo, nephew of Pope Paul II, was the Roman prior of the Order, extensive renovations were carried out with the result that the house took on approximately the same aspect as it has today. It was then that the façade overlooking Piazza del Grillo received its great arch set under a cross-shaped window. In addition, a five-arched loggia was added toward the Forum of Trajan and an elegant front with a trilobed Gothic arched window inserted into a Renaissance cornice was added toward the Forum of Augustus. All this was thanks to Cardinal Barbo, whose name stands out on the inside door of the building at the end of the stairs that lead to the loggia, indicating the year 1470 as the date the work was finished, and flanked by a line from Virgil's *Georgics*,

Supreme Pontiff, with the provision of the Priorate, Marco Barbo, and bishop of Vicenza, priest of the title of St. Mark's Cardinal, restored in more splendid form this building ruined by time).

Cardinal Barbo had restoration work carried out on the Aventine too, which would thus still be considered the seat of the priorate. The change took place at the end of the fifteenth century, leaving this house with the former monastery rented to a timber merchant, a certain Marcantonio Cosciari, who obviously adapted the whole complex to his own needs. The merchant made more rooms out of it, so that this formerly prestigious seat deteriorated into a private residence and carpenter's workshop. The only religious note in the new building was a hall of the former monastery

The splendid fifteenth-century loggia of the Casa dei Cavalieri di Rodi overlooking Via di Campo Carleo. It has five arches with half-columns at the ends and, in the central part, four columns. Flanking the loggia is a charming little balcony in typical Venetian style.

"Felix qui potuit rerum cognoscere causas" (Happy is he who can know the causes of things), placed under a sculpted profile of the Latin poet. This homage recalls the humanism that dominated at the court of Paul II, whose arms recur in the decorative frieze in the adjacent room on the first floor, and who is commemorated in a epigraph celebrating the completed works: "Iussu Pauli II Pontificis Maximi ex proventibus Prioratus M. Barbus Vicentinus Praesul TT S. Marci Praesbiter Car. aedes venustale collapsa augustiore ornatu restituit" (By the will of Paul II,

that Cosciari put himself out to have frescoed with a *Crucifixion* attributed—without foundation—to Sebastiano del Piombo.

Meanwhile the Knights changed their name. In 1522 Rhodes capitulated to the constant attacks of the Turks, and Charles V presented the island of Malta to the Order. Malta was immediately fortified, and was never taken by the Moslems. Thus the Sovereign Military Order of Malta was created. Once the struggle against the Turks was over, the Order became more organized, with a grand master and a series of

The concave façade of the Casa dei Cavalieri di Romi above, closed arcades, tabernae *of c. A.D. 100, overlooking the Forum of Augustus.*

branches throughout Europe, defined by territory as priorates. Only in 1798, when Napoleon occupied Malta, forcing them out, did they move their headquarters to Italy, first to Ferrara, then to Catania, and finally, in 1834, to Rome. Thus, the grand priorate of Rome remains in the complex on the Aventine, while the grand master of the Order resides in a mansion on Via dei Condotti.

The ancient seat in Piazza del Grillo had meanwhile been lost. In 1566 Pius V gave it to the Istituto delle Neofite delle Domenicane della SS.

Annunziata, under whose care the whole complex was fortunately restored to its earlier religious aspect, redeeming it from the degradation into which it had fallen as carpenters' workshops. The same pope undertook its physical restoration, entrusting the work to Battista Arrigoni da Caravaggio. The church of San Basilio which stood in the area of the Forum of Augustus was restored, reconsecrated, and dedicated to the Virgin Annunciate. The former monastery and the house became a religious house once more, this time for nuns. There was a specific difference, however: in this institution were accepted converts from the Jewish faith who wished to embrace the religious life and who could not otherwise become nuns since the other female orders in Rome did not accept them.

The old House of the Knights of Rhodes eventually became the general house of the

The fifteenth-century Salone d'Onore (Hall of Honor), with eight standards bearing the insignia of the eight langues *(tongues) of the Order, each with the cartouche of its flag.*

Dominicans up to the early part of the twentieth century, when the Dominicans moved to San Martino ai Monti.

During the course of 350 years, then, these premises maintained a monotonous existence, throwing up no stories of particular interest, but illuminated, evidently, by faith. It was an atmosphere of prayer and silence, destined in the end to a silence that was eternal. When archaeological work was carried in the area in 1926, the church and the convent

were demolished and the house overlooking the forums was abandoned, seemingly condemned to ruin. It became the property of the Commune of Rome which, however, made no use of its excellent location, with views over the restored archaeological area.

In 1946 therefore it was handed back to the Sovereign Military Order of Malta which, after four centuries, took possession of it once again. The complete reconstruction of the building, with the transformation of an ancient Roman *domus* (house) into a chapel, has enabled the palazzo to resume its fifteenth-century appearance. In the fifty or so years following the return of the building to the Knights of Malta, the Casa has returned to its existence as the customary place for meetings and ceremonies for the ancient Order of Knights.

These are secret quarters, closed to the public by right of extra-territoriality, where impressive celebrations of splendor and religious tradition take place. It should be seen in such a perspective. The porter's lodge leads into two *tabernae* (Roman shops) from which the staircase leads up to the fifteenth-century Salone d'Onore (Hall of Honor). Here are two great maps, one of the islands of Rhodes and Malta and the other of the ancient territorial possessions of the Order. Inside the hall are eight standards with the colors of the eight "tongues" of the Order, each with a cartouche relating to the standard. In the old entrance hall, which gave onto the landing in the time of Barbo, there is now a staircase called the "Stairway of the Crucifix" after the fresco of the *Deposition*, previously in the convent's parlor. The Sala della Loggetta or delle Cariatidi Hall of the Loggia or the Cryatids follows, with its stupendous little balcony with the escutcheons of Paul II, of the cardinal of the time, and of the Order. Then comes the so-called Bizantina (Byzantine Hall), a hall rich with relics from the ninth and tenth centuries. A fireplace with jambs and architraves in travertine is flanked by two bas-reliefs taken from the excavations of the Imperial forums. One then sees the main gallery on Via di Campo Carleo with its elegant cross vaults, loggia, and, finally, the chapel dedicated to St. John the Baptist and the sacristy annex, with a relic of St. Antimo. But it is the chapel, completely rebuilt, that is the most important part of the house; with its sumptuous adornments between the red hangings and the rectangular red flag cut through the center by the eight-pointed white Maltese Cross, it is now a suitable ambience for the religious ceremonies held within its sacral walls.

Here the grand master, in red dress uniform, sits regally on the gold-plated iron throne with knobs on the arms and the back representing stylized pomegranates, and upholstered in purple velvet. Next to him is the patron cardinal of the Order and before them, in a spectacular scene, standing by the benches, are representatives of the three classes of knights, all in dress uniform: the religious knights of the first class wearing black mantles with the white octagonal cross, knights of justice and conventual chaplains, bound to the Order by a solemn vow of obedience, chastity, and poverty; the laymen of the second class, in red jackets with a black diagonal sash, dress sword, and black trousers with a gold band down the whole length, knights of obedience and donors of justice in accordance with the sacred promise they have given; then the dames, most of them wives of the knights, from whom it is required that "they should comport thousand-year-old ethos of the Knights radiates outward and is put into practice. It is from this house, a place of refuge for those seeking political asylum, that the spirit of social and medical assistance offered by the Order is sent to ninety nations, to hospitals and clinics, homes for the aged and the handicapped, kindergartens and refugee camps. Thus this House

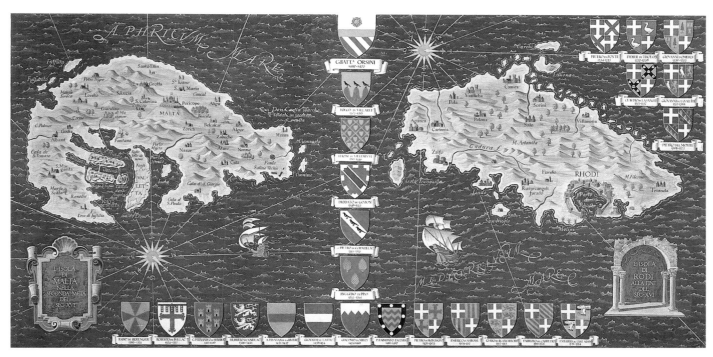

The great maps frescoed in the Salone d'Onore (Hall of Honor) by Di Gerolamo. Above, the ancient possessions of the Order in Europe and bordering the Mediterranean. Below, the islands of Rhodes and Malta, the historic bases of the Sovereign Military Order of Malta, correctly, the Order of the Knights Hospitallers of St. John of Jerusalem, of Rhodes, and then of Malta.

themselves in exemplary Christian fashion in both private and public life, contributing in this way to keep the Order's tradition alive and functioning." All this is expressed in the ancient motto "*Tuitio fidei et obsequium pauperum*," (Guardianship of the faith and protection of the poor); in other words, they are a humanitarian mission sent out to the whole world.

From this house, the symbolic center of the Order, this sumptuous but also profoundly mystical place, the of the Knights of Rhodes exudes an atmosphere of ancient moral and religious integrity, renewed daily in a worthy organization that is unique in the world.

CARDINAL
MARCO BARBO

PALAZZO AND PALAZZETTO DI VENEZIA

The original structure of this great architectural complex consisted of a modest medieval house intended as the residence of the cardinals appointed to the church of San Marco. It took on a new layout when, in 1451, Pietro Barbo, son of one of the sisters of Eugenius IV, became cardinal.

It was a fortified building, composed of a half-basement and a mezzanine that functioned as a *piano nobile*, extending over a small area between the basilica and the gate of the present palazzo overlooking the piazza, with a small external tower. It was a building of no exceptional size but was sufficiently dignified as a cardinal's residence so that, even in 1455, Barbo could proudly boast of it, having a commemorative medal struck in its honor. It was notable also because the cardinal enriched his home with the extraordinary collection of art that he had been accumulating since his youth. It was an exceptional collection, the most sumptuous seen in Rome since the fall of the Roman Empire, with coins and bronzes, gems and crystals, textiles and silverware.

In 1464 Pietro Barbo became Pope Paul II. For this modest cardinal's palace, this was indeed a change in fortune. The new pope did not leave his home but continued to live there and at the same time make it worthier of its new image. A plan was drawn up which would be carried out in three phases between 1465 and 1469. It projected an extension of the palace over an area that was fifteen times greater than the original building, which, nevertheless, remained as the point of reference of the whole complex.

The building was lengthened, pushed upward by another floor, and extended on the area opposite the *platea nova*, the future Piazza Venezia, with the addition of a *viridarium*, a hanging garden placed on an earthwork surrounded by a loggia with stables and service quarters. This was the basis of the future palazzetto, which would function as an annex to the main building, to which it was linked by the tower.

Inside the palazzo were the great reception rooms, the Hall of the Vestments, which contained tapestries and holy vestments, and the Hall of the Pappagallo, a reference to the parrot that the popes liked to keep in their reception rooms. They linked the private

apartments of the pontiff to the state apartment with its rooms with coffered ceilings, the Consistory, and the Sala del Mappamundo with the planisphere made by the Venetian Girolamo Bellavista (destroyed in the seventeenth century). This suite of rooms represented an escalation of grandiose styles that created a sense of reverence among illustrious guests, princes, and ambassadors. Their decoration needed to be refined, but they were already well defined in their structure and furnishings.

The movement to power was expressed also in the space lying in front of the palazzo, the *platea*, onto which the pope looked out so that he could be admired by the people. This occurred during carnival in 1468, when Bacchic processions were set up with

representations of mythological divinities, heroes, and nymphs. Paul II watched the races from his loggia, ordering the start to take place under his windows. One event was "the capture of the barbarians" after a wild race along Via Lata. Once the games were over, he had a great banquet served under the loggia for senators and curators while he threw coins to the crowd who fought over the remains of the meal. This expression of his power renewed the ancient saying "*panem et circenses*" (bread and circuses).

However, from 1469 Paul II was terrified by the discovery of a plot against his person and lost interest in the palazzo, or at least took no further interest in the ongoing construction, supervision of which was managed by his nephew, Cardinal Marco, until 1491.

The principal façade on Piazza Venezia and, at the side, the façade on Piazzetta San Marco with the chuch of S. Marco and, at the back, the Palazzetto di Venezia.

The pope spent much time in the Vatican Palace, but in the end he died in his *viridarium* on July 26, 1471, after dinner, perhaps because he had eaten too much melon, which he often ate greedily.

As an alternative to the Vatican Palace, the palazzo remained a papal residence and served particularly as reception rooms for solemn occasions. Its embellishment was supervised by the cardinals appointed to San Marco who successively lived there. These began with Lorenzo Cibo (1491–1501), who completed the decoration of the Mappamundo and state rooms, and built his personal apartment over Via del Plebiscito, the Cibo Apartment. He also dealt with the road system surrounding the building, and on the side facing the present Piazza San Marco he placed a colossal bust of the goddess Isis, nicknamed

Madama Lucrezia, one of the so-called "talking statues" of Rome.

King Charles VIII of France was responsible for a dark period in the building's history when, in the course of his expedition to Italy to claim the kingdom of Naples, he stopped over in Rome and was accommodated by Alexander VI in the quarter of San Marco. Lorenzo Cibo welcomed the king at the Milvian Bridge on 31 December 1494 and accompanied him to his home with part of the army in his train. An imposing display of artillery surrounded the palazzo, where Charles stayed until 28 January 1495, while his soldiers behaved as if they were the proprietors and committed acts of violence on undefended houses and persons. The monarch held splendid court in the mansion, with the rooms always

The north-western arm of the loggia in the courtyard of Palazzo di Venezia, the unfinished work of Giuliano da Maiano or, possibly, Bernardo Rossellino, with the tower by Marco Barbo dominating it.

61

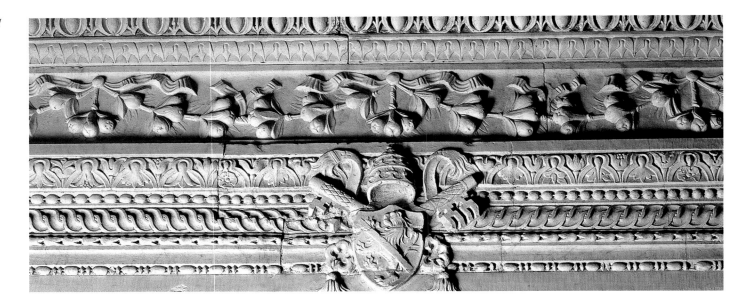

full of Roman magnates and cardinals, diplomatically masking his diffidence toward the Borgia pope, but his soldiers bivouacked in the courtyard, in the garden, and in the basement.

It was a temporary hiatus. With the new appointee to San Marco, Cardinal Domenico Grimani (1503–1523), the mansion again assumed the museum image that Paul II had created with his collection. The cardinal collected antique pieces of marble that had been taken from the pronaos of the Pantheon in the *viridarium* and arranged a library of eight thousand volumes. This treasury of marble and paper was moved to Venice after his death.

After the tragic Sack of Rome in 1527, the palazzo was restored by the Farnese pope, Paul III, who made it his summer residence. He had chapels built, broadened the central window of the façade, and closed the outside arcades of the *viridarium*, linking it with a viaduct to the tower he had built at the top of the Campidoglio.

These were the last years of papal glory for this palazzo, which from 1564 started a new period in its existence. Pope Pius IV, to win the sympathies of the Venetian Republic, gave the mansion to the ambassadors of the Serenissima on condition that a part of the building should be kept as a residence for the cardinals—the Apartment Cibo—and that the Venetian Republic should provide for the building's maintenance and future restoration.

The staircase, courtyard, and state rooms were to remain in common use, which caused numerous controversies in future years, while the pope could continue to reside there whenever he wished. This situation continued until the accession of Pope Clement VIII, with the last Consistory in 1597.

With continuous disagreements between the Holy See and Venice, the palazzo suffered the consequences of this cohabitation, which resulted in a restriction of restoration to the strictly indispensable. Relations finally broke down in 1711, with ambassador Lorenzo Tiepolo instructing the architect Carlo Fontana to design a division of the main rooms. The project was implemented under the supervision of the new ambassador, Niccolò Duodo, who had the great Sala del Mappamundo halved, making nine rooms on two floors. This action, an architectural outrage, involved moving two windows. In 1714 a balcony was added to the central window (destined to become notorious when Mussolini made speeches from it). In 1727 ambassador Pietro Cappello replaced the ceilings in the arcade of the *viridarium* with vaults, and Niccolò Erizzo closed off all the loggias, giving the building an appearance similar to that of the palazzetto.

The cardinals did no less. In 1734 Cardinal Angelo Maria Quirini had a covered passage created on the patrol path of Via degli Astalli, making a link to the small house built on one of the towers of Cardinal Barbo, and had new windows put into his apartment.

The precarious state of the building, aggravated by some of these different construction projects, did not prevent the holding of celebrations and receptions. All sovereigns and important individuals who passed through Rome were welcomed here in great splendor with balls and banquets, from the elector of Cologne to Leopoldo of Tuscany, from Joseph II of Austria to Gustavus III of Sweden. In 1724 Benedict XIII took formal possession of the palazzo in the midst of an outdoor party organized in the courtyard, where a temporary stage-set representing the seven hills of the city hid musicians and performers. In 1758, for the newly elected Clement XIII, ambassador Pietro Correr placed over the façade an artificial elevation with a loggia for fifty musicians. At the sides of the portal, two fountains issued jets of wine for the shouting crowds in the piazza. These were the last flashes of splendor, small demonstrations of power.

After the fall of Venice, with the treaty of Campo Formio in 1797, the palazzo passed to Austria, albeit for a very short time: The triumph of Napoleon, made it the property of the Kingdom of Italy, and an Academy of Fine Arts was inaugurated there under the direction of Antonio Canova. With the Restoration in 1814, the building became Austrian again, as the ambassador had his residence there. Life moved on monotonously and with no particular commitments apart from diplomatic ones.

After a complete survey of the building from the point of view of its structural soundness, the edifice was reworked and consolidated to stabilize it. But the palazzetto was sacrificed, demolished between 1909 and 1911 to make room around the Vittoriano. An imitation was built near the chuch of San Marco in 1913. The palazzo remained in Austrian hands until August 1916, when it was confiscated by the Italian state. Between 1924 and 1930 it was restored a number of times.

The mansion lived up to its image during the Fascist period, when it became the headquarters of the head of government and of the Gran Consiglio del Fascismo (Great Fascist Council). Mussolini had his office in the Sala del Mappamundo, and the balcony on which he appeared to make speeches to the cheering crowd was the center of attention in Rome and in Italy for about twenty years. The aura of power, reemerging from the past, lasted until July 24, 1943.

Subsequently the culture and art that had been a characteristic part of the complex flourished. The building's use as a museum and its precious library had already given a different function to the palazzo. The palazzetto, now the seat of cultural institutions, has cancelled every trace of its past. The Barbo coats of arms on the walls were certainly not impressive enough to restore the past to life.

VATICAN PALACE
(PALAZZO APOSTOLICO VATICANO)

Every Sunday the pope recites the Angelus from the penultimate window in the corner of the top floor of this palace, which looms over the colonnade of St. Peter's Square. This is his home. The floor below, the second floor, is reserved as the formal ceremonial apartment. The building is called the Sistine Palace (Palazzo Sistino), after Pope Sixtus V (1585–1590), who had it built in the farthest part of the Vatican Palace, arranged within two massive rectangular buildings united by a structure in the form of a loggia, overlooking the large courtyard called the Cortile di San Damaso. The residence of the reigning pope had not always been in this building but had once been located elsewhere, in buildings that formed the western part of the complex and constituted the original medieval nucleus. The latter was created when

Eugenius III (1143–1153) laid the foundations for a building to the north of St. Peter's. Construction work continued under Clement III and Celestine III, but it was under Innocent III (1198–1216) that the building was enlarged and given a fortified tower. This was the nucleus of the fortress-like palace used by Nicholas III (1277–1280), the first pope actually to live in the Vatican. Pope Nicholas was the real founder of the Vatican Palace: he had the building designed on a rectangular plan with corner towers and had the *viridarium* set next to it, the basis for the future Vatican gardens. He also bought the hilly land and the valley to the north, which would also be useful for any future expansion of the building and all around the area he had a new wall constructed, inserted into the pre-existing walls built by Pope Leo, and reinforced with towers.

View of the St. Peter's basilica, preceded by the spectacular colonnade by Bernini. On the right, around the Cortile di San Damaso, is the complex of the Sistine Palace, featuring the loggias and, in the centre, the Sistine Chapel.

The building, however, was not finished because soon afterward the pope and his successors, during the so-called Great Schism, were forced out of Rome to Avignon. The unrest in Rome that lasted until the first half of the fifteenth century resulted in the abandonment and deterioration of the building, despite interventions by Gregory IX and Boniface IX. Nevertheless, the *passetto*, the fortified passageway connecting the palace with Castel Sant'Angelo, was built in this period, giving the building an even clearer appearance as a fortress, so well protected by its walls that it appeared to be a single entity.

It was Nicholas V (1447–1455) who brought to fruition Nicholas III's conception of the Papal Palace, maintaining the imposing appearance of the existing exterior architecture with the addition of a large new tower. The interior, however, took on a more splendidly luxurious appearance, from the three rooms of the first floor to the six of the upper floor with their frescoes by Benedetto Bonfigli, Andrea del Castagno, and Piero della Francesca. Fra Angelico decorated the pope's personal study, now called the Chapel of Nicholas V.

Sixtus IV (1471–1484) continued the construction, putting the walls around the buildings and adding to the two existing towers the small fortress of the Sistine Chapel, which protrudes from the main body of the building and is crowned with its distinctive battlements.

Innocent VIII (1484–1492) designed an alternative to the fortress complex. Three hundred meters from it, at the end of the garden, he had a small villa built as a summer residence, the Belvedere; it consisted of two rooms with a loggia for strolling. But privacy was not easily reconciled with the fortress-like nature of the entire building. To partially solve this problem, Alexander VI (1492–1503) had a tower built, the Torre Borgia, and within it created a large papal apartment.

The first floor of the Papal Palace was enlarged, from the original three rooms of Nicholas V to the other three in the new tower. These six rooms currently house the papal collection of modern religious art, established by Pope Paul VI in 1973, but they made history in the Vatican residence as the first suite of rooms with the appearance of a royal palace.

The apartment became notorious as the setting for a dark period in the history of the papacy, with Alexander VI and his children—Juan, Cesare, Lucrezia, and Jofré—his women—Vannozza de' Cattanei and Giulia Farnese—and an entire entourage of courtiers, mercenaries, and hired assassins. At that time the apartment was the site of corruption and crime. Numerous books have been written about it, with fictional twists and embellishments that nevertheless have a basis in reality.

Thus when one looks at the frescoes by Pinturicchio that adorn these rooms, it is not at all difficult to recognize in the holy figures portrayed there the perpetrators of these evil machinations. The pope kneels in his pontifical robes in the lunette of the *Resurrection* in the Sala dei Misteri della Fede (Room of the Mysteries of the Faith), and neither the lascivious Jofré, in the part of a melancholic youth in armor, nor the cruel Cesare, another kneeling figure, are convincing. Vannozza, the mother of the pope's four children, is shamelessly portrayed as the Madonna in the *Annunciation*, as is Giulia Farnese in the *Madonna with Child* on the door of the Sala dei Santi (Hall of the Saints), a blasphemous interpretation of the nickname she was given as the pope's concubine, "the bride of Christ." Again, in the *Disputation of St. Catherine of Alexandria with the Philosophers*, Juan is fairly realistic as the youth on horseback in Oriental dress, fond as he was of picturesque costumes, but the fourteen-year-old Lucrezia is not very credible in the role of the saint; she had already been through an unhappy first marriage and was possibly the willing victim of her brother Cesare's depravity.

On 12 June 1493 Lucrezia's first marriage at the age of thirteen was celebrated in this apartment. With great pomp and splendor, she married Giovanni Sforza, count of Pesaro. The ceremony was attended by all the Roman aristocratic women, including Giulia

The second loggia, overlooking the Cortile di San Damaso, called the Loggia of Raphael after the frescoes of the great artist and his studio.

Farnese, the notables of the city government, the diplomatic corps, and twelve cardinals, as well as by the pope—naturally, on his throne. The reception was lavish, followed by dances that degenerated into ribald games. Stefano Infessura wrote that "the pope presented fifty silver cups filled with sugared almonds which, as a sign of great joy, were poured into the breasts of many of the women." In the unrestrained atmosphere that followed, Juan proposed a contest to see which woman could take the greatest quantity from the cups with her breasts. The beautiful Giulia won and received a silver basin as a prize.

The carnival atmosphere that prevailed was confirmed by the festivities preceding Lucrezia's third marriage, to Duke Alfonso d'Este. Burchard, the papal master of ceremonies, wrote in his diary that on the evening of 31 October 1501, Cesare organized a huge party in the pope's apartments, inviting "fifty honest harlots, those known as courtesans. . . . When dinner

was over they danced with the servants and other people there, at first dressed, and then nude. After dinner the candelabras with the lighted candles that had illuminated the table were placed on the floor, where chestnuts had been strewn. The naked harlots picked the chestnuts up, passing between the candelabras on their hands or on their feet. All this took place in the presence of the pope, the duke, and

The spectacular ceremonial staircase, the Scala Regia, created by Bernini, leads to the Sala Regia and the great reception rooms of the Palazzo Apostolico.

Lucrezia. Finally silk capes, sandals, hats, and other gifts were displayed that would be given to those who had the largest number of carnal relations with these harlots. With whom, in that same room, under the eyes of the others, everyone did as he pleased, after which the prizes were distributed to the winners."

These excesses of the Renaissance era were tolerated by the pope in an attitude that was hardly apostolic. The apartment was also contaminated by violent death, for the most part attributable to one person, Cesare Borgia. It was he who killed a certain Pedro Calderón, Lucrezia's presumed lover, in the throne room in March 1498. Lucrezia's second husband, Alfonso of Aragon, duke of Bisceglie, was killed by two of Cesare's hired assassins in the Sala delle Sibille (Hall of the Sibyls) on 18 August 1500.

The Sala Regia, the most splendid area of the whole pontifical apartment, entirely frescoed by Francesco Salviati and Federico Zuccari. At the end and on one side, the entrances to the Sistine Chapel and the Pauline Chapel with the frescoes by Michelangelo.

Even the death of Alexander VI has been attributed to assassins but it is unlikely that the pope fell victim to poison. He died of malaria in this apartment on 18 August 1503. His son Cesare caught it, but survived, in time to send his thugs to his father's study, the Sala delle Scienze e delle Arti Liberali (Hall of the Sciences and the Liberal Arts), to seize the keys to the treasury before the cardinals could get their hands on them. This was the last crime to be committed by a Borgia in the Papal Palace.

The successor of Alexander VI, Pius III, lived in this apartment, but only for the twenty-six days of his brief pontificate. Julius II (1503–1513) succeeded him and stayed until 1507. During his pontificate the Belvedere once again became important. Two long parallel corridors designed by Bramante connected the Belvedere to the palazzo to make a unified complex. The small villa was transformed into an enormous courtyard with three terraces joined by monumental salons. The scenic courtyard of the Belvedere was created, destined for theatrical events, parties, and tournaments. Society life flourished there for the whole of the sixteenth century.

Among the numerous events, the most magnificent took place under Pius IV (1559–1565), a tournament fought on March 5, 1565, during the marriage of Ortensia Borromeo, a relative of the pope, to Annibale Altemps. Twenty Italian and Spanish knights participated and, as a chronicler of the period wrote, the celebrations reached a climax when "in a single moment a great number of candles were lit in many lamps that were placed with consummate skill in all the arches. After a brief moment all the trumpets sounded at once." The celebration ended with a banquet for more than a thousand people, at the end of which, "with many dances and symphonies that came in between, and the different music that was played, the sentence of the judges was pronounced," and the bride rewarded the winning knights.

The Sala Ducale with the imaginative solution devised by Bernini. With imposing fake drapery in marble and stucco, united the original two rooms into a single one, with great spatial and decorative effect.

The courtyard of the Belvedere was later divided into two with the construction of the library and then into three when the so-called *terzo braccio* (third arm) was built. Thus it lost the purpose for which it had been created. In any case, the Belvedere was not to have anything more to do with the actual Papal Palace since Julius II placed several treasures of ancient sculpture there as decoration, the statue now known as the *Apollo Belvedere,* the *Venus Felix*, and the *Laocoon*. It was to become the nucleus of the Vaticani Museums, which would become a growing series of buildings until they finally took over the Papal Palace itself.

In the end, Julius II installed his apartment in Pope Nicholas's old complex on the floor above the Borgia apartment, where all the successive popes would reside up to Sixtus V, each adapting it to his temperament, to the extent of having himself portrayed as the protagonist of the frescoes that adorned the rooms, with clearly narcissistic overtones.

This was an apartment made to order for the pope. It was developed during Julius's pontificate from the rooms that had been built by Nicholas V. Pope Julius, however, had them frescoed by Raphael and his pupils, and included the Chapel of Pope Nicholas as the private chapel of the pope. These rooms constituted the official part of the apartment, beginning with the Sala degli Svizzeri (Hall of the Swiss Guards), the guardroom, and the Sala dei Palafrenieri (Hall of the Grooms), with its function as first antechamber. Next was the Sala dell'Incendio di Borgo (Hall of the Fire in the Borgo), so called for its fresco depicting the fire in the Borgo in Rome of 847. This was the dining room, but Leo X used it as a music room. The Sala della Segnatura (Signing Hall) came next, thus called because it was later used for signing briefs, but at the time it was decorated it housed the pope's study and library. This room was followed by the Stanza di Eliodoro (Hall of Heliodorus), after the fresco depicting the treasurer of the king of Syria being expelled from the temple of Jerusalem. This room was used as a private antechamber for the apartment. Finally came the Stanza di Costantino (Hall of Constantine), with its frescoes celebrating the first Christian emperor, which was used for receptions and ceremonies.

The subjects for the frescoes decorating these rooms chosen by the various popes that lived there are significant in that they reflect their specific interests and personalities. Julius II wanted his policy of the restoration of papal power to be reflected there. Thus *Gregory IX Receiving the Decretals* in the Stanza della Segnatura portrays justice with particular harshness. In the Stanza di Eliodoro, the *Mass at Bolsena* recalls the miracle from which the institution of Corpus Domini derives. Showing Julius II kneeling in front of the altar, it alludes to the vow he made during his first expedition against Bologna, when he stopped to pray in the cathedral at Orvieto in adoration of the corporal. The *Expulsion of Heliodorus* refers to Pope Julius' crusade to expel the foreign powers from Italy.

When Leo X entered the apartments, the work had already begun. He adapted to his predecessor's style but was not to be outdone. Thus on the walls of the Stanza di Eliodoro, he had himself glorified in the *Liberation of St. Peter*, alluding to his own liberation from prison when he was a cardinal, after the battle of Ravenna. In the *Leo the Great Repulsing Attila,* Leo's face was already supposed to appear among the cardinals attending Pope Leo the Great, who was to be depicted with the visage of Julius II. Instead, upon his succession, Leo X had his own portrait put on Leo the Great, and thus appears twice in the same painting. But this Medici pope also managed to have himself immortalized in the Stanza dell'Incendio di Borgo in the faces of two popes with his name, Leo III and Leo IV. In the *Coronation of Charlemagne*, he is portrayed as Leo III while Francis I is portrayed as the emperor, in commemoration of the agreement between the Church and France stipulated in Bologna in 1515. The *Oath of Leo III*, in which he is portrayed as the pope who defends himself in St. Peter's from the calumny of the nephews of Hadrian I, alludes to the Lateran Council of 1516 and the papacy's dispute against the theses of Martin Luther. And again in the *Battle of Ostia*, the celebration of victory over the Saracens refers to the crusade proclaimed against the Turks by Leo X, portrayed here as Leo IV.

The next to be glorified was Clement VII (1523–1534), in the Sala di Costantino. These paintings, conceived as propaganda, glorified the apotheosis of the Church in two pseudo-historical scenes, "genuine frauds," that were frescoed by Giovanni Francesco Penni: the *Baptism of Constantine*, (the Emperor had in fact been baptized by an Arian bishop a few days before his death), and the *Donation of Constantine*, an adaptation of the forged document that purported to grant great temporal power to the papacy.

These rooms led to the Loggia, on three floors overlooking the Cortile di San Damaso (Courtyard of San Damaso), which simultaneously separates and unites the older building of the Papal Palace and the newer. These thirteen spans were frescoed with biblical scenes by Raphael and a throng of assistants, while in the lunettes and on the pillars and pilasters were painted grotesques inspired by the decorations in the "grottoes" of the Domus Aurea (Golden House). At the end of the Loggia a door opened onto the *cordonata*, a ramp with low steps originally built to be used by horses.

Pius V (1566–1572) had a small two-room apartment built to the west of this apartment beyond the present Sala Sobieski, along with a small chapel at the end of a gallery, above two other chapels. This was a house as a place of prayer, reflecting the deeply pious spirit of this holy pope of the Catholic Reformation. The large reception rooms were added later: the Sala Ducale, originally divided into two parts but then brilliantly unified by Bernini, and the Sala Regia, created to accommodate the envoys of kings and emperors.

In his bloodthirsty zeal against the followers of the Reformation, and to mark the horrendous massacre of St. Bartholomew in Paris on 23–24 August 1572, Gregory XIII (1572–1585) commissioned Vasari to commemorate a few scenes permanently on the walls of the Sala Regia. These three frescoes, together with that of the *Battle of Lepanto*, an event which had taken place only two years before, were intended to renew the prestige of the Church by immortalizing historical episodes—a glorification on the walls that seemed to loom menacingly over the representatives of sovereigns in the long wait before their audiences with the Holy Father.

With Sixtus V (1585–1590) the third wing of the Cortile di San Damaso was created, that is, the structure dominating the colonnade. This was begun by Ottaviano Mascherino and completed by Domenico Fontana, and was destined to be the Papal Palace of modern times, developed as it was from a plan by Clement VIII (1592–1605), with the rooms that make up the present private apartment of the pope on the third floor and the official ceremonial apartment on the

second. All of the older structure of the building became part of the museums, with the exception of the top floor where the secretary of state is installed.

The Sistine Palace has been the pontifical residence uninterruptedly only since 1870. From the seventeenth century, the popes considered it only for ceremonial use, preferring the Quirinal Palace, which was evidently considered more regal. Until 1903 the · secretary of state was on the third floor. Leo XIII (1878–1903) slept in one of the not very comfortable small rooms on the first floor, with wooden ceilings. This pope, Vincenzo Gioacchino Pecci, was not particularly interested in having a perfect apartment since he was more interested in the gardens, which became a new element in the context of a pope's residence. The old *viridarium* had seen a period of glory under Paul IV and under Pius IV, who had loved to rest in the greenery of the gardens and had had a lodge built by Pirro Ligorio in 1561. Leo XIII had the gardens taken care of, creating flower beds between the paths and ramparts, and setting a large aviary in an orange grove with pheasants, peacocks, turtle doves, and ducks. In a fenced area he even placed deer and gazelles.

Pope Leo XIII loved to walk through this triumph of flora and fauna, but in the end he wanted to live there as well. He had an annex built to the Papal Palace, adapting the largest of the round towers of the original walls, near the Fountain of the Great Eagle. He had a sort of chalet with battlements added to the tower facing Monte Mario, a small masonry pavilion where he took his coffee and which, for this reason, was given an English nickname, the Coffee House. He also had a small villa built on the other side of the tower, a carefully designed building for himself and his small court. In practice, the Papal Palace had become a villa, and Leo XIII ended up living more in this annex than in his apartment. Moreover, he had a cement reproduction of the Grotto of Lourdes set up there, which French Catholics had sent him as a gift, to protest against the anticlerical policy of the Italian government. There was everything he could want in those gardens—and indeed he spent most of his life there.

Pius X (1903–1914) did not follow his predecessor in this. He gave the annex over to the observatory and did without the garden residence. Instead, he changed places with the secretary of state, settling his private apartment on the third floor, where it has been ever since, even if it has changed with the different habits of each successive pope. Pius X did not choose the top floor out of any particular sense of ambition but simply because people had to pass through the first floor to get to the other floors, and the pope wanted to spend his days modestly and in peace and quiet. He had the bed that had been used by Pius VII, regilded for the occasion, an historic antique that had belonged to the pope who had stood up to Napoleon—but still second-hand. "Nice," he commented, "but I'm going to have to die on it." The novelty of Pius X's papacy was that he did not want to eat alone, as had been the tradition for the other popes. He ate with his two

The vault of the first Sala dei Foconi (so-called because of the custom of keeping large burning braziers, foconi, *there to heat the apartment) with frescoes of St. Gregory the Great by Lorenzo Sabbatini.*

camerieri segreti (private secretaries) and, at times, with his sisters.

The same was true for his successor, Benedict XV (1914–1922), who ate with his sister, Countess Persico. During his pontificate the history of the pontifical apartment was not particularly eventful. Benedict XV loved gardens, and these came back to life with a series of works beginning with the woods which, as Arturo Lancellotti tells us, "once again had to become a place of delights, with cliffs, fountains, waterfalls, ponds, and pleasant gravel paths." Benedict even had a chapel built to the Madonna della Guardia in memory of the Genoese sanctuary of the same name, where he had been bishop.

Pius XI (1922–1939), the pope who built the Vatican City, brought the Papal Palace back its former prestige, but in a very simple way. He prevented any access to "outsiders." "He received no one," wrote Silvio Negro, "he even met his closest relatives in the ceremonial apartment. On the third floor were allowed to enter only his two '*camerieri segreti partecipanti*,' who acted as his secretaries, and the '*aiutanti di camera*,' friars who took care of the wardrobe and the kitchen. The '*facchino di camera*' and the '*scopatore segreto*,' traditional figures among the members of staff who lived closest to the pope, did not go up to the apartment on the third floor unless they were called. The only outsiders who entered were the barber and, when needed, the doctor, and they went up the service stairway or used the elevator because the door that opened onto the main staircase was always locked."

The situation became worse with Pius XII (1939–1958). Eugenio Pacelli was even more solitary than his predecessor, abolishing the posts of the personal secretaries and turning their room into a personal library. Everything that concerned the daily needs of the apartment was handed over to the tertiary Franciscan sisters of Meuzingen, who lived in one wing of the apartment under the direction of Sister Pascalina Lehnert, who regulated life in the house of Pius XII. The apartment was remodeled. It was wallpapered in purple with great curtains at the windows. A dentist's and doctor's surgery were set up, as well as a gym and a room for viewing films. All these additions were secrets that leaked out very slowly from those rooms, obstructed energetically by Sister Pascalina. It was also she who kept in contact with the pope's relatives, who were received only once a year, at Christmas, in front of the Nativity scene set up there.

With John XXIII (1958–1963), things were altogether different. The apartment did not change, but certainly Angelo Giuseppe Roncalli did not use the gym. He found an outlet in the gardens and had one of the medieval towers of the ancient walls furnished for him, but since the resulting apartment was quite lavish he ended up not going there. There were no secrets in his rooms, and what there was to know became known in his own lifetime, contributing to the creation of the myth of the "good pope."

The apartment changed again with Pope Paul VI (1963–1978), who wanted his home to be elegant but austere. The purple wallpaper disappeared, to be replaced by pastels, which would then characterize all the Vatican offices. On the walls, numerous paintings by Lombard painters and avant-garde artists filled all the rooms of the apartment. A hanging garden was created on the large roof-terrace of the building because Paul VI did not particularly like gardens. Again this floor of the Papal Palace was filled with mystery, and the life inside it was secret once more.

A new spirit has been brought to the pontifical apartment by John Paul II. The Lombard atmosphere has been eliminated in favor of a bare but functional environment. Beyond the rooms of his personal secretaries is the pope's private study, the penultimate window of the façade dominating Piazza San Pietro, where the pontiff stands every Sunday for the Angelus. On the corner is his bedroom, with a window on the southern façade and two more on the eastern. Toward the eastern side then comes the bathroom, the dentist's surgery, the dining room, the kitchen, and the pantry. On the northern side are the wardrobe and the larders.

This apartment no longer holds any mysteries. The private library is occasionally transformed into a television studio for the filming of messages and encyclicals. Even if privacy still reigns, the secrets of these rooms have been captured by the mass media to such an extent that they no longer seem closed off to the world.

The ceremonial apartment on the second floor has had quite a different history. Comprised of a series of thirteen rooms, it did not change until the time of John XXIII. Each room had its precise function in relation to the presence of lay or military dignitaries on duty there. The floor opened with the Sala Clementina, where the picket of the Swiss Guards was stationed, and continued with the Sala dei Sediari (Hall of the Chairbearers) or del Candelabro (of the Candelabra), as an antechamber. There followed the Sala del Gendarme with two gendarmes in full-dress uniform, after which the Sala d'Angolo (Corner Room) led through to the Sala degli Arazzi (Tapestry Hall), with the duty officers of the Swiss and Palatine Guard together with the *Bussolanti* (attendants). The Sala delle Guardie Nobili (Hall of the Noble Guards) followed, then the Throne Room, used for audiences with important personages and heads of state, the private antechamber with the *camerieri di Spada e Cappa* (literally, servants of the Cape and Sword) and the *Esente di Guardia Nobile*, the commander of all the guards of honor. Then came the Sala dei Papi (Hall of the Popes), so called because of the busts of the popes displayed there, the rooms of St. John and the Small Throne, and finally the pope's library.

With Paul VI the purely honorary offices were eliminated and with them the high-sounding names of some of the traditional rooms, so that a new denomination was required for the structure. They are now called the rooms of St. Ambrose, the Sculptors, the Painters, the Evangelists, the Redeemer, the Madonna, St. Catherine, and Sts. Peter and Paul. The library remains, with its splendid landscape frescoes, the chapel, a large study, and the Throne Room, no longer magnificent as in the past but consisting only of a marble seat with the statues of the apostles Peter and Paul. The antechamber leads into the Sala del Concistoro (Hall of the Consistory), frescoed by Giovanni Alberti and Matthijs Brill, with a ceiling famous for the beauty of its exquisite golden inlay. Here the pope convenes the College of Cardinals and receives groups in audience.

These rooms have been made familiar to the general public through television, thus diminishing the aura of mystery that certain ceremonies traditionally had. It can be said that if once this Papal Palace was created to the measure of a pope, today it is arranged, with great openness and accessibility, to the measure of man.

THE PALAZZI ON THE CAMPIDOGLIO

Panorama of the Campidoglio and Aracoeli, with the monument to Vittorio Emanuele II on the left. Around Piazza del Campidoglio, with its characteristic design of crossed stars, are, from the right, Palazzo dei Conservatori, Palazzo Senatorio and Palazzo Nuovo.

The Campidoglio is on the southern side of the lowest of the legendary seven hills of Rome, the Capitoline hill where in ancient times the temple to Jupiter Optimus Maximus stood, where the consuls ascended in their solemn triumphal processions, and where the state archive was kept in a special building, the *Tabularium*. It was the perfect example of a public place, aimed at maintaining in perpetuity the offices governing the city in its thousand-year history and

used as a synonym for the municipal administration of Rome to the extent that it became a universal symbol.

This authentic historical, political, and administrative center is above all an urban jewel designed by Michelangelo to take the best advantage possible of the geographical position of the hill. The ellipse on the ground, with its extraordinary star design worked out by the genius of the artist (but actualized only in 1940), was inserted into the great

trapezium of one of the most beautiful piazzas in the world. The equestrian monument of Marcus Aurelius stands at the epicenter of an unrepeatable impressive setting. This uniqueness is confirmed by the changing perspectives that one sees as one gradually ascends the shallow steps leading up to the piazza, with the first appearance of the bell tower of the Palazzo Senatorio (Senate) followed by the sight of the full building in the background with its majestic double flight of steps forming a wide triangular shape and the two wings of the symmetrical Palazzo dei Conservatori (Curators) on the right and the Palazzo of the Musei Capitolini (Capitoline Museums) on the left.

The Palazzo Senatorio stands where the *Tabularium* was originally located. In 1143, over the ancient remains of the state archive, a building was erected as a Senate building, that is, as a gathering place of a dignified assembly of fifty citizens of the Roman middle and artisan classes, headed by a nobleman. This was the myth of the *renovatio senatus* (new senate) in the mystical vision of Arnaldo da Brescia, right up to the figure of the single senator who had to juggle the city feuds between baronial struggles and papal claims.

The Palazzo Senatorio took the shape, therefore, at the end of the thirteenth century, of a three-storey battlemented building with large apertures that allowed the onlooker to see what was happening inside, a prototype of a building aiming at political and administrative "transparency." The people here were called to parliament by the Patarina, the bell stolen from the Commune of Viterbo. Under the vaults toward the Roman Forum was the prison, and on the flight of steps, death sentences were carried out; on the square in front, emperors submitted their powers in a purely formal ceremony to the Roman people. This building lived through its golden age midway through the fourteenth century, when the popes were in Avignon. It triumphed in the poetic crowning of Francesco Petrarca (Petrarch) and in the republican adventure of Cola di Rienzo. The motto "Senatus Populusque Romanus" (Roman Senate and People) was lived out fully until papal authority was reinstated with the definitive return of the Apostolic See.

The side of the Campidoglio with two statues of the Dioscuri defining the entrance onto the Piazza. At the bottom, the gigantic "speaking statue", the "Marforio", which decorates the fountain in the courtyard of the Palazzo Nuovo.

The pope combined in himself all the different powers with a state legislative apparatus before which the senator took on a symbolic value only with representational functions, while alternative municipal magistracies acquired importance as delegated by the pope in a decentralization of power. Thus, the *caporioni* (local district leaders) became important; they took control of the social and economic life of the district where they acted as municipal policemen outside the Palazzo Senatorio. Similarly, the *conservatori*, effective

a large ground-floor arcade where there was also room for an art collection set up with donations from Sixtus IV in 1471. However, the palazzi were small for such institutions and a complete rebuilding was needed, in a style that would exude prestige and accord well with an overall plan for the "monumentalization" of the Campidoglio. The design was Michelangelo's.

The new regularization of the Palazzo Senatorio started in 1536 when the bronze statue of Marcus Aurelius, taken from the Lateran, was placed in the

heads of the Commune's bureaucracy, dealt out justice directly inside the palazzo and presided over the public and secret councils, deliberative bodies set up to consider a variety of problems. The Palazzo Senatorio was adapted to provide the structures needed by the new features of the municipal center: the square was embellished by towers erected by Popes Boniface IX, Martin V, and Nicholas V between 1393 and 1453.

The *conservatori* obtained their own headquarters in a building to the right of the Palazzo Senatorio, with

excavated piazza in line with the center of the Palazzo. This was outlined by part of the double staircase, the two reclining statues of the Nile and the Tiber, and a standing statue of Minerva in an alcove. However, this was not the way Michelangelo wanted, and the two lateral buildings of the piazza remained at the drawing stage only.

The Palazzo Senatorio was completely finished between 1582 and 1605 by Giacomo Della Porta. The double ramp was finished and the new façade was

The end wall of the Sala degli Imperatori in the Palazzo Nuovo, with the background of the Gallery where the Athena Giustiniani is kept, found at Velletri and a copy of an original of the fifth century BC.

Portrait of a woman of the Imperial period over a sepulchral memorial stone with the inscription "Dis Manibus Antoniae Pancrotis. L. Helenes," and, next to it, a portrait of the Emperor Maximinus in the Sala degli Imperatori in the Palazzo Nuovo.

DIS MANIBVS
ANTONIAE
PANEROTIS·L·
HELENES

View of the Sala dei Filosofi in the Palazzo Nuovo. In the foreground, the statue of a seated magistrate, probably Marcellus.

installed—with its rich portal into which Michelangelo's had been incorporated—up to the cornice with the escutcheons of the Aldobrandini pope Clement VIII (1593–1605) and the balustrade. The new bell tower rose, the work of Martino Longhi the Elder, in place of the old one, which had not been centered and had been destroyed in part by lightning. Under the steps a fountain was placed, and the large Minerva in her alcove was replaced by a smaller one in porphyry and marble, transformed into the Goddess Roma by Giacomo Rainaldi. Two marble basins, placed one above the other, stood next to her when the Acqua Felice reached the Campidoglio.

Work on the Palazzo dei Conservatori proceeded at the same time. Actual construction started in 1563, when Michelangelo was still alive, and was continued by Guido Guidetti and Giacomo Della Porta up to 1568. The façade had the balustrade and statues as features, while the arcade was decorated with plaster figures and trophies. It bore six doors with the titles of the most important corporations of artisans who had their offices there, such as pharmacists, sellers of cloth, butchers, carpenters, blacksmiths, and innkeepers (the latter's hall nowadays is used for weddings). The work on the interior went on until the end of the eighteenth century, with the decoration of the rooms on the first

Portico of the Palazzo dei Conservatori with the colossal statue of Roma, dating back to the time of Hadrian.

On the following pages: Hand, arm, and head of Constantine II in the courtyard of the Palazzo dei Conservatori, which came from the 12-meter high acrolithos which was once in the apse of the Basilica of Maxentius in the Roman Forum; the Spinario, *a statue in bronze of the first century B.C. in the Sala dei Trionfi; the* Esquiline Venus, *a first-century A.D. copy of a work by Praxiteles.*

floor all intended as reception rooms and offices of the *conservatori*. These included the Sala della Lupa (Room of the She-Wolf), originally a loggia, with the sculpture of the legendary *Capitoline Wolf* (which gave the room its name), the Sala degli Orazi e Curiazi frescoed by Cavalier d'Arpino with scenes from the birth of Rome, the papal throne room, then called the Sala degli Arazzi (Tapestry Room), and the Sala dei Capitani, which took its name from the five marble statues representing the captains of the Church: Marcantonio Colonna, Alessandro Farnese, Carlo Barberini, Gianfrancesco Aldobrandini, and Tommaso Rospigliosi. Then came the great courtyard with the portico erected by Alessandro Specchi in 1720. Remnants of ancient marble statues and reliefs were gathered here, including pieces of a colossal statue of Constantine, so that the palazzo gradually came to be used as a museum, and finally the very offices of the *conservatori* were moved. This was a cultural operation that began in 1748 with alterations to make a picture gallery on the second floor of the building; this renovation was implemented by Ferdinando Fuga. A new salon was subsequently added under Benedict XIV (1740–1758) to house a precious collection of art, which remains there today and which finally brought the palazzo to a high cultural level.

In contrast to the extensive new façade added onto the exterior and the alterations done on the interior of

View of the Sala dei Capitani in the Palazzo dei Conservatori, which takes its name from the five marble statues representing the captains of the Church: Marcantonio Colonna. In the foreground, Alessandro Farnese, Carlo Barberini, Gianfrancesco Aldobrandini, and Tommaso Rospigliosi. On the walls are frescoes by Tommaso Laureti with scenes from the early Republican period, such as Mucius Scaevola before a Porsenna on the left-hand wall.

The Sala degli Orazi e Curiazi with marble statues of Urban VIII in the detail at the bottom, the work of Bernini and assistants, and, on the end wall, Innocent X in bronze by Alessandro Algardi. On the walls, frescoes by Cavalier d'Arpino with the Discovery of the She-Wolf *(1595–96) and, on the left, in the foreground, the* Duel between the Horatii and the Curiatii *(1612–13) which gives the room its name.*

the Palazzo dei Conservatori, the Palazzo Senatorio—apart from restoration work—never changed in appearance either outside or inside and, in substance, it kept to its original purpose. Up to 1870 it continued to be the residence of the senator of Rome. The senator presided over the civil and criminal courts in what became the Council Hall of the Commune, with its great statue of Julius Caesar from the time of Trajan which gave the room its name. The senator was assisted in the functions of his post by two judges appointed "a latere" (ancillary) and a captain of appellation. No other functions pertained to this post, in a clear limitation of power which partly came about in 1847 through the *motu proprio* of Pius IX, in the context of the modern Commune with 100 councilors, 8 conservatori, and, of course, the senator. It was a brief history, cancelled by the reactionary politics of the Mastai pope Pius IX after the "adventure" of the Roman Republic of 1849.

However, it was just these revolutionary events that gave life to the otherwise flat existence of the Palazzo Senatorio. There was a scandal when, on 15 February 1798, the tree of Liberty was erected by the Jacobins in front of the staircase and the meetings of the triumvirs Mazzini, Saffe, and Armellini were filled with illusions. These took place in the Sala delle Bandiere (Room of the Flags), so called because it housed the flags of the district's civic guard, which was instituted by Pius IX at the request of Ciceruacchio, and other historical banners such as the one representing St. George as he transfixed the dragon that the tribune Cola di Rienzo waved during the attack on the Campidoglio in 1347. On that scarred wooden table, built by Roman master craftsmen in 1842, rested the hand of Giuseppe Mazzini who, when preparing his proclamations of Republican faith, decreed "in the name of the sovereign people." Here too sat the mayors and magistrates of the municipal

councils of Rome which have met at the Campidoglio since 1870 and which continue to meet there.

After the fateful September 20, the palazzo became the seat of the Commune and the Hall of Julius Caesar was occupied by the benches of the town and municipal councils in austere but impressive state, with the banners of the Commune and of the twenty-two districts on the walls amid the crests of popes and senators, ancient emblems of the city, and historical inscriptions. However, the Commune took possession, obviously, of the Palazzo dei Conservatori too, and these offices became municipal reception rooms, though care was taken to safeguard the museum image that the building had partly taken on in the past—indeed this image was increased with the incorporation of two neighboring edifices, thus producing an enlargement of the building as a real museum. These were the Museo Nuovo (New Museum), constituted in 1925 in the Palazzo Caffarelli, and the Braccio Nuovo

(New Arm), which connected the two palazzi and was opened in 1950. In this way, the second great area of the Musei Capitolini was defined, which was originally located in the Palazzo Nuovo, built as twin to the Palazzo dei Conservatori opposite.

The Palazzo Nuovo ideally dates back to the project designed by Michelangelo, who had intended to build on this side of the piazza only a façade—without a constructed body—as a screen for the retaining wall to the land of the Aracoeli. It should have been similar to the façade of the Palazzo dei Conservatori, with a balcony acting as a loggia and with an identical portico. It was not carried out, and remained as the retaining wall until, in 1655, Innocent X wanted a proper palazzo. This was built by Girolamo and Carlo Rainaldi, who completed it under Pope Alexander VII (1655–1667) whose crest is placed above the arcade. It is in every way similar to the Palazzo dei Conservatori, with the courtyard in

On the following pages:
Hannibal on the Elephant, *a fresco by Jacopo Ripanda in the Sala della Lupa.*

EXACTO PRIMO BELLO PVNICO
PACIS INITAE
CVM CARTAGINENSIBVS
PER
Q LVTATIVM CATVLVM CONS
IN FORO
PACTA SANCIVNTVR
ANNO AB VRBE CONDITA
DXII

which the fountain of the talking statue of Marforio was placed in 1679, while to the right, after lengthy restoration, was placed the equestrian statue of Marcus Aurelius, which until 1980 stood on the piazza.

The Palazzo Nuovo is the principal center of the Musei Capitolini and as such does not have any particular part to play in the political and administrative context of Rome; rather, it has its place in Rome's artistic and cultural world. Its intended use had never been clearer than in 1734 when the precious

collection of Cardinal Alessandro Albani was acquired. Since then there has been a continuing increase of materials on display, the results of various archaeological discoveries throughout the city. Undoubtedly, many more still remain to be brought to light.

The She-Wolf Suckling Romulus and Remus by Rubens (1617–1618) with the aid of Jan Wildens for the landscape and Frans Snyders for the animals, in the Pinacoteca Capitolina. Opposite, a fresco by Jacopo Ripanda in the Sala di Annibale, representing Lutatius Catulus Negotiating with Hamilcar *or, according to others,* Atilius Regulus before the Carthaginian Ambassadors.

PALAZZI MASSIMO

The Palazzi Massimo comprise the complex of buildings that were developed on Corso Vittorio Emanuele II, between Piazza di Sant'Andrea della Valle and Piazza San Pantaleo, and Piazza dei Massimi at the back, following the curving line of the ancient Odeon of Domitian on which the buildings were originally erected.

The Massimo family was the most ancient noble family of Rome. Its origins supposedly went back to

The Palazzo dei Massimo, nicknamed Istoriato, decorated with grisaille pictures by the school of Daniele da Volterra, which still exist in part, on Piazzetta dei Massimi where the cipollino column stands which came to light in 1938 and which probably belonged to the Odeon of Domitian.

the Roman dictator Quintus Fabius Maximus, called Cunctator, the Delayer, for his tactics against Hannibal in 217 B.C., and who himself, according to legend, was descended from the mythical Hercules. The family's presence in Rome is documented historically from at least 999, the year indicated on a sepulchral stone for a Leone de' Massimi immured in the cloister

G. Vasi dis. sc.
1. Palazzo Santobono, 2. Chiesa di S. Pant

92

of the convent of Sant'Alessio on the Aventine; but the historian Panvinio indicates that the pope and martyr Anastasius I (399–401) was a member of this family, thus suggesting an even more ancient origin.

The Massimo houses along the Via Papalis (Papal Way)—of which a stretch corresponds to the present-day Corso Vittorio Emanuele II—were recorded in 1159, constituting a compact nucleus in an actual quarter, crossed by a main road called Via dei Massimi, which led into the piazzetta of the same name. On this piazzetta stood an older building, later called *istoriato* (decorated), while on the road was a *domus antiqua* (ancient house) that featured an arcade and therefore was called the *casa del portico* (house of the arcade), flanked by a *domus nova* (new house) and two other houses. There is no documented evidence of the Massimo family's life in these houses, only names, such as Giovanni in the twelfth century and Alessandro in the thirteenth, but it seems clear that the family had gradually become prominent in the city, filling important civil positions: for example, Massimo was leader of the Parione district in 1447 and Capitoline curator in 1454. These houses were medieval structures that were restored in 1462, as we learn from the *Commentarii* of Pius II, and they assumed the appearance of Renaissance palazzi, complete with symbols of patronage. The Massimo family seemed to be open to cultural developments since in 1467 Pietro accommodated the printing press of the Germans Arnold Pannartz and Conrad Schweynheim in his house on the piazzetta.

Palazzo Maſsimi, detto delle Colonne
...zzo della medesima Famiglia Maſsimi, detto di Pirro, 4. Strada Papale verſo il Palazzo Valle

Palazzo Massimo, called alle Colonne, an etching by Giuseppe Vasi taken from the first book of Delle Meraviglie di Roma Antica e Moderna *published in Rome in 1752. The print portrays also the so-called Palazzo di Pirro, marked with the number two, after the more famous building featuring columns.*

The beautiful loggia of the courtyard of Palazzo alle Colonne seen from the inside, opposite, and from the outside, on the left. It is supported by small columns and pilasters with Ionic capitals, and has an architrave decorated with stucco palmettes. It is an exceptional example of pure Renaissance architecture.

The paterfamilias between the end of the fifteenth century and the beginning of the sixteenth was Domenico, son of Pietro, who enjoyed the confidence even of Alexander VI, otherwise so hostile to Roman nobility. He became so wealthy that he could boast 160 people in his service, needed because his wife, Giuseppina Maddalena Capodiferro, bore him eighteen children. A true patriarch, he settled his children in the various houses of the quarter, adapting them as needed and planning improvements to the buildings that concerned not only their comfort but also their splendor.

The first building to be restored was the oldest on the piazzetta. At this time it assumed the characteristics that still allow it to be described as *istoriato*. On the occasion of the marriage of Angelo Massimo and Antonietta Planca Incoronati in 1523, the façade of the building was wholly decorated with grisaille paintings that are still somewhat visible. They represent scenes from the Old and the New Testament. A nineteenth-century restoration brought to light a stone indicating that a certain Nicolò Furlano was the painter.

During the Sack of Rome in 1527, all the houses were badly damaged, but Domenico was too old to plan new repairs, and he had also lost some of his children, among them Giuliano, who had been killed during the hopeless defense of Rome. When Domenico died in 1532, the property was shared among the remaining children, each of whom took care of the rebuilding of his own house.

On the following pages: One of the rooms of the piano nobile of Palazzo Massimo alle Colonne, reached by a staircase adorned with marble sculpture, a statue of Aesculapius with its traditional serpent wound around the staff, and a ceiling with engraved lacunars.

The splendid ceiling of the salon on the piano nobile *of the Palazzo alle Colonne, by Daniele da Volterra. He also made the frieze beneath it that recounts the life of Quintus Fabius Maximus, the ancient Roman dictator known as the "delayer" in the war against Hannibal, to whom the Massimo attribute their origin.*

The two groups of houses on Piazza San Pantaleo were incorporated into a single building, eventually constituting an extension of the nearby palazzo, the *domus nova*, while remaining separate from it and going its own way without particular historical or architectural interest. Its moment of glory came in the nineteenth century, when Prince Camillo Carlo Alberto and his wife Francesca Luccherini lived there. Their terracotta family crests stand out among the garlands on the façade.

The *domus nova* was completely rebuilt between 1532 and 1536 for Angelo Massimo by Giovanni Mangone di Caravaggio, a pupil of Antonio da Sangallo. During the foundation work there came to light a statue of Mars with a cuirass decorated with elephants, wrongly identified as a portrait of Pyrrhus, king of Epirus. This made the palazzo's fortune and also bestowed upon it the popular name Palazzo di Pirro. The statue was displayed in the splendid courtyard until in 1738 it was bought by Pope Clement

XII for the Campidoglio. The magnificent salons of the piano nobile were frescoed by Perin del Vaga and represent the mythical tales of Dido and Aeneas, the prehistory of the glorification of the Massimo family's Roman origins. The narrative continued in the frescoes of the rooms opening onto the adjacent Palazzo del Portico, which became Palazzo alle Colonne. In 1874, Prince Camillo Carlo Alberto had the two buildings unified so that all together there was an impressive suite of richly decorated rooms.

The Palazzo del Portico was completely rebuilt for Pietro Massimo by Baldassare Peruzzi in the same years as the restructuring of the Palazzo di Pirro, and became "alle Colonne" because the new portico, which kept the convexity of the earlier one, utilized six Doric columns that combined to produce an impressive architectural effect. This new portico was the emblematic image of the palazzo; it reflected an element of nobility that derived from this classical feature and that was enriched in the interior in the decorations culminating in the Massimo family crest and in the copy of the *Doryphorus* by Polyclitus. It was a motif that characterized the entrance hall too, between lunettes and decorative panels that evoked ancient myths, up to the first of the two courtyards, enriched by archaeological remains and groups of columns, and where, notably, in 1620 a nymphaeum was installed, decorated by Giovanbattista Solari. The structure of the palazzo had its crowning in the seventeenth century with the opening of the second courtyard, in connection with the palazzo *istoriato*, where two granite columns stand which came from the Temple of Isis in the Campus Martius, another symbol evoking the Massimo family's connection to the world of ancient Rome.

This building thus became the key to the whole complex, combined as it is with the Palazzo di Pirro and the palazzo *istoriato*. The story of the Massimo family is all concentrated here, finding its highest affirmation in the frescoes of the piano nobile, from the *Histories of Fabius Maximus* on the ceiling of the entrance hall to the *Founding of Rome* in the Salone Rosso, and the *Labors of Hercules* immortalized in the Flemish tapestries.

It was here that five centuries of the life of the Massimo delle Colonne family were spent, starting with Fabrizio, son of Angelo, builder of the Palazzo di Pirro. The family were barons of Pisterzo from 1544, marquises of Roccasecca from 1558, lords of Arsoli from 1574, and, finally, princes of Arsoli from 1826. It was a life that ran parallel to that of the Massimo d'Aracoeli who originated with Tiberio, brother of Fabrizio; they resided in a palazzo opposite the Campidoglio steps, marquises of Ortona in 1685 and dukes of Rignano and Calcata from 1828, merging at the beginning of this century with the Colonna. However, it is in the Palazzo alle Colonne, where the Massimo family still live, that the most famous personalities and the most intriguing stories of the dynasty are recorded.

These rooms contain the memories of the tragic events of the end of the sixteenth century. The protagonists were the sons of Lelio Massimo who killed his second wife because they could not bear to have a stepmother "of doubtful reputation," but they themselves had tragic ends. The second son Marcantonio poisoned his elder brother Luca and was executed, Girolamo died fighting the Turks, Alessandro was killed at the walls of Paris, and Ottavio was overcome by a jealous rival.

The palazzo was also witness to royal weddings, like that of Camillo Massimiliano Massimo VIII (1770–1839), prior of the *caporioni* and captain of the company of Parione, who married Princess Christine of Saxony, and those of their children: Giuseppina married Ottavio Lancellotti Ginetti, prince of Lauro, and Camillo Vittorio wed Maria Gabriella Caterina Antonietta di Savoia Carignano.

The most memorable event in the history of the palazzo must certainly be that linked to little Paolo, the fourteen-year-old son of Fabrizio Massimo. On 16 March 1583, the dying boy asked for Filippo Neri, who arrived at his bedside only after the boy had died. After saying some prayers, the saint brought the boy back to life. Since Paolo asked to be confessed so that he could go to heaven and join his sister Elena who had died a few days earlier, Filippo carried out his wish, blessing him while the boy died again. This event was considered to be a miracle, and the room was transformed into a chapel. Every year, on March 16, a religious ceremony is carried out in remembrance: the columns of the arcade are decorated with red damask as a sign of celebration, and the palazzo is open to anyone who wishes to visit it. This sacred rite once again exalts the noble air that all can breathe between these walls.

Female busts in ovals of precious stucco in Palazzo alle Colonne. The lines of the faces, clothing, and coiffures evoke the appearance of ancient Romans, emphasizing the princely and ancient noble family name.

The Sala Egizia in Palazzo alle Colonne, following the fashion that influenced art after the Napoleonic campaigns in Egypt. In the panels are frescoed views of the Nile and the pyramids, flanked by stylized figures of pharaohs and sphinxes against a background of starry skies.

100

VILLA FARNESINA

CHIGI DELLA ROVERE

Detail of the Sala della Galatea in the Villa della Farnesina with overdoor landscapes by Gaspar Dughet and, in a lunette, the head of a youth by Sebastiano del Piombo.

This marvelous villa, set between the Via della Lungara and the Tiber embankment, was built at the beginning of the sixteenth century as the luxurious home not of a nobleman or a cardinal, but of a banker from Siena, Agostino Chigi (1466–1520). Chigi moved to Rome at the age of twenty and was a genuine capitalist, thanks to his dynamic banking activities, based on two financing companies with numerous foreign branches, and his commercial business for which he had privileges obtained from popes and the king of Naples. In fact, he had the contract to supply grain and to exploit alum mines and salt. Pope Julius II then came onto the scene and granted him the right also to use his arms and his name so he was called il Magnifico (the Magnificent) because of the splendor with which he liked to surround himself and because of his patronage.

In the villa he enjoyed life according to the ideals of the period: celebrations and banquets, culture and beautiful women, like the courtesan Imperia and then Francesca Ordeaschi, who bore him four children and whom he married a year before his death. It was a villa designed to be a center of Renaissance life, a life of intellectual and material pleasures, synonymous with the *delizie* (delights), a name given in that period as the maximum expression of a sumptuous home. The villa, designed by Baldassarre Peruzzi, was built between 1505 and 1518, mostly as it still appears today: a palazzo created in the context of Italianate gardens "with that beautiful grace," wrote Vasari, to whom it did not seem "built of bricks, but actually born," of refined proportions, of sharp planes from the arcaded loggia to the numerous windows and the elegant frieze with festoons and putti inspired by the bas-reliefs in the Pantheon.

The interior contained a gallery frescoed by Raphael with the famous story of Cupid and Psyche and the Sala di Galatea, which took its name from the fresco of the same name, also painted by Raphael, and for which Imperia, of course, had been the model. On the vault, which can be considered the glorification of Agostino Chigi, was the astrological representation of his horoscope of good fortune with episodes of mythology created by Peruzzi. Jupiter was in Aries, the Moon in Virgo, Mars in Libra, Mercury in Scorpio, the Sun in Sagittarius, Venus in Capricorn, and Saturn in Pisces, all favorable positions of the planets at the moment of Chigi's birth at 7 a.m. on 1 December 1466. This is why this great man of business believed firmly in astrology and wanted his horoscope, which revealed such extraordinary good fortune, to be visible to all who took part in the *delizie* of the villa.

In the summer months, in the shade of the Sala di Galatea, with the cool breeze that rose from the Tiber, Chigi's friends the humanists Sadoleto, Colucci, Inghirami, and Pallai, as well as Raphael and Sebastiano del Piombo, who created scenes from Ovid's *Metamorphoses* in the lunettes of the vault, and, of course, Peruzzi, all spent hours in his company. They read works of the Latin poets, discussed philosophical questions and planned further embellishments for the villa, while Biagio Pallai sat listening and taking mental notes for the poem he would write to describe the magnificence around him.

They relaxed with intimate suppers, sensuous prologues to the amorous pleasures for which each guest was solicited by refined courtesans, ideal company for these drinking parties. Among these, Imperia stood out, Agostino's mistress, destined to share his bed of gold and ivory studded with precious stones in the Sala delle Nozze (Wedding Chamber), which took its name from Sodoma's fresco of *The Marriage of Alexander and Roxane*. So it was, at least, until the "divina etera" (divine courtesan) committed suicide in August 1512.

Parties and sumptuous receptions for the official world were also celebrated in this villa, held in ostentatious display and luxury in the daylight. On 30 April 1518 a fabulous banquet was organized for Leo X and his train of fourteen cardinals in the northern part of the building, in rooms where the walls were covered in tapestries and the floors hidden by precious carpets. So luxurious was it that the pope rebuked his host for his excessive splendor, only to be answered that his devoted friendship toward the pope was demonstrated by the modesty of the place—and, so saying, tapestries and carpets were removed showing the stables beneath. This was really a sort of

residence and were part of the sumptuous context of the whole villa.

A famous banquet was given for Roman nobles in 1518 in a loggia that gave onto the Tiber. The culminating moment came at the end, when Chigi had his servants throw into the river all the gold and silver plate used during the meal. Such theatrical waste was a trick, however, because nets had been spread in the river before the banquet and once the guests had left, all the silver was pulled in again without any damage.

The Sala delle Prospettive, with its extraordinary frescoes by Baldassare Peruzzi. On the left, a view of Rome between paired columns and the frieze in fifteen panels, separated by hermes, showing myths by Ovid and Vulcan's workshop over the fireplace, also all by Peruzzi.

challenge to Riario, the owner of the villa opposite, to whom Chigi wanted to prove that the stables of his residence were more luxurious than the Riario drawing room which was in the process of being built. In any case, it was quite true that these stables were luxurious quarters where not only Chigi's one hundred horses were kept, but where the staff also lived. Chigi wanted them to inhabit rooms that were not inferior to his

Another extraordinary banquet was held on St. Augustine's day in 1519 to celebrate Chigi's marriage to the mother of his children. It took place in the presence of the pope and twenty cardinals in the Sala delle Prospettive (Hall of Views) on the upper floor, against a background of illusionistic landscapes and views of Rome, among *trompe l'œil* allegorical statues painted on the walls and gods that looked down from above. It was a theatrical fiction for his wedding, indeed, but it was also the reading of his will, a prophetic announcement of his death, which occurred the following year.

His heirs were not able to administer their enormous patrimony nor care for the property. During the sack of Rome in 1527 they did not risk defending the villa and probably offered money to the invaders, as did owners of other great houses. They took away what they could and fled the camp. The Imperial soldiers sacked Rome and left their signature on the

had a splendid palazzo on the other bank of the Tiber, the famous "Dado". They planned to link the two residences with a bridge of boats but did not carry it out. They did not appreciate the beauty of the villa and neglected it, much as they neglected the building in Via Giulia. Yet it was they who left the name of Farnesina on this amazing complex, and it is by this name that it is commonly known.

In 1704, after the wedding of Elisabetta Farnese to the Bourbon Philip of Spain, the villa became the property of the Bourbon family of Naples who, in

Sala delle Prospettive. On the frescoes can be read, "Why should I who write not laugh: the soldiers have made the pope run" and graffiti was left on the bell tower in the corner of the wall with the fireplace, with the word "Babylon," referring to Rome, carved in Gothic letters.

The Chigi squandered their fortune and finished up by selling the villa in 1590 to the Farnese, who already

1714, used it as the seat of the Accademia di Napoli. No more than that. The demolition of the stables was the obvious sign of how far the villa had by then been abandoned: its degradation affected the whole complex.

In 1861 Francis II, having lost the kingdom of Naples, took refuge in Rome and went to live in Palazzo Farnese, the restoration and maintenance of

Detail of the Sala delle Prospettive with a door surmounted by a splendid decoration on two levels, with winged cupids and the figure of a divinity.

which were already creating problems. The Farnesina was an "extra," and the king gave it to the ambassador of Spain at the court of Naples, the prince of Ripalda, Salvador Bermudez de Castro, who in 1863 finally restored the villa, rebuilding the fallen ceilings and fixtures, and replacing doors that no longer existed.

In 1870 Bermudez de Castro cancelled the rent and the villa passed to his daughter. The commitment to maintain this masterpiece of a villa remained intact, but the building of the walls removed the historic loggia of Agostino Chigi that had overlooked the Tiber—along with all its memories of symposia.

In 1927 the villa was bought by the Italian state, and between 1929 and 1944 it was put at the disposal of the Accademia d'Italia. Subsequently, the Farnesina housed the official delegation of the Accademia dei

Lincei, which has its headquarters in Palazzo Corsini, and, from 1950, the Gabinetto Nazionale dei Disegni e delle Stampe (National Cabinet of Drawings and Prints). Culture has returned to the villa, even if only in the official and academic terms of state institutions; the Renaissance adventures of the Farnesina's founder cannot be repeated.

The sumptuous gallery with the myth of Cupid and Psyche frescoed by Raphael, Giulio Romano, and Francesco Penni. The festoons of flowers and fruit are by Giovanni da Udine.

PALAZZO FARNESE

CARDINAL
ALESSANDRO
FARNESE

Palazzo Farnese, known as the "Dado" (dice) on account of the compact solidity of its architecture, was considered in its day one the "four marvels" of Rome, together with the Borghese *Cembalo*, the grand staircase at Palazzo Ruspoli, and the great portal of the Sciarra Colonna. It remains one of Rome's most beautiful mansions, occupying the whole side of the piazza to which it has given its name. The focus of an urban stage set, it is placed among well-defined,

artists of the Renaissance and finally was revealed as anything but a family home. It was more an archaeological museum, an art gallery, or an architectural prototype of an autonomous royal palace, an historical monument, a symbol of the aggressive insertion into the papal city of a "foreign" family such as the Farnese. They never considered it an actual family mansion, but more a showplace, as was the Villa della Farnesina alla Lungara on the other side of the Tiber.

The imposing façade of Palazzo Farnese overlooking the piazza of the same name. The "Dado" (Cube), as it was nicknamed because of its shape, was built between 1515 and 1589 and designed by Antonio da Sangallo the Younger, extended by Michelangelo, added to by Vignola on the back façade, and completed by Giacomo della Porta. The building is crowned by a splendid cornice with Farnese lilies.

Opposite:
A corner of the courtyard with five arcades on each side, separated by Doric half-columns and surmounted by a cornice with metopes and triglyphs, in a gallery of great effect, repeated on the first and second storeys with closed arcades as windows.

harmoniously proportioned buildings that contribute toward making its massive structure even more prominent.

Built as the residence of the Farnese family by its most important member, Cardinal Alessandro, before he became Pope Paul III (1534–1549), the palazzo took on its magnificent appearance thanks to the work of major

Better, they thought, actually to live within the orchards on the Palatine, or at Caprarola, with the greenery of its gardens, or even in Parma, capital city of the duchy held by the family from 1545 until 1731, until the absorption of the Farnese into the Bourbon line.

This is a palazzo conceived for the glorification of the Farnese family. The family in truth was of modest,

though ancient, origins; it goes back to around the eleventh century, to the small fief of Castrum Farneti in the area of Viterbo, which expanded in the following two centuries in the zone around Lake Bolsena. The prime mover of the family's political and economic growth in Rome was Ranuccio the Elder (1375–1460), a man of arms, defender of the papal state, and senator in 1417. With his son Pier Luigi, husband of a lady of the Caetani family, the Farnese entered the Roman nobility, but it was with the two sons born of this marriage that the family made its real leap in status. Giulia "the beautiful" married an Orsini, thereby strengthening the relationship with the highest echelons of the aristocracy, but it was her position as mistress of the Borgia Pope Alexander VI, an authentic "uxor Christi" (bride of Christ), according to the court gossips, that ensured the taking of the cardinal's hat for her brother Alessandro in 1493. He was known as the "cardinal gonnella" (skirt cardinal) because he obtained his appointment thanks to the amatory arts of his sister and also because of his own amatory adventures, making him the father of four children, Pier Luigi, Paolo, Ranuccio, and Costanza. He recognized them as his own, made no secret of them, and went to live with them in Campo de' Fiori, which was then the business center of Rome, buying a building from the Augustinian friars of Santa Maria del Popolo.

The palazzo took shape over this building along the lines of the project designed by Antonio da Sangallo the Younger, who worked on it from 1515 until his death in 1546. Although the work proceeded slowly on this new structure, the cardinal continued to live there with his growing retinue of family members and servants. According to a census held in 1527, the number of people living there amounted to 366 "mouths," despite Paolo's very early death, Costanza's marriage to Bosio Sforza II in 1517, Ranuccio's fighting for the French (and subsequent demise in 1529), and Pier Luigi's presence in the imperial army of Charles V. Pier Luigi thus took part in the Sack of Rome in 1527, then went to live on his personal fief of Ronciglione, where his father had "acquired" the vicariat for 2,000 gold ducats.

The election of Alessandro as pope in 1534 instigated faster progress in the work in order to make the palazzo worthy of its owner's new role. The façade and the courtyard were enlarged, but the construction did not proceed beyond the ground floor. The pope, it seemed, had too many political pressures to be able to follow the progress of the building, so it was supervised by Pier Luigi, who had become duke of Castro and Nepi, and from 1545, duke of Parma. It was he who had the travertine brought from the quarries at Tivoli and the huge rafters for the ceilings from Carnia in the Friuli region. A determining factor, however, was the replacement of Sangallo by Michelangelo who, between 1546 and 1549, raised the height of the second storey and created another above it, capped by a superb cornice. This was done in such a way as to define the elegant and compact façade, now centered on the great loggia, on an axis with the portal, framed

The impressive atrium of the Palazzo, the work of Sangallo, is divided into three aisles by two rows of granite columns. The central aisle (left) has a barrel vault while the side aisles show a flat covering, as can be seen in the top picture opposite. In the niches are a series of antique Roman busts. In the bottom picture opposite is the side vestibule of the colonnade that runs around the square courtyard.

by four green columns from the baths at Acque Albule and the architrave with the escutcheon of Paul III and the Farnese lilies. This was as much as the pope was able to see before he died, though the interior of the building was already defined by its splendid square courtyard, impressive arcades, and large rooms giving onto the piazza. It was Vignola who, between 1569 and 1573, supervised the work on the façade with the two loggias at the back of the house, facing Via Giulia, and Giacomo Della Porta who finally concluded the architectural work in 1589.

The greatest glory of the palazzo, though, was its interior, with its frescoed ceilings and walls commissioned by the different family members who

came to live there. The first Farnese to resume permanent residence was the cardinal of Sant'Angelo, Ranuccio (1530–1565), who had his bedroom decorated by Daniele da Volterra with scenes from mythology and started to have the Sala della Loggia, also called the Sala dei Fasti Farnesiani, frescoed by Francesco Salviati. The iconographic program of the latter was designed to glorify the family through a commemorative depiction of the exploits and achievements of Ranuccio the Elder and the papal acts of Paul III. In the salon, an area of 300 meters built to a height of two floors, the decoration was limited to adorning the ceiling with shields and rosettes and the fireplace with escutcheons. The size of the room already made it impressive, and the colored marbles added a variegated light to the busts and tapestries on the walls.

Cardinal Alessandro (1520–1589), brother of Ranuccio, lived there and continued the work, having the frescoes of the Fasti Farnesiani finished by Taddeo

and Federico Zuccari so that the apotheosis of the family was complete. It was he who gave thought to the upkeep of the mansion, took care of the furnishings, and made the interior definitively into a palace. One of the rooms was the extraordinary library, with a collection of texts started by Paul III and increased by two brother cardinals, so that there were finally 238 Greek manuscripts and more than one thousand printed volumes of historical and scientific texts of great rarity. Every so often, between 1586 and 1592, the great condottiere Alessandro, duke of Parma, came to live there. When he was not fighting wars, he obviously resided in his own capital city, and yet he too took the trouble to have the decoration completed of the rooms on the second storey overlooking the Via Giulia.

The person who really achieved the final completion of the palazzo as a regal residence, however, was Cardinal Odoardo, who came to live there shortly before the death of his father Alessandro, staying there until the end in 1626. He retained the usufruct of the mansion since the "owner" was his brother, yet another Ranuccio, who preferred living in his native Parma. Odoardo started giving attention to the outside of this jewel of a building, decorating the piazza with two fountains, decorative elements in a scene that seemed predestined to be the theater of celebrations and processions. He had other buildings erected opposite the rear façade, the so-called external Camerini (little rooms) giving onto the courtyard; these were all frescoed by the Carracci. The masterpiece is in the gallery: the theme is the Triumph of Love, shown through scenes from Greek mythology. The painting is one of the most significant works of the seventeenth century, created at the dawn

of the Baroque era. Nowadays the palazzo really looks like a museum: to actually live there might seem to be a sacrilege or an excess of luxury and, above all, very difficult to keep up. In fact, this is what would create problems for this masterpiece a few years later.

In 1626, when Cardinal Odoardo died, no other Farnese wanted to live in the palazzo, which then remained practically deserted. The maintenance expenses were enormous and the new duke of Parma, Odoardo, decided to lease the building to France, which made it the site of its embassy. It may seem strange, but it was then that the palazzo began to really come alive. The ambassadors who succeeded each other there opened salons and rooms for receptions, parties, and guests, which all brought improvements to the whole area surrounding the diplomatic seat. Weddings and births of the French royal family were reasons for celebrations that colored the piazza with the help of sumptuous *macchine* (apparatuses to produce special effects) in the triumph of the ephemeral Baroque.

From Cardinal Alphonse de Richelieu, brother of the famous minister, to the duke of Créquy, from the duke of Chaulnes to the duke of Estrées and the marquis of Lavardin, the mansion displayed the living image of a royalty that contrasted with the papacy: diplomatic immunity permitted violence and abuse, outrage and arrogance. The palazzo unknowingly gave its hospitality to a "devil" in the person of an ambassador who embodied the "long hand" of the Sun King, who blinded the pale light of the papal government and conducted himself as master. Thus, the jewel lost its luster; it became a den of intrigue that the dances and celebrations could not conceal.

It was here that Christina of Sweden felt at home when she came to Rome after her abdication and conversion to Catholicism. Ranuccio Farnese had no problem accommodating her from December 1655 until July of the following year, since the palazzo was temporarily free of its lease to France on account of the aftermath of the war of Castro and the Thirty Years'

The small sloping courtyard on the first floor of the internal staircase is decorated with stucco and antique sculpture from Villa Madama, which belonged to the Farnese family until 1731. Two protoma are placed, the one on the right on fragments of a cornice over a sacrophagus with the nine muses, and the one on the left on the front of a sarcophagus representing Diana and Endymion, in turn over a strigilated sarcophagus with a portrait within a shield. Beside it, a group of antique remains, picturesquely arranged in Piranesi style.

117

On the previous pages: The ceiling of the famous Gallery decorated with frescoes by Annibale Carracci, assisted by his brother Agostino, del Domenichino, and del Lanfranco, based on the Alexandrian tales of Greek mythology. The detail shows the myth of Polyphemus and Galatea. The walls of the Gallery are faced with extraordinary stucco decorations which frame a series of frescoes and statues.

Triumph of Bacchus *in the middle of the Gallery vault.*

War (1618–1648). Christina set up court there, installed an academy, and was "at home" every Wednesday, allowing nobles, clerics, and artists to admire the marvels of the palazzo which had always been closed to all. Thus the Dado became the Roman center of literary, artistic, and fashionable society.

Behind this fine façade, however, intrigue and crime were still in waiting. The court was manipulated by unscrupulous secretaries to the queen, the brothers Santinelli and Rinaldo Monaldeschi, "three angels from hell," according to a chronicler of the period. They installed a gambling house on the ground floor, used the service area to prostitute eunuchs who were highly sought after by certain enthusiasts, and sold furniture, books, and precious objects. In short, Palazzo Farnese became a real den of thieves. This nasty story was not hidden by the fireworks regularly displayed on the piazza at the parties held in honor of

Christina. Even if her stay there lasted only seven months, it was enough to soil the image of one of the "four marvels" of Rome.

In the meantime, the palazzo began to lose its objects of value. Between 1662 and 1663 numerous works of art and precious furnishings left Rome for Parma. The well-known statues decorated by the Carracci were destroyed and only a few canvases were saved. The Farnese had no further interest in Rome and

dismantled a palace that they felt was no longer theirs; they even had the family crests removed from the palazzo's façade.

When, in 1731, the Farnese family became extinct and was absorbed into the Bourbon family with Elisabetta, wife of Philip V of Spain, their Roman property passed to their son, Charles, and through him to the Bourbons of Naples. In this way, what was left of the library made its way to Naples, along with all the statues and art works, which were transferred to the palace on Capodimonte in Naples, (now the Museo di Capodimonte) and the royal palace at Caserta.

The Bourbons were not interested in Palazzo Farnese, going there occasionally for short stays that coincided with visits to the pope. This is how Ferdinand II and Maria Teresa Isabella in 1834

transferred yet again the last pieces of antiquity to Naples. The palazzo was the residence of the administrator of the former Farnese property who certainly did not take the trouble to convince the sovereigns to restore the great rooms that were literally falling into ruins. It still functioned as a stop over for the king's minister during his diplomatic journeys, but

he did not report the degradation of the building, a degradation based on real ignorance. Suffice it to say that the rooms of the Camerini that had been frescoed by the Carracci were being used as kitchens.

When the Bourbons lost their throne in Naples and took refuge in Rome in 1861, the Dado risked becoming a royal palace again when the sovereigns

Francis II and Maria Sofia were accommodated in a building where the interior was falling to pieces. Some restoration work was carried out under the direction of the architect Cipolla, but more time and more money were needed.

The work was limited, therefore, to the strictly necessary. Some rooms on the first floor were

decorated, though not always with scientific techniques and artistic know-how: some of the ceilings were damaged through hasty whitewashing. The best work was done in the so-called Sala delle Prospettive (Hall of Views) and the Sala del Trono (Throne Room) between friezes and splays on the windows, with landscapes of the Kingdom of the Two Sicilies. The escutcheons of Cardinal Ranuccio and Paul III on the façade were renewed, and the empty gallery was filled with busts from the villa at Caprarola.

For the Bourbon family it was a bitter exile in a sad palace which had retained its regal nature mainly on the outside. Here, in 1869, the queen mother Maria Teresa died, and on that fateful 20 September 1870, after Francis II and Maria Sofia had left for Paris, only the count of Caserta and the count of Bari, brothers of the king, were left in the palazzo. They had the door closed and raised the Prussian flag. However, nothing happened. In any case, it no longer made sense for the Bourbons to live there; the palazzo was no more than a skeleton, and the restoration of the whole building was urgently needed.

When in 1874 France again asked to lease the palazzo as its legation, then its embassy, the Bourbons could hardly believe their luck. On the second floor the historic École Française de Rome was installed, which immediately restored the cultural atmosphere that had inspired the Biblioteca Farnese, over and beyond the

One of the reception rooms, featuring frescoes with mock panels on the walls and rich stucco decoration in the frieze, of marked manneristic stamp— evidence of the lengthy work carried out in the Palazzo over a long period, until the end of the sixteenth century.

The short side of the great Gallery with rich wall decoration. Above the door, the Lady with the Unicorn *by Domenichino.*

The impressive salon is built to the height of two storeys of the Palazzo. On the walls, under the rich coffered ceiling, are a series of tapestries reproducing the frescoes by Raphael in the Vatican Stanze, and a monumental fireplace, flanked by the statues of Abundance *and* Peace *by Guglielmo della Porta.*

A corner of the Sala dei Fasti Farnesiani (Hall of Farnesian Magnificence), which took its name from the frescoes by Francesco Salviati and Taddeo Zuccari aimed at glorifying the origins and historical lineage of the Farnese family.

museum context which by now had gone for ever. In 1911 the lease was transformed into a sale for three million francs with the right of redemption by Italy within a period of twenty-five years. This right was exercised in 1936, when the Italian state acquired the palazzo, but Italy immediately ceded it back to France for ninety-nine years and a nominal rent.

It is thanks to France that a series of restorations has renewed its magnificent rooms and brought the Dado back to its original decorative condition. The palace has found itself again and has returned to being a "marvel."

Opposite:
Detail of the fresco in the Sala dei Fasti Farnesiani of the Entry of Charles V in Rome *by Francesco Salviati.*

PALAZZO MATTEI DI GIOVE

MATTEI

Below and opposite:
Details of the second floor of
the first courtyard of the
Palazzo, with the loggia and a
wall covered with antique busts
and bas-reliefs and a wealth of
stucco decoration.

Giacomo Leopardi did not like this palazzo because of "[its] dreadful untidiness, confusion, nothingness, unbearable pettiness, and unutterable shabbiness, and the other frightful qualities that reign in this house." He wrote these words to his brother Carlo on 25 November 1822, in truth only three days after his arrival in Rome for a stay with his uncle, Carlo

Teodoro Antici, owner of the mansion at that time. The poet did not change his mind even at the end of 1823, when he returned to an opinion evidently weighed upon by his state of innate melancholy and solitude, aggravated by the idea that "these immense structures" the noble mansions of Rome in general "are so many spaces thrown among the people, instead of being

A corner of the loggia with an antique bust and the iron grille of a window, surmounted by a bas-relief.

spaces that contain people". There was also the fact that he was obliged to spend "two hundred hours in bed" in that room on the third floor on account of an injury to his foot. Nevertheless, those five months of Giacomo Leopardi's sojourn there became something of a boast for this palazzo, which is one of the buildings of the *isola Mattei* (Mattei block) and the last of the complex to be built, brushing out of its way some of the houses owned by the dukes of Giove.

It was built by Asdrubale Mattei, son of Alessandro, who was responsible too for the building next to it, known as Caetani. Asdrubale, who lived here while his own house was being completed in time for his marriage to Costanza Gonzaga, entrusted the architectural design to Carlo Maderno in 1598. The work lasted twenty years although the section linking it to the family mansion was already finished in 1613.

From 1618 it rose imposingly on the corner of Via Caetani and Via dei Funari, with its façades in bricks and travertine, its ashlar angle irons, a cornice with the heraldic devices of the Mattei and the Gonzaga families, and a covered roof-terrace with a loggia that looked down onto the Sant'Angelo district.

The courtyard, however, was the main feature of the palazzo. It was literally covered with side walls of antique bas-reliefs, busts, and statues, and had a two-storied open loggia that was also filled with plaster statues and busts of emperors. This courtyard opened

Interior of the loggia and, opposite, a complete view of the loggia of the courtyard with the arcade below giving entry to the stairs. The wealth of sculpture decorating the courtyard forms part of what was one of the most valuable private collections of antique marble existing in Rome. Most of it is now in the Vatican Museums.

128

The landing on the stairs with a stucco vault and walls richly decorated with antique sculptures in niches and crossed bas-reliefs in stucco. All the decoration was carried out by Donato Mazzi between 1606 and 1611. Opposite, detail of elegant bas-relief.

onto a second, garden courtyard with a fountain featuring a grotesque mask that poured water into a sarcophagus with leonine protomes. From here four flights of steps, decorated with marble figures between plaster cornices, led to the upper floors.

It was really an entrance hall in the form of an archaeological gallery, even though the antique relics represented only a part of the large Mattei collection, which also occupied space in their villa on the Caelian hill, the present-day Celimontana public park. Sold by Giuseppe Mattei to Pope Clement XIII in 1766, the

Solomon by Pietro da Cortona. These are treasures that are still linked to the palazzo today, not having undergone the fate suffered by the archaeological collection, and they can be considered an accurate reflection of the religious faith of the Mattei family that survived even beyond their own dynasty.

In fact, the palazzo does not have any particular stories to recount other than those tied to the intense papal fidelity of its owners. No fewer than four Mattei cardinals started their lives in this mansion in the persons of Girolamo (1546–1563), Luigi

collection of marble figures was in fact the only patrimonial wealth, apart from the palazzo furnishings, of which the family could boast, a sign above all of an austere splendor which was nevertheless in line with their very reserved nobility, one that had never indulged in excessive pomp on account of the family's profound religious beliefs.

It was probably for this reason that the themes chosen for the frescoes in the rooms were not of secular character but concentrated on biblical events. They were the work of the most famous artists in Rome in 1615 and include *Stories of Jacob* by Francesco Albani and Domenichino, *Stories of Joseph* by Giovanni Lanfranco and Pomarancio, and *Stories of*

(1702–1758), Alessandro (1744–1820), and Lorenzo (1748–1833). The spirit of this noble residence did not change much when, once the Mattei di Giove line was extinct, the property passed in 1802 to the Antici family as a result of the marriage of the only daughter of Giuseppe Mattei, Maria Anna, to Marquis Carlo Teodoro Antici of Recanati.

The Antici too were very religious, with a Giambattista as bishop in the eighteenth century and a Tommaso appointed cardinal by Pius VI in 1789. Their inheritance from the Mattei family certainly elevated them to the first level of Roman nobility, but without it turning their heads and with a rigorous respect for religion in a life that was probably monotonous.

Detail of the refined and elegant bas-relief.

The decoration of the Gallery was carried out by a group of painters including Pietro da Cortona and Pietro Paolo Bonzi, called il Gobbo. The latter was responsible for the representation of the Mattei estates in the lunettes, like Maccarese on the right. In the cornice below runs a rich frieze of gilded stucco with Bacchante putti playing with the heraldic symbols of the Mattei family, by the French artist Jean Maszriet.

One of eight gilded monochrome clipei inserted above the lunettes, on subjects taken from the biblical Book of Kings; they are held by a couple of youthful nudes, partly reclining on the cornice.

Opposite:
The middle part of the vault with a fresco by Pietro da Cortona, the Meeting of King Solomon and the Queen of Sheba, alluding to the second marriage in 1595 of the Marquis Asdrubale Mattei to Costanza Gonzaga of the Counts of Novellara.

132

Part of the side façade of the first courtyard with antique statues and craters on high Renaissance pedestals. On the one supporting the statue is sculpted an eagle crowned with the coat of arms of the Mattei di Giove family.

Culturally they had little to offer Giacomo Leopardi when he stayed there, considering that the literary claims of his uncle went no further than a translation of the *Life of Jesus Christ* by Friedrich Leopold Stolberg. The poet reached the point of telling his brother Carlo that as far as "life at the Antici residence … ; which we two discussing together did not know … if it can be called life, in any case" was concerned, he found "the devil was much worse than the one painted." For him, "instead of pleasure there is nothing but boredom to be had," which he tried to escape by reading—even if Rome was "a literary dunghill." He himself in his room did not manage to write anything of importance,

only frivolous pieces that were published in a newspaper.

One evening in bed during the carnival season, he thought again about a woman he had seen dancing on the Via del Corso and confided by letter, as usual, to his brother, that a woman when dancing "seems to communicate something inexplicable and divine to her form, a special strength to her body, a faculty that is more than human." In short, it was not the religious spirit of those rooms and their biblical stories that gave the poet his inspiration.

Life in the palazzo went on for the Antici family along the lines reported by Leopardi, but it bore fruit in the context of pontifical Rome. Giacomo's cousin, Matteo, was elected senator of Rome in 1859 and took the surname Mattei. His son Tommaso was inscribed in 1868 among the Roman princes and obtained a number of titles that gave prestige to the palazzo. Matteo was prince and marquis Antici Mattei, count of

the suitably restored beautiful rooms a series of institutions that would certainly have stimulated Leopardi's interests in a livelier stay.

Now housed in the palazzo are the Istituto Storico Italiano per l'Età Moderna e Contemporanea (Italian Historical Institute for Modern and Contemporary

Castel San Pietro and of the Sacro Palazzo Lateranense, lord of Pescia, knight of Malta, confidential server to His Holiness and Grand Cross of San Gregorio Magno. The palazzo derived considerable glory from his wife Carlotta too, inasmuch as she was a Gallarati Scotti of the dukes of San Pietro in Galatina and of the princes of Molfetta.

Less than two generations passed before the Antici Mattei family put the mansion up for sale in 1938, and it probably lost the reasons for its noble and pious image. However, it gained others in line with a certain innate austerity, which gave rise to firm cultural objectives. The Italian state bought it and installed in

History); the Biblioteca di Storia Moderna e Contemporanea (Library of Modern and Contemporary History) with at least 300,000 books and journals; the Discoteca di Stato (State Recording Archive), with its collection of rare sound reproduction equipment and a library of 45,000 volumes; and the Centro Italiano di Studi Americani (Italian Center of American Studies), which boasts the most complete library in Europe on this subject.

Two more antique statues on the side of the courtyard opposite the loggia, with a passage to the second courtyard which has an entrance onto Via Caetani, featuring luxuriant vegetation.

PALAZZO SACCHETTI

SACCHETTI

The architect Antonio da Sangallo the Younger in 1542 bought a series of plots of land in the Florentine quarter at the beginning of Via Giulia, the splendid straight line that ran between the districts of Ponte and Regola. He wanted to set up house there, so that he too, after building so many great houses for nobles and cardinals, would have his own real mansion where he could live with his family. "He completed it successfully," wrote Vasari, spending on it "thousands of scudi" in the stretch of road that precedes those characteristic "*sofà,*" curious plinths of the Tribunal which was designed by Bramante but never built. The *domus Sangalli*, which was similar to the nearby Palazzo Farnese, would have needed greater finishing and larger structures to have competed with the Dado, but the brilliant architect did not have the means to incur further expenditure. He died in 1546, and only six years later, his son Orazio sold the unfinished mansion to Cardinal Giovanni Ricci di Montepulciano for 3,145 scudi. The cardinal had no such problem

Front elevation of the Palazzo on Lungotevere Sangallo with a loggia decorated with antique sculptures, two masks and a female head with diadem, perhaps Juno, the background to a beautiful orchard of citrus trees. Above right, a bust in the Audience Room of Cardinal Giovanni Ricci di Montepulciano, one of the owners of the Palazzo before the Sacchetti family; opposite the family coat of arms, carved into the ceiling of the Dining Room.

committing himself to an enlargement of the building so that it would appear important enough to be suitable for him, since he was treasurer to Pope Julius III and certainly did not need to economize. He entrusted the project to Nanni di Baccio Bigio, under whose direction the building reached more or less its present dimension.

The decorations of the apartments on the main floor were splendid. In the audience chamber of the cardinal, which was also called the Chamber of the Mappamundi, Francesco Salviati frescoed the *Stories of David*, which remains one of the marvels of the palazzo, a masterpiece of Roman Mannerism. In the other rooms were landscapes, grotesques, and mythological and biblical scenes, the work of French and Italian artists, including Fantino, Sordo, and Veneziano.

After all this embellishment, obtained at huge expense, the cardinal ceded the property in 1557 to the Genoese financier Tommaso Marino di Terranova.

Eleven years later, however, in 1568, Cardinale Ricci bought back the mansion in order to enjoy it until his death in 1574, when his nephew Giulio inherited it. Two years later it was sold again, to the Pisan banker Tiberio Ceoli.

It seemed to be a property that nobody wanted—or more probably that was too costly, so that its buyers were forced to resell it continually in order to get back the money spent in expansions or decorative work. The very wealthy Ceoli family did not hesitate to undertake new work. In the little more than thirty years that they owned it, they brought a series of alterations to the building that were so substantial as to give to the palazzo an entirely new dimension. This started with the raising of a floor, a cornice decorated with their heraldic star emblem, and a new block toward the Tiber, including a garden and a loggia-nymphaeum overlooking the river, with a painted façade, which in time, unfortunately, would lose its color. The Ceoli enriched the palazzo with their precious collection of

The Dining Room built by Cardinal Ricci in 1573, with the splendid ceiling carried out by Ambrogio Bonazzini. It became a gallery for the rich marble collection of the new owners, the Ceoli, who entrusted the decoration of the walls to Giacomo Rocca from Salerno. The frescoes represent sibyls and prophets, copies of the series by Michelangelo in the Sistine Chapel. Under the Sacchetti family, two frescoes were added by Pietro da Cortona, a Holy Family *and* Adam and Eve.

138

Decorative detail of the frieze and the floor of the sixteenth-century rooms of the piano nobile, one of which is reproduced below. They were decorated with landscapes and mythological scenes by a group of French and Italian artists, including Maître Ponce, Marc Duval, Nicole de Bruyne, Fantino, Marco Marcucci, Giovanni Antonio Veneziano, Stefano Pieri, and G.A. Napolitano.

145

antique sculptures, which were placed in the courtyard; the building thus became a sort of museum. The family was also responsible for decorating, with a fountain representing a putto between dolphins, the façade on the corner of Vicolo del Cefalo, a street name which justly commemorates them.

In 1608 the Ceoli family moved out. They sold the sculpture collection to Cardinal Scipione Borghese, except for a third-century A.D. relief representing an episode in the life of Emperor Septimius Severus, which remains in the entrance hall of the palazzo. The palazzo was sold to Cardinal Ottavio Acquaviva d'Aragona, who had a small chapel built on the left

side of the courtyard, which was entirely frescoed by a pupil of Pietro da Cortona, Agostino Ciampelli. The cardinal's heirs could not keep up with the expense of maintaining the building and sold it in 1649; it was bought by the Sacchetti family, who had originated in Florence and moved to Rome because of their conflicts with the Medici. The Sacchetti gave it up to no one and are still the owners today.

Even though the building was fairly well defined in terms of its structure, and leaving aside the splendid frescoes by Pietro da Cortona in the dining room of the gallery and the restructuring of the nymphaeum, probably by Rainaldi, it was the Sacchetti family who gave the palazzo its greatest prestige by maintaining its artistic features right up to the present time.

The family's greatest stamp on the building derived without doubt from Cardinal Giulio (1583–1663), papal legate to Ferrara and Bologna, where he gathered a large collection of paintings that enriched the palazzo until 1748, when the collection

was bought by Pope Benedict XIV to form the nucleus of the Capitoline Gallery.

A lover of the verdant, Giulio also bought Villa della Rufinella at Tuscolo, renamed Sacchetta, which was sold in the eighteenth century to the Jesuits, the estate at Pigneto, which was sold to the Torlonia family in 1861, and the estate at Castel Fusano, which was reclaimed and improved with approximately 30,000 pines, then sold in 1755 to the Chigi family; it is now the property of the Commune of Rome. The palazzo in Via Giulia played a special role in botanical history: the garden there was the first place in Rome where oleanders, at the time very rare, were grown and cultivated. The plant was the *nerium oleander*, popularly called "amazza l'asino" (donkey-killer).

In line with this real patriarch who made his family fortune thanks to the wealth deriving from his ecclesiastical appointment, the Sacchetti family always maintained its support of the papacy, and this indisputably bore fruit, also in the person of another family cardinal, Urbano (1640–1705). Bishop of Viterbo, he lived the last years of his life in this palazzo, and was buried in the nearby church of San Giovanni dei Fiorentini.

However, the prestigious titles in the history of Rome that marked the pride of the Sacchetti family, marquises of Castel Romano, were those of curators of the Campidoglio and Forieri Maggiori. Thanks to this post, which was hereditary in the family from 1794 with Scipione (1767–1840), the Sacchetti have carried out the functions of prefects of the papal palace, having the responsibility, among other things, to direct the route of the papal chair in solemn ceremonies. Sacchetti loyalty to the pope has remained unswerving over the centuries, so much so that in 1932 Pius XI conferred on them the title of "princes of the Baldacchino," authorizing them to bear the papal title, still used by them, of "Don" and "Donna."

This palazzo also has a literary curiosity attached to it, thanks to the French writer Émile Zola, who set part of his novel *Rome*, written in the last years of the nineteenth century, in this very building, renamed "Boccanera" for the occasion. Prince Dario, one of the main characters in the novel, died from eating poisoned figs that had been intended for his uncle, Cardinal Boccanera. According to the literary fiction, a drama of passion upset these walls with an assassination organized in the Vatican, but this does not diminish the aristocratic and cultural atmosphere of the building and its real owners.

The Sacchetti are open to cultural initiatives in their own drawing rooms and, in a spirit of patronage that does them honor, they have opened their courtyards and the palazzo itself to the general public.

VILLA MADAMA

MADAMA
MARGARET OF
AUSTRIA

View of the Palazzina from Villa Madama, and, opposite, the interior of the loggia 'of Raphael', with the frescoes of classical myths by Giulio Romano, in the splendor of the cupola and the large niches, decorated with shells and festoons by Giovanni da Udine.

Aristocratically alone and aloof at the foot of Monte Mario, this villa evokes the noble and reserved personality of the sixteenth-century lady from whom it takes its name, Madama (Madame) Margaret of Austria, the illegitimate daughter of the Emperor Charles V, who owned it and used it as a country home during the period of her residence in Rome, from 1538 to 1550. Its construction, however, dates back to the period when Leo X was pope (1513–21). Cardinal Giulio de' Medici, his cousin, had it built as a country *vigna* (vineyard) to go along with his city mansion (now the seat of the Senate), the latter in the Sant'Eustachio quarter. By a strange coincidence, this is also called "Madama."

The cardinal was motivated by a desire to emulate his cousin, like himself a believer in the Renaissance ideals of art, literature, and nature, who had a villa *fuori porta*, outside the gates of the city, in the Magliana area. Here the pope often passed entire days immersed in plays, poetry readings, sumptuous banquets, and falconry. The cardinal was not willing to follow his cousin in the "train of cardinals, the swarm of poets, the host of barons and princes, all making such a racket that they seemed to be part of a Bacchanal," as Gregorovius wrote. He wanted a quiet place where he could spend time with a few close friends in a refined artistic environment.

The cardinal used the services of the greatest artists of his time. According to Vasari, Raphael made the drawings and his student Giulio Romano supervised the building work, which, however, he would never complete. Others wrote that the idea for the complex originated with Antonio da Sangallo the Younger, whose original drawing still exists. This involved a series of loggias, colonnades, exedras, terraces, and walkways that were to be developed in scenic succession along the slope of the hill down to the Tiber.

This plan was only partially carried out, perhaps on account of the unstable nature of the terrain, but the vicissitudes of the city of Rome at the time when Cardinal Giulio de' Medici became pope must have played a role as well. Taking the name of Clement VII, the new pope had to face a serious political and military crisis culminating in the Sack of Rome in 1527. Certainly the completion of the villa was the last thing on his mind, although it had nevertheless become an elegant house in the meantime. The stairway opened onto a sort of amphitheater, with an Italianate garden in front of a fishpond. A vestibule opened onto the loggia known as the loggia of Raphael, with frescoes by Giulio Romano evoking classical myths. It had a splendid dome and niches decorated with shells and festoons. A series of rooms opened up from there, their walls illuminated with the exploits and heraldic symbols of the Medici family, culminating in the room named after Giulio Romano, with a complex frieze of exotic animals in the triumphant Medici coat of arms. Among the curiosities of the garden was Giovanni da Udine's marble fountain portraying the head of the elephant Annone, which had been a gift of the king of Portugal to Leo X in 1514 and which had become the pet of the Roman populace owing to its good nature and intelligence. Another curiosity consisted of two stucco giants by Baccio Bandinelli placed as guardians at each side of the doorway that led from the terrace to the rustic garden, a secret place reserved for the owner and his guests.

Giulio de' Medici was able to enjoy this bucolic environment when he was a cardinal and in his first years as pope, where he could pass the time without being surrounded by too many people. He reserved it mainly as a place for quiet reflection, reading, and relaxed conversations with artists and scientists. Here he surely must have savored *Arcadia* by Jacopo Sannazzaro, who also dedicated a poem to him, on the birth of Christ, in 1526. Here in 1533 he had the Copernican system explained to him by the learned

Johann Albert Widmanstadt. And on the fateful day of 5 May 1533, Margaret of Austria, still only a girl of ten, arrived here on her way to Naples where she would wait to be of age to marry Alessandro de' Medici, duke of Florence. She was not greeted here by the pope but by the papal steward and a number of nobles who would make up the procession bringing her to the Vatican to be received by Clement VII. In retrospect, we could say that when the young Margaret kissed the pope's slipper, it was as if she had sealed the deed that would give her the villa on Monte Mario when she became "Madama."

When Clement VII died in 1534, the villa effectively passed to the Medici family. The first to inherit it was the young cardinal Ippolito, who went to live there, but only briefly. The exiled Florentines, determined to oust Alessandro de' Medici from the throne of the grand duchy of Florence, appointed Ippolito to take an embassy of protest against the atrocities of his vassal to Charles V in Tunis, where the emperor had led an expedition against Turkish pirates. Ippolito, Alessandro's step-brother, did set out to make

the voyage, but at Itri, near Gaeta, while he waited to embark for Tunis, he was poisoned and died. It was thus Alessandro de' Medici himself who inherited the villa. He married Margaret on 19 June 1536. The marriage did not last long. The grand duke was assassinated only six months later. Margaret, a widow at only fifteen, was not neglected by her father, Charles V, who wanted to see her finally settled at an aristocratic level. As a widow, she had no right to the house of the Medici and was thus forced to marry the fourteen-year-old Ottavio Farnese, grandson of Pope Paul III.

Margaret was back in Rome again and spent her first day, 3 November 1538, at the villa on Monte Mario before making her ceremonial entry into Rome. The Senate and Roman nobility paid her homage, offering her a dinner at the villa. By then the procession and the reception by Pope Paul III in the Vatican must have become routine for her. Moreover, she was experiencing bitter apprehension at the thought of the marriage her father was forcing on her but which she did not want. She felt degraded by a husband whose only title was duke of an obscure duchy, Camerino. What was even worse, he was still a child. Margaret refused to consummate the marriage, slamming the door in her husband's face in Palazzo Cesi in Borgo, where she was obliged to live, because the various claimants to the Medici inheritance made both the palazzo in the city and the villa outside it unavailable.

That year Margaret obtained the villa on Monte Mario and the usufruct of the other property. She moved to the villa and her husband went with her, but she was still determined not to yield to him, and Ottavio stayed outside Rome much of the time, in Castro, the fief where he recently had become duke. It is not difficult to imagine the thoughts that must have passed through her head in the loggia of Raphael, the unhappy thoughts of an unsatisfied woman, cheered only by the presence of a few Florentine friends. Her deep religious faith sustained her in this difficult period, and she dedicated herself to charitable activities and missionary work. For the people she was "Madama."

In the long run, however, Charles V's pressure persuaded her—together with the compensation of the considerable income she was due from the Medici—to change her mind about her husband. In 1543 she consummated her marriage and twins were born, Carlo and Alessandro. This birth was a source of great emotion for their grandfather, Pope Paul III, who did not feel up to participating in his grandsons' baptism and the reception afterward in the palazzo in Sant'Eustachio, but spent the day in the vineyard on Monte Mario, already known as Villa Madama.

Margaret remained in Rome until 1550, a few months after the death of Paul III, and then she joined her husband in Parma where he had succeeded his father Pier Luigi as duke. Nevertheless, she continued to be the owner of the villa on Monte Mario, even though she never saw it again. It is probably justifiable to think that she continued to have a soft spot in her heart for this mansion, having understood its spiritual meaning. Perhaps it is for this reason that she offered it to the poet Giovan Battista Guarini, who may have found the bucolic inspiration for his *Pasto Fido* there. But a long period of neglect was already beginning for Villa Madama because the owners hardly ever used it, preferring to use it as a place to house their guests.

On Margaret's death in 1586 the property passed to the Farnese family, the dukes of Parma and Piacenza, who already owned the Farnesina on Via della Lungara as an alternative to their splendid Dado, near Via Giulia. They gave over the villa to literary and music academies, so much so that in 1672 the Accademia degli Sfaccendati for music and theater was founded there. In 1731 it passed to the Bourbon family of Naples who never came to Rome and who accommodated writers and artists there as guests. Between 1786 and 1787 Goethe came frequently to admire the marvelous sunsets, with the view of a solitary pine on the slope of Monte Mario which later became almost legendary. He immortalized it in drawings of the scene that for him was evocative of Olympian fantasies.

These were the last moments of the villa's splendor. It was later turned into an agricultural warehouse complete with hayloft. It was then used as a barracks for the troops during the Jacobin Republic in 1799, during the Napoleonic occupation, and again during the Roman Republic of 1849. By then, it was in a state of total abandon. As Gaetano Moroni wrote in 1860, "It no longer has the form of a villa, with no traces left of magnificence." The Bourbons were in Rome at the time, exiles from their previous kingdom that was now annexed to the unified Italy, but they had enough to do restoring the dilapidated Palazzo Farnese to a state of decent habitation to be able to even think about restoring their mansion on Monte Mario.

Villa Madama would have to wait another fifty years to return to life. In 1913 an engineer from Toulouse, Maurice Bergès, bought it and carried out a series of restorations on a design by Marcello Piacentini. These were finished by the following owner, Count Carlo Dentice of Frasso, who acquired it in 1925. The building was restored to its former splendor—only then was it finally completed, following the original unfinished drawing as closely as possible, closing the loggia and lengthening the building. In 1937 the villa was rented by the Ministry of Foreign Affairs; in June 1941 it was bought by the Italian state and used as the headquarters of the ministry.

Curious fountain in the gardens, created by Giovanni da Udine and showing the head of the elephant Annone, which was presented to Leo X in 1514 by the King of Portugal, and became the pet of the Roman population because it was so good-natured and intelligent.

The "rustic" garden of the Villa, featuring rows of cypress trees lining the paths, rustic fountains, and enormous pots with plants. Opposite, the hanging labyrinth garden in front of the loggia, with the statues of the two Colossi by Baccio Bandinelli, guarding the entrance gate to the 'rustic' garden.

VILLA MEDICI

THE GRAND DUKE
OF TUSCANY

The façade overlooking the gardens is made up of a central body opening onto a Serlian loggia squeezed between two avant-corps surmounted by roof-garden towers. A feature are the splendid decorations of antique bas-reliefs between theatrical masks that cover it completely. On the sides are mythological scenes and sumptuous garlands from the Ara Pacis and in the center, scenes of sacrifices, soldiers on the River Danube, and the struggle of Hercules with the Nemean lion.

The location of this villa, at the top of the Spanish Steps, is legendary. In ancient times, Lucullus had his villa here. His is a name that recalls not only luxurious living, banquets, and legendary voluptuousness, but also a fabulous library. It was here that Messalina ended her days; assassinated by order of the emperor Claudius, she still wanders with his ghost in the woods, or so the legend says, when the moon is full. Then the site was a vineyard and convent.

In 1540, however, Cardinal Marcello Crescenzi bought the vineyard with a rustic house, "a cube on two floors with a tower"—nothing luxurious, just a resting place especially for walks on the hills in the company of the Olivetan monks whose protector he was. When he died in 1552, it was inherited by his son, "his Magnificence Don Camillo Crescenzi, Roman nobleman," who did not know what to do with it since he did not have the ecological spirit of his father. He kept the property for twelve years, then sold it to "their Magnificences Don Giulio and Don Giovanni Ricci," nephews of Cardinal Giovanni Ricci of Montepulciano, the same cardinal who had built a beautiful mansion in Via Giulia, now known as Palazzo Sacchetti. The Ricci family restored the house and the vineyard. Indirectly it was the cardinal who took care of them, and he charged Nanni di Baccio Bigio with the task of building a larger residence, taking advantage of the existing structure. The result was a building on two floors with a loggia and a tower. The rooms on the piano nobile were decorated with the family crest, a chestnut and the sun, carved everywhere. The garden took shape with the raising of its level to hide the vault of a Roman cistern, and the whole complex looked more dignified, boasting a monumental entrance on Via di Porta Pinciana and the creation of the Salita di San Sebastianello, thanks to the purchase of some neighboring vineyards.

In short, the villa acquired substance, but when the cardinal died in 1574, his nephews showed no interest in maintaining the property. They sold it two years later to Cardinal Ferdinando de' Medici, a young man passionately interested in art and nature, who wanted to build himself a luxurious residence. The villa in its present state was not enough for him, and he instructed Bartolomeo Ammannati to enlarge the whole complex.

The central part of the building was altered, creating a master apartment underneath the loggia and adding another wing intended to house the gallery. The gardens were designed Italian-style in front of the façade of the palazzo, which was rich with carvings, busts, and antique statues bought from the Valle and Caprarica collections. It was a suitable background for the culture that the cardinal wanted to represent as a genuine patron. The beauty of Venus and Cupid and the expressive force of divinity and emperors spread over the boxwood and myrtle pathways up to the Parnasso, the hill on the remains of the Temple of Fortune, and resounded to the music of players and singers that the cardinal had brought with him from his native Florence.

However, the villa was a mine of ideas. Gregory XIII often came here to walk about the grounds, debating with his cardinal, and the two of them created institutions of renewal like the Congregatio de Propaganda Fide (Congregation for the Spreading of the Faith) and the Stamperia Orientale (Oriental Press) which served to strengthen Catholic faith throughout the world. The cardinal became responsible for these

View over the gardens of Villa Medici from the loggia made up of columns of cipollino and Egyptian granite, flanked by two lions and delimited by the balustrade with the Mercury Fountain in the center.

Detail of the loggia with a flight of steps and a marble lion with a ball under its paw, evoking the coat of arms of Cardinal Ferdinando de' Medici, who carried out improvement works on the Villa between 1576 and 1587.

Opposite:
Fountain with obelisk in the center of the gardens in front of the loggia, a vast flat space broken up only by the flower beds, which have been remade recently in accordance with the original design. In the background are the woods with a gazebo in the place where an antique temple to Fortune used to be.

Two views of Villa Medici frescoed in the frieze of the small study of Cardinal Ferdinando de' Medici, which is on the edge of the park in a hanging garden above the Aurelian walls. The frescoes, carried out, like all the decoration, by Jacopo Zucchi between 1576 and 1577, do not offer a very realistic picture of the villa as they differ, even from each other, in a number of details, leading to the supposition that they reproduce architect's drawings known to the painter.

On the following pages:
The ceiling and a corner of the pavilion of Federico de' Medici. The decoration of the vault, representing a pergola populated by a multitude of birds and concealed in the eighteenth century by several layers of plaster, has been brought to light recently. The grotesque-style vestibule, with allegories of the seasons and some of Aesop's Fables, gives three views of Villa Medici along the frieze over the door.

161

The statue of the goddess Rome at the furthest point of the park bordering the Passeggiata del Pincio. This colored statue was recovered from the area of Monte Cavallo and bought by the Cardinal d'Este for his garden at the Quirinale. It was later donated by Gregory XIII to the Cardinal de' Medici, who placed it here in front of the entrance to Via di Porta Pinciana, in the opening of the boundary wall, embellished by two masks.

One of the masks that have always decorated the wall of the statue of the goddess Rome. In 1822 the sculpture was moved by Valadier to the area in front of the loggia, but it was later brought back to its original site.

missionary activities and organized them from the villa as an authentic manager. He even established the technical means of distribution and the ability to print in the various alphabets (Syriac, Arabic, Coptic, Persian) needed to translate the books that were the basis of the Christian faith. The villa became a center for oriental culture, a place of preparation for

missionaries and researchers. As in other times Roman intellectuals had rushed to the library of Lucullus, so now scientists crowded around the collections at Villa Medici in order to discover the Orient. The villa was a reference point for Catholic Europe and the Counter-Reformation, and the cardinal could say with pride that he had raised the place to the glory of his family, leaving there an indelible stamp, immortalized in his own apartment by the decoration of Jacopo Zucchi.

These were the rooms above the loggia, dedicated to the Elements, the Muses, and the Loves of Jupiter, where the ceilings glorified the culture and patronage of Ferdinando with a sort of talisman that protected his glorious future. Female figures displayed the attributes of Muses and planets with zodiac signs of precise astrological value formed a horoscope which prophesied power—power that for a cardinal could be identified only in the papacy, even if in fact this is not what transpired.

In October 1587, during a hunt near Florence, Ferdinando's brother, Grand Duke Francesco, died. The following day Francesco's wife Bianca Cappello also died. Rumours of poison abounded, and suspicion fell on Ferdinando who was the absolute and only beneficiary since there were no male children of the marriage. It was a disgrace for the upright cardinal: the autopsies declaring that Francesco had cyrrhosis of the liver in its final stages and that his wife had a tumor in the breast served him little. Two sudden deaths taking place within twenty-four hours left public opinion incredulous. Ferdinando had, in any case, to take the succession. He would not become pope, but he did become the third grand duke of Tuscany. The power indicated by his horoscope in his room in the Roman villa still did come true.

In a ceremony marked by its solemnity, Ferdinando resigned from his cardinal's office and succeeded to his throne. He never returned to his residence on the Trinità dei Monti. Another Medici cardinal, Alessandro, went to live there. He was a distant relative but still a cardinal, capable of honoring the place that had reached exceptional social and cultural heights. The only problem was that Alessandro was not a man of culture. He liked the scientists and protected them, but he was not one of them. He was a simple man. Nevertheless, with him the villa was further enriched by new marvels, including the Venus, later named after the Medici. Brought to light during excavations at Hadrian's villa in Tivoli, it would reign in the loggia until Innocent X, scandalized, judged it unsuitable for the residence of a cardinal and sent it to Florence. With Alessandro de' Medici, fifteen sculptures of Niobe came to light from Porta San Giovanni, as well as vases, sarcophagi, and obelisks. Then too, there was the fountain, a masterpiece by Annibale Lippi, which became the emblem of the villa in the piazza in front of the heavy gate of studded oak. Alessandro lived among these splendors for sixteen years until 1 April 1605, when the Sacred College chose him as pope. He was named Leo XI and ruled for only twenty-seven days. The villa, however, in a mysterious link with power, continued to bring good luck to those who lived in it.

Perhaps it for this reason that Grand Duke Ferdinando made over the property to his third son, eleven-year-old Carlo, who was intended for the ecclesiastical life. He did in fact became a cardinal and deacon of the Sacred College. Though he exercised considerable influence in the Vatican, he never become pope. With him the chain linking the villa's inhabitants to power snapped.

From then on, the villa did not have a permanent resident. It was considered the summer residence of the Medici ambassadors to Rome and sometimes lodged members of the family who were passing through Rome, or other important personages. In 1610, the second son of Grand Duke Ferdinando, Prince Francesco, commander of the Medici army, stayed there for a few days; in 1618 the grand duke of Mantua, Ferdinando Gonzaga, was accommodated there for a week while he was busy trying to persuade the pope to grant an annulment of his brother Vincenzo's marriage; in 1627 the seventeen-year-old Grand Duke Ferdinando II resided there during his travels to Rome to gain experience of life before starting to govern; in 1633 Galileo was detained there between June 26 and July 7, after being sentenced by the Holy Office and before being moved to Arcetri; in 1630 and 1650, the painter Diego Velázquez resided there, precursor of the scholars of the Académie de France who would also live there, and left the masterly strokes of his brush in portraits of Gian Lorenzo Bernini and of Innocent X.

The arrival in Rome in 1655 of Christina of Sweden brought about the change on the Lippi

fountain from the lily holding a jet of water to a cannonball: it was the one "shot" by the queen from Castel Sant'Angelo with the intention of "knocking" at the gate of the villa where she was awaited. Since she was late for her appointment, she wanted to prove her punctuality in this way—and the cannon ball was subsequently used to decorate the fountain.

There was no further direct Medici participation in the life of the villa, which eventually was almost abandoned and, in part, was left to fall into ruins. History records no more official visits or important guests for more than a century. Activities were so few that there was no documented reaction to the passing over of the property in 1736. In that year the Lorraine family succeeded the Medici family as heirs to the

In the garden and the woods at Villa Medici there were once many fountains and nymphaeums watered by the Acqua Vergine. Many of these featured female statues, particularly in the attitudes of the goddess Venus, like this fountain, said to be of Faustina, evoking ancient Lucullan times in this place.

grand duchy of Tuscany, and they became also the new owners of the "royal Villa of Monte Pincio," as it was now called, even though this name did not eclipse its former denomination—today it is still known as the Villa Medici.

The villa recorded a few days of glory in 1769 when from March 6 to April 27 its legal owner, Grand Duke Leopold I, stayed there accompanied by his brother, Archduke Joseph, the future emperor. Their presence in Rome was for the election of the new pope: in the gardens and among the marble statues of Venus, political conversations and intrigues between diplomats and cardinals intertwined. The conclave was managed from outside the Vatican, and the fate of the Society of Jesus came into play, with the selection of a pope who would be favorable to its suppression. Gian Vincenzo Ganganelli, who took the name of Clement XIV, was elected, and the Order of Jesuits was dissolved within a few years (1773).

The villa lived through a splendid event in 1776 when Archduchess Marie-Christine of Austria and her husband, Duke Albert of Saxony Teschen, were guests

there. In a ceremony of great solemnity the papal decoration of the Golden Rose, an object in solid gold, was conferred upon them in recognition of the faithfulness of this royal couple to the Church of Rome. To confer it upon them, in the name of Pius VI in the salon of the villa, was the Vatican's master of ceremonies, Archinto, together with the holy relics of St. Augustine and St. Christine. This was to be the last sighting of Roman magnificence in the twilight of eighteenth-century gallantry. After that it came close to total extinction. Between 1780 and 1788, the Lorraine family moved part of the collection of ancient sculptural masterpieces to the museums in Florence and tried to sell the villa. But they found no buyers.

With the advent of Napoleon, they lost both the grand duchy and the villa. Napoleon placed the young Luigi, son of Bourbon Duke Ferdinand of Parma, on the throne of Tuscany in 1801, and it became the kingdom of Etruria. The youth was sickly and governed under the control of Napoleon, who was greedy not only for the Villa Medici but also for the *Medici Venus*, which he wanted to place next to the

Apollo Belvedere, already in the Louvre. In January 1803, the young king gave in to France's requests even though they had in reality already taken possession of the villa a year earlier. The historic Académie de France, founded in 1666 by Louis XIV, and housed until then in Palazzo Mancini on the Corso, was then moved to the Villa Medici. At the end of the loggia appeared the notice: "A Napoleone il grande le arti riconoscenti" (The arts are grateful to Napoleon the Great).

Suitably restored, the villa began a completely new life in the name of culture, creating a scholastic atmosphere that was not exclusive but was a great attraction to the city. The Académie did not limit itself to offering young French artists the opportunity to perfect their art in Rome with what would later be called the "Prix de Rome," consisting of a stay of years in the city, but also developed cultural initiatives such as exhibitions and concerts that brought brilliance to the very appearance of the villa with celebrations and society receptions. It was all dependent on the directors of the Académie, or rather, on their organizational skills and the artistic interests and

quality of their scholars. Thus in the nineteenth century it shone with the director-painters Horace Vernet and Jean-Auguste Dominique Ingres, creators of splendid cultural initiatives, when artists such as the painters Bouguereau and Carpeaux, the architects Baltard and Garnier, and the musicians Berlioz and Debussy were welcomed there.

In the twentieth century, a certain academicism prevailed, and this was reflected in the villa in a tendency toward a monotonous life without any particular interest, which in turn caused a certain degradation of the complex. A leap in quality occurred in the 1960s under the direction of the painter Balthus when the villa was restored and the gardens redesigned with copies of the statues that had decorated the villa before 1780. The activities of the Académie were no longer limited to scholars only but included exhibitions, concerts, film showings, and conferences, in lively artistic exchanges between France and Italy. This is the road where the villa's light shines brightest, faithful to the cultural imprint of its origins.

A marble sculpture of Niobe and her children evokes their tragic myth in a sort of war dance in the garden at the edge of the wood, separated from it by a high box hedge.

VILLA GIULIA

POPE JULIUS III

When Giovanni Ciocchi del Monte, better known as Pope Julius III, had this mansion built at the beginning of his papacy in 1550, the area just outside the walls of the city was still countryside, covered in vineyards and farms. The del Monte estate stretched from the Aurelian walls to the Milvian Bridge. It covered the entire area close to the Tiber and inside Via Flaminia, which crossed it, along the hills in front of Villa Borghese and the Monti Parioli. In fact what today is called Villa Giulia, a building set amid courtyards, nymphaeums, and gardens, is only one of the three that made up the original complex. Today not only are the outbuildings that once surrounded it missing, but so is its former rural context.

Villa Giulia, in the strict sense, was divided into three villas. The oldest of these was called *vigna vecchia* (old vineyard). It led to the building with the public fountain that still exists on the Via Flaminia, later to become the *casino*, or lodge, of Pope Pius VI (1560–1565), and extended to the foot of Villa Borghese behind it with what was later to become the part of Rome called the Borghetto Flaminio. The second complex, called the *vigna del porto* (vineyard of the port) was situated between Via Flaminia and the

Detail of the façade overlooking Viale delle Belle Arti, with the imposing ashlar-work on the portal, Doric columns, and lateral niches simulating a triumphal arch and acting as base to the loggia with niches between Corinthian pilasters.

Polychrome terracotta with Gorgon on the left, and a Maenad, of the sixth century B.C. These are two stupendous finds in the Etruscan Museum housed in the villa, the most important in Italy.

Tiber. As indicated by the architect Bartolomeo Ammannati in a description of the area, "it is a comfortable house, with a portal a full thirty palms in height and all richly made in stone. And there is a vaulted or, rather, arched pergola that extends as far as the river, covered in greenery, eighty canes long. At the end is the port, built so that when Pope Julius came to relax in this beautiful villa he could disembark comfortably." The third complex was centered on the building currently called Villa Giulia. It extended from the large square as far as Via Flaminia and onto the hilly area rising to the right of the building. Connected to the mansion was a spacious garden with high walls covered by ancient sculptures and inscriptions and, further up, another garden with ancient marble busts. In the green area in front were a series of loggias for

The internal façade of the villa, opening onto the courtyard in a wide semicircular theatrical setting, with the arcade under the atrium in the form of a parquet and the street as the stage.

169

relaxing, while two other buildings rose on the hill, one of which, "with its rich ornamentation would in itself be enough for any great prince, due to its many statues and paintings, as well as its beautiful gardens decorated with espaliers and wonderful paths." This complex has completely disappeared.

The only structure remaining is the palazzo that Pope Julius had built to his own design. He had Michelangelo look over the drawing and improve it and subsequently had Vasari, Vignola, and Ammannati enlarge it and supervise its construction between 1551 and 1555.

It is a perfect building set in its valley, with an impressive combination of corridors, stairways, and colonnades, connected by flower beds, lawns, and

terraces. Structurally, the building is still basically the same today as it was then, with its succession of rooms opening onto one another, from the splendid portal made to resemble a triumphal arch to the semicircular colonnade leading to the truly theatrical courtyard, with a walkway that functions as a proscenium, the colonnade as a parquet, and the loggia as the stage.

A second courtyard opens up from the loggia, and here is a second theatrical set, with access from two ramps that lead down to the scenic three-tiered nymphaeum with loggias. At the bottom is the greenery of the Fontana della Acqua Vergine (Fountain of the Acqua Vergine), an actual "water theater," decorated with busts, caryatids, and sculptures of the Arno and the Tiber.

This masterpiece has gradually been despoiled over the centuries and has lost much of its decoration, including the gilded stuccoes and the sculptures that embellished the exterior and interior. Prospero Fontana's and Taddeo Zuccari's splendid frescoes that have survived in the rooms next to the entrance hall

The theatrical nymphaeum designed by Ammannati and executed by him with antique marbles and statues. It opens onto two levels with loggias supported by hermes as caryatids, visible in the detail, and in the background of the river divinities, Arno and Tiber.

and in the main hall on the first floor give us an idea of the splendor that has been lost.

Julius III did not wait for the work to be finished to enjoy his creation. The work was interrupted by his death, leaving the third courtyard unfinished. The pope was here from the beginning of construction and continued to come once a week, often with a train of cardinals, organizing parties with music, singers, and acrobats.

On his death, the entire villa with all its buildings passed to his brother Baldovino, but when the latter died in 1556, Pope Paul IV confiscated the property of the del Monte family, considering it to have been bought with money from the Apostolic Chamber. In many ways this signaled the beginning of the villa's

Rome. Reduced to a mere accessory, few of its rooms were being used, and its glory and pomp had become a thing of the past. The archives do not speak of important people being received there. They evidently were, but probably not with any particular ceremony.

There is only a mention of Christina of Sweden's brief stay there in 1655. She had been housed in the Palazzo Apostolico when she arrived on December 12 and then was transferred here on the evening of December 23 so that she could make her official entry into Rome. She was offered a "*rinfresco di confetture*" (sweet refreshment), after which she awaited the arrival of the steward of the pontifical court "in a room under the canopy." Here she received the gifts of Pope Alexander VII, consisting of a carriage, a sedan chair,

The semicircular colonnade faced on the vault with "à grillage" frescoes by Pietro Venale and on the walls, with grotesques and mythological figures.

decline, since there was no longer a person with an emotional tie to it and a direct interest in its upkeep. Finally it was broken up when Pius IV gave the *vigna vecchia* on Via Flaminia to his Borromeo nephews. The place was then restored and a chapel built. At the same time a large number of statues, busts, and fountains disappeared from Pope Julius's villa and were used to decorate the Vatican and its gardens.

After that, the palazzo was used as a place where sovereigns, cardinals, and ambassadors were housed before making their official ceremonial entrance into

and a caparisoned mule, which she could use for her solemn cavalcade to St. Peter's. Christina chose the mule, which she rode sidesaddle "in the manner of women" in a procession along the Via Flaminia, passing through Porta del Popolo and leaving Villa Giulia behind her—where, in fact, she would never have occasion to return.

The image of the villa did not change even with the completion of the third courtyard in the middle of the eighteenth century, when the end of its use for receptions was decided. Pius VI (1775–1799) had the few sculptures that were left brought into the Vatican and closed the aviary, which had already been unused for some time, turning it into quarters for the gardeners. A few years later, even the gardeners were sent away and the building was completely abandoned, left to be used in ways that could only make it deteriorate further. Thus it became a hospital, a military barracks, and under Leo XII (1823–1829), a veterinary school, and finally a storehouse. In 1876 it became military property and was again used to house soldiers.

Later, the great Villa Giulia disappeared, as the Flaminio *quartiere* was created and the green area broken up into lots. Only several small villas cut out of the foot of the hills were spared. A series of apartment buildings rose along Via Flaminia, and Viale delle

Thus the palazzo of Pope Julius has come to its cultural conclusion, reflecting the ideals and spirit of the Renaissance in which it was conceived. With the artifacts deriving from the main archaeological digs in Tuscany and Latium, and the rich contributions from the renowned Barberini, Castellani, and Pesciotti collections, it is the most important Etruscan museum in Italy. Precious works of art such as the Ficoroni cista, the *Bride and Groom* sarcophagus, the Faliscan Aurora crater, and the *Hercules Fighting Apollo* make the Villa Giulia a priceless treasury of art.

Belle Arti was opened, isolating Pope Julius's palazzo. This coincided with its redemption, however, when in 1889 the villa became the Museum of Etruscan Art. At that time the outer walls of the two side gardens were built and the entire building renovated for its new function, restoring some of its former dignity. The gardens were also restored; the garden on the right was entrusted to Count Alfonzo Cozza to build a hypothetical reconstruction of the Italic temple of Alatri, in perfect harmony with the Etruscan setting with which the villa was finally identified.

Detail of one of the lunettes in the atrium attributed to Prospero Fontana, with putti and birds in an exultation of green in imitation of a pergola.

PALAZZO ALTEMPS

ALTEMPS

Palazzo Altemps in Piazza Sant'Apollinare, currently seat of an important section of the Museo Nazionale Romano. Opposite, two niches of the internal courtyard, with antique statues.

This building's massive size, reminiscent of a fortress, brings to mind the Palazzo della Cancelleria. Perhaps this connection is not purely accidental: in both cases, the name of the Riario family was involved at its origin, a family that owed its fortune to Pope Sixtus IV (1471–1484). In 1480 it was built by Count Girolamo Riario, a general of the Holy Roman Church, the son of the pope's sister Bianca della Rovere, and husband of Caterina Sforza. Nevertheless, the count never went to live there because construction went too slowly and he preferred his villa on the Lungara, which would later, in the eighteenth century, become the property of the Corsini family.

The palazzo thus had a sad beginning. It was unfinished, uninhabited, and neglected by Girolamo's son, Ottavio Riario Sforza. It came to life only around 1520 when it was rented to Spain. It became a residence for the Spanish ambassador, creating a Spanish oasis, thanks to its extra-territorial status, in Piazza di Sant'Apollinare which lay before it. The building was then completely renewed, and the splendid courtyard, with its colonnade and loggia designed by Baldassare Peruzzi, was added.

A few years later, the Spanish embassy moved to Piazza Navona with its own headquarters in the buildings around the church of San Giacomo. The palazzo, once again abandoned, was the victim of plunder and deterioration. The Riari family decided to get rid of it. They sold it to Cardinal Francesco Soderini, who put it back in order, giving special attention to details of the finishings in order to turn it into a residence worthy of his rank. The façade was decorated in *chiaroscuro* by Polidoro di Caravaggio and Maturino da Firenze, who also frescoed some of the rooms. But the cardinal never had the chance to enjoy his new residence. He died in 1568 and his nephews sold it to Cardinal Marco Sittico Altemps.

This turned out to be good luck for the palazzo for the new owner had dreams of grandeur. The cardinal was the son of Chiara de' Medici, sister of Pope Pius IV (1559–1565), and Count Wolfgang Hohenems, who came from an illustrious German family that had changed its name in Italy to Altemps. His dream was to turn his mansion into a palace. Martino Longhi the Elder was employed to direct the renovations, and he created a great covered roof-terrace with arcades, surmounted by four small obelisks and a small cupola with a heraldic marble ram rampant, the device of the Altemps family. The courtyard was decorated with splendid classical statues and a colored mosaic fountain with the crest of Cardinal Marco Sittico Altemps.

The palazzo became the image of prestige for the wealthy cardinal, who bought fiefs in Sabina such as Gallese, Soriano, and Rocchetta complete with the title of duke, as well as land in Tuscolum, where he built the splendid villa at Mondragone. This estate was not inherited by Marco Sittico's brothers and their sons at his death because the cardinal had legitimized his natural son, Roberto, and even though his would be considered a cadet branch of the Altemps family, the title and property went to him.

he was relegated to Avignon and essentially was unable to enjoy his inheritance. But his son, Giovan Angelo, second duke of Gallese and considered Duke Altemps *par excellence*, was able to enjoy it fully.

The first twenty years of the seventeenth century, under Giovan Angelo, were the golden age of the palazzo. Its great salons witnessed extravagant parties for Rome's high society, and carnival-like events, concerts, and melodramas were performed in a theater complete with balcony and gallery that he had built in the basement in the back of the

One side of the arcaded courtyard, the work of Martino Longhi the Elder, with four sculptures belonging to the Altemps Collection.

The first duke of Gallese tried to use his wealth and his marriage to Donna Cornelia Ursina, sister of Giovanni Antonio, duke of San Gemini, to enter Roman society but as a result of "certain youthful excesses" that are not better specified in the chronicles,

building toward Via dei Soldati. The duke also collected works of art and set them up in the villa at Mondragone and in the Roman palazzo, where he also established a rich library, buying, among other things, the collection of Cardinal Colonna, which was later partly passed on to the Vatican and partly sold separately at auction in 1908.

Duke Giovan Angelo also received the relics of Pope Aniceto (155–166) from Clement VIII in 1604. These had been found in the catacombs of San Callisto and were then placed in an antique yellow urn, in which, legend had it, the bones of Emperor Alexander Severus had been kept. The urn was deposited in the palazzo chapel, decorated for the occasion by Pomarancio and Ottavio Leoni.

of cadet branches which, through marriage, tied the Altemps increasingly to the Roman nobility. The family tended to cancel out its Germanic origins in favor of the Italian, and particularly Roman, aristocracy. Even the sale of the villa at Mondragone to the Borghese family and the art collection to Cardinal Ludovico Ludovisi, nephew of Pope Gregory XV, had this intention, that is, to earn the favor of two families at the highest level of the pontifical aristocracy.

However, the Altemps had financial problems, and at the end of the seventeenth century they had to rent

Giovan Angelo's first marriage was to Maria Cesi, daughter of Federico, duke of Aquasparta, and his second was to Margherita Madruzzi. His eldest son married first a Medici and later a Lante. Their numerous sons and daughters went on to form a series

out the palazzo. This indicated a downward course in the aspirations of the family and was a loss of face for their home. Any ostentation was left, naturally, to the tenants, the first of whom was Cardinal de Polignac, ambassador of the king of

The entrance atrium to the stairs, decorated at the ends with stucco heraldic goats. On the left, the torso of a colossal late Hellenistic statue of Neptune.

In December 1997, over two
hundred antique sculptures
from the Boncompagni
Ludovisi Collection were
placed in Palazzo Altemps,
since it had become one of the
homes of the Museo Nazionale
Romano. They are splendid
statues, Roman copies of
original Greek work, restored
at the beginning of the
seventeenth century by artists
such as Gian Lorenzo Bernini
and Alessandro Algardi. On
this page is the statue of
Aesculapius, the god of
medicine, an elaboration of the
Hellenistic age, restored by
Algardi who remade part of the
head, all the right arm, and the
staff with the serpent.

France. The palazzo came alive again with him and was partly rebuilt.

The Roman nobility thus had the occasion to have contact again with the home of the Altemps, thanks to the parties and theatrical representations put on by the French cardinal. On two occasions the courtyard itself was used as a setting for the festive commemoration of great events. In 1725 celebrations were held in honor of the wedding of Louis XV and Marie of Poland, and in 1729 fireworks, dances, and games celebrated the birth of the dauphin. For the latter, a cantata by Metastasio put to music by Leonardo Vinci was performed, and in the adjacent Piazza di

some way and to keep the duchy of Gallese in the family. Lacking available cousins, Lucrezia gave her heart to a French petty officer who was her junior, Jules Hardouin, son of a modest watchmaker of Caen. Hardouin was stationed in Rome with the French army supporting Pius IX and lived in a rented room on the ground floor of Palazzo Altemps; he was not the type to let such good luck pass him by. The two fell in love and their marriage was celebrated in 1851, evidently with the blessing of the old Duke Giuseppe. They had a daughter, Maria, and with her the future of the family line seemed assured. In 1854 the family attained their long-awaited aspiration and were entered in the

Detail of the frieze frescoed by Giovanni Francesco Romanelli in one of the reception rooms, once the Audience Room of the Duchess Isabella Lante Altemps, representing stories of the gods such as this Birth of Venus.

Sant'Apollinare a fountain was made to spout wine, much to the joy of the citizens.

But there was no glory for the Altemps. Their only resources were the palazzo and the title of dukes of Gallese, which they would not give up for anything in the world. But even leaving these in inheritance turned out to be a problem. In the middle of the nineteenth century the main branch of the family risked dying out with Duke Giuseppe, who had no children, even though he did return to live in the ancestral home. He wanted to die in peace, leaving his title and home to a relative, so he named his cousin Marco as his heir, who was married to another Altemps, his cousin Lucrezia, in a crossing of cadet branches that seemed to be the last hope for this family line, which was otherwise destined to die out.

This marriage did not last long. Lucrezia was left a widow and childless, and it was necessary for her to remarry in order to have the family line continue in

Roman patriciate by Pope Pius IX. But it seems that the Altemps were not born under a lucky star. Between 1857 and 1860, Jules Hardouin saw the last three representatives of the family die: his wife Lucrezia, his daughter Maria, and Duke Giuseppe. And although he was not an Altemps, and not even a Roman, he was nevertheless the only heir to the palazzo and the title, and this was officially recognized by Pope Pius IX on 8 March 1861.

Naturally, Jules Hardouin remarried, thus strengthening his tie with the Roman aristocracy. His second wife was Natalia Lezzani, Princess Giustiniani and niece of Marquis Bandini. The two had a whole brood of children, male and female, and one of the daughters, Maria, was courted by the poet Gabriele D'Annunzio, an up-and-coming figure in the great world of Rome under Umberto of Savoy, king of Italy. Jules Hardouin evidently knew well what type of person his future son-in-law was (not yet called "the divine" but already much gossiped about in aristocratic salons), and he tried unsuccessfully to dissuade his daughter from the marriage. The marriage was celebrated in the chapel of the palazzo in 1883 and was the last magnificent event to take place in that ducal home. Donna Maria, soon abandoned by the poet for other loves, returned to her paternal home, a situation considered a disgrace in those days and in any case a sign of crisis for the family. It coincided with the end of the Altemps residence. In 1887 the Hardouins of Gallese sold the prestigious mansion to the Holy See.

At this point, the spirit of the building changed completely. The cultural institutions it was then to

dialect and changed its name to "Romanesco." It closed in 1911. When it reopened in 1958, it was again named after Goldoni, but finally it was turned into a piano bar and closed definitively in 1982.

The closure coincided with the sale of the entire building by the Holy See to the Italian state. It was assigned to the Ministry of Cultural Heritage to be made into a museum. Over a period of fifteen years the palazzo was completely restored, bringing the original decoration of the rooms to light and thereby restoring at least part of the building's former image.

On exhibition are more than two hundred sculptures from the great Roman collections, most

house, however noble, canceled out its exclusiveness as an aristocratic dwelling, which it no longer was. It became only a great building for schools, academies, and colleges. Many rooms were restructured to suit these various functions. Here, in different periods, were housed the Ateneo Leoniano, the Accademia Pontificia dei Lincei, the Accademia Archeologica Cristiana, and the Pontificio Collegio Spagnolo.

And yet, a bridge to the past seemed to be made in 1879 when in the basement where there had once been the Teatro Altemps, a new theater was built opening onto Via dei Soldati and named after Goldoni. A fine ceiling decorated with allegorical figures and an elegant foyer pointed hopefully to a refined management ideally suited to the lavish productions of the past.

But it was an illusion. The theater offered only an inferior repertoire, to the point that it was nicknamed "the trap." It ended up specializing in performances in

importantly that of the Ludovisi, which in turn had received a significant contribution in the middle of the seventeenth century from the purchase of the Altemps collection, and then the Del Drago, Mattei, and Brancaccio collections. Thus, on balance, not all the splendor of the Altemps has been lost.

Opposite:
Another masterpiece of the
Boncompagni Ludovisi
Collection, *the* Crouching
Aphrodite, *which is enthroned
in the room frescoed by
Romanelli.*

*The god Pan with the shepherd
boy Daphnis, mythical inventor
of bucolic poetry, a Roman
copy of the masterpiece created
by Heliodoros in 100 B.C. It is
in the room frescoed with
obelisks.*

The splendid statue of Mars, god of war, resting, his shield placed on the ground. The Ludovisi family had it restored by Bernini, who remodeled the hilt of the sword and sculpted a little putto in the form of an angel between the god's feet. Recently it has been identified as Achilles, part of a complex of several statues spread over different collections. Opposite, detail of the Ludovisi Sarcophagus, showing a battle between Romans and barbarians, dating back to 250 A.D.

CAETANI

PRINCE
RUSPOLI

PALAZZO RUSPOLI

The main feature of this palazzo was its great staircase. Each of its four flights was made up of thirty monolithic marble steps that rose from the portico on the side facing Largo Goldoni. It was popularly considered one of the "four marvels" of Rome, along with the Borghese *Cembalo*, the Farnese *Dado*, and the portal of the Sciarra Colonna. It was built in 1640 by the Caetani family, the third owners of the building which at that time already had its own history.

The original structure dates back to 1556 when Francesco Iacobilli had it built on the area at the corner of Via del Corso, Via della Fontanella Borghese, Via del Leoncino, and Piazza San Lorenzo in Lucina. The architect was probably Nanni di Baccio Bigio. Construction proceeded slowly while the Iacobilli were living there, alternating with their residence in Foligno where the family had numerous interests. Francesco, moreover, was the treasurer of Umbria, a hydraulic engineer who reclaimed the swamps in the valley of Foligno, and was also *caporione*, the local leader of Campo Marzio. This did not give him much time to enjoy his Roman palazzo. Apart from being away for these professional engagements, he also suffered the death of his son Bernardino, who was buried in San Lorenzo in Lucina. When Francesco Iacobilli died in 1575, he left his heirs free to sell the Roman property, which was unfinished even if its extension was already clearly laid out and the part surrounding the courtyard was complete.

It was bought eight years later, in 1583, by Orazio Rucellai, a member of the noble Florentine family that had made Rome the center of its financial policies in the train of Cardinal Piero Rucellai, thanks to the two Medici popes, Leo X and Clement VII. The Rucellai family already owned another building on Via del Corso, opposite this one, on the corner of present-day Largo Goldoni, and so were able to create their own private block. Orazio naturally had his architect friend Bartolomeo Ammannati finish the work on the new palazzo, which he did in 1586, defining the edifice with a long façade on the Corso and enclosing two courtyards within, but without adding a concluding element to the rear facade. Ammannati also changed the internal configuration of the rooms, making them larger, and found space on the piano nobile for a long

G. Vasi dis. sc.

1. Strada dei Condotti verso Piazza d

gallery. It was here that Jacopo Zucchi, between 1589 and 1592, added the brilliant new decoration depicting pagan gods and kings of ancient Rome that would become the backdrop for many banquets and diplomatic meetings.

When Orazio Rucellai lived in this building with his wife and children, he was engaged in the social life that his rank as diplomat required. Having served as the plenipotentiary minister for Ferdinando I, grand duke of Tuscany, he was given sensitive assignments in Rome, including the delicate negotiations for the transfer of Palazzo Madama from Catherine de' Medici to the grand duke. Later he took on the difficult position of intermediary between Clement VIII and the king of France, Henri IV, regarding the abjuration of the king in favor of Catholicism in 1593. In fact, it was precisely diplomatic interests vis-à-vis France that helped determine the appearance of the palazzo. When Orazio Rucellai died and the house passed to his sons, Luigi, in the service of Marie de' Medici, and Ferdinando, the building's links to France were strengthened.

The enormous residence was excessive for the two unmarried brothers, and offering hospitality, with or without rent, became a social obligation. In 1605 Cardinal Jacques Davy du Perron lived there, and between 1605 and 1609 a great part of the mansion became the headquarters of the French representative to the court of Rome. Ambassador Charles de Neuville d'Halincourt, marquis of Villeroy, and his successors

Palazzo Ruspoli sul Corso
a. Detta verso Ripetta, 3. Palazzo Ottoboni, 4. Palazzo S. Marco, e Torre del Campidoglio.

Palazzo Ruspoli in an etching by Giuseppe Vasi in book four of Delle Magnificenze di Roma Antica e Moderna, *published in Rome in 1754. The print shows the building with its unique platform, the so-called "scalinone", a kind of observation point overlooking Via del Corso used for watching passersby and, in turn, to be admired while sitting there. The platform was demolished around 1830.*

ATLAS

de Brèves and the duke of Nevers also lived there. In 1611 Cardinal François de Joyeuse lived there as "protector" of France. The last illustrious person to be given hospitality by the Rucellai was Cardinal Gaspare Borgia, the Spanish ambassador, who had a retinue of ninety-two people, as well as eight priests. He lived there from 1618, and his presence gave the building a religious tone that overshadowed its diplomatic one. During this time Cardinal Borgia was intensively engaged in assisting the poor of the city.

Since the palazzo was too big for the needs of the Rucellai, they did not fully enjoy its beauty and in 1627, two years after his brother Luigi's death, Ferdinando Rucellai sold the great mansion to the Caetani of Sermoneta for 51,500 florins. This old family, which boasted prelates, men of arms, and diplomats among its members, had some economic problems but was effectively forced to buy the palazzo. The lower floors of their homes on the Tiber island and at Tor di Nona were continually subjected to flooding because of the overflowing river and had become uninhabitable. Thus the house on the island was rented out and the other sold to pay the first installment on the new property in 1629, when the Rucellai allowed the Caetani family to enter. The castle on the island was also sold in order to finish paying for the palazzo in 1634, when the final papers were signed.

Despite their continuing financial problems, the Caetani family maintained a high standard of living and wanted the palazzo to reflect their dignity. They enlarged it to place their personal stamp on it. The family's financial stability was finally restored and the commitment to restructure the building renewed, thanks to Cardinal Luigi Caetani, the first to live there with the thirteen people in his service, followed by the brothers Onorio V and Francesco IV with all their families and servants, a total of more than one hundred people.

Under the direction of architect Bartolommeo Breccioli, the palazzo was finished between 1633 and 1637 with the addition of a new façade on Via della Fontanella Borghese, a majestic cornice, and an elegant covered roof-terrace. In 1640 Martino Longhi the Younger designed and built the marvelous grand staircase, which became the Caetani family's mark on the building and a legend in urban architecture. The interior was arranged more rationally into apartments, concentrating more on enlarging the spaces inside than on decorating them. All decoration was focused on the magnificence of the famous stairway that led to the apartments. Nevertheless, the new rooms were richly furnished and included tapestries sent from the family mansions in Naples and Caserta.

Despite all the work they did to renovate this palazzo, the Caetani family preferred to live in Sermoneta and ended up considering this Roman home more as an official residence. Their occasional presence did nothing to raise the tone of the building, therefore, and during the eighty years that they owned it, it was lived in by the less "noble" members of the family. Filippo II (1620–1687) killed Count Beroaldo

The vault of the gallery on the piano nobile was decorated by Jacopo Zucchi between 1589 and 1592, and evokes pagan divinities and some of the kings of Rome, among signs of the zodiac and constellations. On this page is the allegorical group of Atlas between the zodiac signs of Sagittarius and Scorpio, with the constellations of Eridian and Orion in the lunettes, and a Hare in the grisaille tablet.

On the following pages: Detail of the vault with allegorical groups of Vesta and Pluto between the zodiac signs of Libra and Leo. In the panels, on the left is Mars in a chariot of war drawn by wolves, and on the right is Jupiter in a chariot drawn by eagles.

VESTA

Opposite:
The lower end of the gallery,
frescoed by Jacopo Zucchi for
the Florentine Orazio Rucellai.
In the center of the wall at the
end, an allegory of Florence
under the crest of the
Marzocco.

Allegory of Rome, with the
symbols of spiritual and
temporal power, frescoed on
the entrance wall of the
gallery.

and his servant, so that he was forced to live in exile. Ruggero III (1632–1706) was a libertine who mostly found space for his adventures outside pontifical Rome. Gaetano Francesco (1656–1716) was involved in a plot against Filippo V of Naples. His property in Caserta and Sermoneta was confiscated, and he ended up living in Vienna.

In 1713 the nobility of the palazzo was again enhanced when it was rented by the Ruspoli family, who were of Florentine origin but had been in Rome since the fourteenth century. They were the marquises of Cerveteri, and, from 1709, princes, starting with Francesco Maria (1672–1731). The Ruspoli were financially secure when they bought the property, concluding the sale in 1776 and starting improvements

on it immediately thereafter. It was with the Ruspoli family that the most refined and triumphant period of its history would take place.

In 1715 the apartment on the ground floor was decorated by a host of painters under the direction of Domenico Paradisi. This decoration, however, was executed too quickly and ten years later already needed to be restored. For this, excellent Mannerist painters were called in, such as Giovanni Reder and Paolo Anesi. In 1727 the painted decoration was completed on the second floor by Michelangelo Cerruti, with a series of hangings that were "finti e fatti a guazzo" (false and made of gouache) to accompany Rubens's precious tapestries. The architectonic arrangement was completed, transforming the loggia overlooking the garden into a gallery and unifying the ground-floor apartment, setting up a direct sequence of rooms. All these works were supervised by the architect Giovan Battista Contini.

Francesco Maria Ruspoli intended to turn his mansion into a palace for parties, literary meetings, and musical performances that would truly bring it to life and enhance the magnificence of the family. The Ruspoli, politically involved in diplomatic support for the pope's policy on the War of the Spanish Succession, made their home a reference point in the mediation of relations between France and Spain, also

making use of the culture of patronage, along the lines of the Accademia dell'Arcadia.

This policy bore fruit with the sons of Francesco Maria. Bartolommeo rose rapidly through the ecclesiastical hierarchy, from apostolic protonotary to secretary of the Propaganda Fide and cardinal, and was on a number of commissions in the Curia. He also became a knight of the Order of Malta and then grand prior, which brought considerable prebends. His brother Alessandro developed the family's inclination to patronage, increasing the number of performances and parties in the house. These took place in the ten rooms of the mezzanine floor, which were embellished with ephemeral decorations painted in various ways up to the gallery, where the orchestra gave concerts, and up to the garden amid real and artificial fountains and greenery.

One party held there became legendary. It was given on 17 March 1769 in honor of Joseph II and his brother Peter Leopold of Austria, Grand Duke of Tuscany, followed on March 27 by the great spectacle of the carnival with the "race of the barbarians," watched by guests from a platform built outside the

palazzo for this purpose, with an orchestra playing on either side. Another memorable party was that of 10 July 1775 in honor of Archduke Maximilian of Hapsburg. This event was also enlivened by a similar race, especially organized in honor of the guest, since it was not carnival at the time. It was watched from a new loggia with gold carvings.

It was in this same period that the building was extended along Via della Fontanella Borghese and Via del Leoncino, as designed by the architect Giuseppe Barberi, the gifted scenographer of the festivities in the Ruspoli house. In 1782 the *piano nobile* was finally decorated with an allegory of the fine arts and mythological themes, which reflected a glorification of the Ruspoli family in its symbolic references to the military valor and diplomatic qualities of Prince Francesco, ambassador to Naples and Venice.

The palazzo was distinguished, moreover, by a singular feature. It was built on a platform eighty centimeters high that extended for the whole length of the façade along Via del Corso. This *scalinone* (large step) was part of the construction but became a sort of observatory onto the street, useful for watching

Bust of Cardinal Galeazzo Ruspoli (1627–1726), by the Bernini school, in the entrance salon of the main floor in front of a seventeenth-century Flemish tapestry representing Queen Zenobia of Palmyra Captured by Emperor Aurelian. On the left, a marble bust of the Emperor Vitellius in the Gallery decorated by Jacopo Zucchi. This is part of the series of twelve Caesars arranged along the long walls and framed by grisaille paintings that record their virtues and faults.

passersby and, in turn, for being gazed at and admired while sitting there. The Ruspoli made this parquet available to nobles and members of the middle classes, and at carnival they also offered chairs to their guests, thus increasing the prestige of their mansion, which more than ever became a reference point along Via del Corso. "It is here," wrote Goethe in his *Italian Journey*, during the carnival of 1788 "that high society takes its place, and all the seats are either taken or reserved. The most beautiful ladies of the middle classes allow themselves to be gazed at avidly by the passersby. Everyone who happens to pass stops to contemplate that seductive parquet. Everyone is curious to guess who the women are among the numerous figures of men that seem to be there and to discover, perhaps in the uniform of an elegant officer, the object of their desires."

With the coming of the Jacobin Republic and the subsequent Napoleonic imperial rule, the palazzo fell into the same critical situation as the Roman aristocracy. In particular, the Ruspoli family suffered from the extortionate bank interest rates and taxes, as well as from the cost of maintaining the French generals billeted in their house. Not only were no parties held there any more, but even the dignity of the household began to suffer. The situation did not improve when pontifical power was restored. The Ruspoli lost their feudal rights over the territories of Cerveteri, Vignanello, and Riano, with all their economic benefits. They were left with their titles—and the problem of maintaining them.

They saved their dignity by intensifying their international diplomatic connections, particularly with the court of Vienna, and by expanding their cultural interests. Prince Alessandro Ruspoli, the king's chamberlain, took it upon himself to pursue this policy. He supported himself by taking advantage of his various appointments in the Church and in the confraternities, with their corresponding economic advantages.

But these were not enough. In order for the palazzo to resume its former role of receiving ambassadors and important people, it was necessary for the Ruspoli to rent out portions of the building. This policy saved the palazzo and is still being followed today. As early as 1812 the prince rented the ground-floor apartment and the garden to a Roman café proprietor, Antonio Bagnoli. The legendary rooms of the eighteenth-century balls became a public coffeehouse called Caffè Nuovo, which would remain open until 1870, when this part of the palazzo would be taken over by a bank, causing the building to assume a distinctly bourgeois identity and ruining most of the frescoes. The *scalinone* became a place to meet and exchange gossip, used even by people of the lower classes, and in the end it was demolished.

Also starting in 1812, other apartments in the palazzo were rented to a series of important personages, first to the family of Napoleon's imperial procurator, Giuseppe Lopodinec, two years later to the Neapolitan Prince Carlo Doria, in 1820 to the Milanese Count Giuseppe Cambarano, chamberlain to

the emperor of Austria, and finally to Ortensia Beauharnais. Daughter of Empress Josephine, she was the former queen of Holland, separated from her husband Count Louis Bonaparte. She lived in the palazzo from 1827 to 1828 and between 1830 and 1831. The palazzo increased its prestige thanks to her and her social gatherings and literary salons, parties, and concerts, behind the scenes of which were hidden political intrigues for the future of her sons, Napoleon Louis and Louis Napoleon. The latter became Napoleon III. Renting was a means of economic survival for the building, and it allowed the Ruspoli, who still live there today, to maintain a high standard of living and to display the presence of important guests.

This was the case with Prince Emanuele (1838–1899), who participated in the second war of independence and was in the provisional government when the temporal power of the pope finally ended. He sat in the right wing of Parliament in various legislatures and was mayor of Rome several times, from 1878 to 1880 and from 1892 to 1899.

His son Eugenio (1866–1893) had the soul of an adventurer and went to Somalia to explore Ogaden. He collected zoological and botanical speciments there and contributed to the confirmation of the Italian protectorate in the region of Burgi; he was killed by an elephant. His nephew Carlo (1892–1942) followed in his footsteps and explored Ethiopia. He died fighting in Egypt. Alessandro (1869–1952), the seventh prince of Cerveteri, a scholar and enthusiastic follower of the Futurists, grand master of the Sacred Hospice under Pius XI and Pius XII, lost an eye in a hunting party and wore a black eye patch, which distinguished him from then on.

The palazzo and the Ruspoli princes maintained their nobility while keeping up with the times and with the requirements of their circumstances. They were helped in this by the establishment in 1975 of a new cultural institution, the Memmo Foundation, in the palazzo. Because of it, the two main floors on Via del Corso were sumptuously decorated with furniture and paintings of the highest quality, some of which already belonged to the Ruspoli family. Two magnificent exhibition spaces were created on the mezzanine and basement floors. The first-floor hanging garden was restored and bloomed again, after being eliminated in 1907 to build the theater Lux et Umbra. This was later rebuilt by Marcello Piacentini and called the Corso; it is now the movie theater Etoile. The abandoned stables on the ground floor on Via della Fontanella Borghese were restored and turned into more exhibition areas, adding one more impressive element to this splendid palazzo.

A room on the piano nobile, restructured by the Fondazione Memmo with furniture and paintings that were partly already the property of the Ruspoli family.

Opposite:
The dining room of the piano nobile of the palazzo. On the walls, an oval painting Capriccio with Roman Monuments *by Jan Frans van Bloemen, called "l'Orizzonte," (1662–1749), and* Marina *by Adriaen van der Cabel (1631–1705).*

PALAZZO SPADA

Central part of the façade of Palazzo Spada facing onto Piazza Capodiferro. Opposite, the courtyard with its splendid decoration in stucco by Giulio Mazzoni.

This delightful Baroque palazzo, which stands in all the splendor of its precious and ornate façade on a piazzetta in the Regola district of the city, dates in its original structure to the middle of the sixteenth century. It originated as Palazzo Capodiferro, and the family name is still preserved in the name of the piazzetta itself, which goes all the way back to the thirteenth century.

This was an illustrious dynasty, linked in particular to the political events in Rome starting from the ascension to the papal throne of Martin V (1417–1431), and involved in particular in the activities of the Commune, so much so that five of its members fulfilled the role of Capitoline curator. The Capodiferro family was also highly esteemed in the field of religion, since it was one of the six Roman families chosen to have custodianship of the Volto Santo (veil of St. Veronica).

In fact it was to Cardinal Girolamo Capodiferro that the palazzo owed its existence. This zealous man of the Church (1502–1559) made his family's fortune. As apostolic nuncio in Portugal and France, he fulfilled the important role of papal treasurer and after being appointed cardinal in 1544, he was nominated bursar of the Vatican, as a trusted confidant of Pope Julius III (1550–1555). These appointments indisputably brought financial advantages to him since in 1548 he had this palazzo built on an area that had previously been occupied by old family buildings, which were then demolished for the purpose. The construction work should have been completed in the course of two years. It was under the direction of an unknown but talented architect—the name mentioned subsequently was that of a Giulio Merisi da Caravaggio and, recently, Bartolommeo Baronino.

The cardinal was able to live in the palazzo for at least eight years until his death, proud of his outstanding achievement, encamped with a dog next to

A glimpse of the courtyard wall, with the frieze of the battle of the Centaurs and the coats of arms held up by nudes. On the left, that of Pope Julius III and, on the right, that of the King of France.

a burning column and the motto VTRO(QVE) TEMPORE repeated at least eight times on the façade, which was then, as now, decorated with plaster figures by Giulio Mazzoni from Piacenza and statues of ancient Romans in niches.

The motto also appears many times in the splendid courtyard, conceived in similar fashion to the façade, with the same decoration. Above the frieze of the battle of the centaurs and statues of pagan divinities together with the Capodiferro family crest of a bull *passant*, the crest of Julius III with its three mountains, and the lilies of the king of France. The latter was in homage to Girolamo's repeated legations at the court of Henri II. It was a blaze of escutcheons, in brief, for the undying glory of the Church and its sovereignty.

Magnificence was evident in the suite of rooms on the *piano nobile*, from the Galleria degli Stucchi, with an endless exaltation of the arms of Julius III and Henri II, to the room of Achilles, with its great frieze evoking the life of the mythical hero, and the room of the Fasti Romulei, with its ceiling carved and gilded with the heraldic symbols of the Farnese pope, Paul III, to whom Girolamo owed his cardinal's hat.

In this blazoned apartment, still dominating the Sala Grande, is a gigantic marble statue of Pompey that was discovered in 1553 in Via dei Leutari and given by Julius III to the cardinal. Standing three meters high, this symbol of the heroic affirmation of liberty is said by tradition to be the statue at whose feet Julius Caesar was stabbed in 44 B.C.

Everything combined immediately to have this palazzo come alive in the style of a cardinal, of diplomacy, and of art, confirmed subsequently by the fact that it became the exclusive residence of cardinals and ambassadors. On the death of Girolamo Capodiferro, his heirs—or rather first his mother Bernardina and then his nephew Pietro Paolo Mignanelli—rented it out. It was inhabited, therefore, by Cardinals Vitellozzo Vitelli, Agostino Cusani, Francesco Guzman de Avila, and Ferdinando Gonzaga. The ambassadors both of the emperor and of the king of France lived there, the latter in the person of the comte de Bethune (1624–1630).

Mignanelli finally sold it in 1632—to a cardinal, of course, in fact to Bernardino Spada. The palazzo then took on the appearance of a palace, with rebuilding under a team of architects, including Paolo Maruscelli, Vincenzo Della Greca, and the great Francesco Borromini. The piazzetta then acted like a mirror to the façade, isolating the building itself. The palace featured an entrance hall, the garden on Via Giulia, a spiral staircase in the extension of the building connecting to a neighboring palazzetto, as well as the scenographic library corridor, with its nine-meter colonnade and a small statue at the far end of the corridor, greatly enlarged by an extraordinary perspectival illusion that makes the corridor seem five times longer than it is in reality.

Created by Borromini, the artist's highly effective visual joke served as a worthy introduction to the splendid gallery instituted by Cardinal Bernardino for a private collection of works of art, which was increased over the centuries by the Spada family, cardinals or otherwise, to the honor and glory of what remained a jewel of a mansion, bearing the indelible stamp of a dynasty.

In fact the origins of the Spada family were modest. They came from Zattaglia, near Brisighella in Romagna, and made their fortune with Paolo, who obtained the contract of the treasury of Romagna, thanks to which he became wealthy. Thus his son Bernardino, born in 1594, could study, ensuring him an ecclesiastical career that culminated in his becoming a cardinal.

Bernardino was the best exponent of a diplomatic personality which was like a mirror to the palazzo which, once it became his property, was renamed

Opposite:
The first room of the gallery, with paintings by Giuseppe Chiari and Vincenzo Camuccini and two portraits of Cardinale Bernardino Spada on the end wall, the large one, in the center, is by Guido Reni (1630), and the one on its right, at the bottom, by del Guercino (1631).

Bust of the Barberini Pope, Urban VIII, attributed to Gian Lorenzo Bernini, in the Corridor of the Bas-reliefs in the piano nobile apartment, now the seat of the Consiglio di Stato.

On the following pages:
A masterpiece by Orazio Gentileschi, David with the Head of Goliath, *in the fourth room of the Gallery, and a corner of the third room with a statue of Aristotle, a sculpture of the Lysippus school. On the wall, a portrait of the Cardinal by Rubens.*

Spada, cancelling, somewhat impiously, the name Capodiferro. Bernardino was apostolic nuncio to the court of Louis XIII and the political spokesman for Pope Urban VIII (1623–1644), who aimed at pacifying the great Catholic powers; it was while he was in Paris, in January 1626, that he received his prize, his nomination as cardinal.

A year later in Bologna as papal legate *a latere* he distinguished himself especially for the initiatives he took during the plague of 1630. From 1631, however, he was permanently in Rome and a year later bought the palazzo which became his small court. From here he administered his duties as bishop of Albano from 1648 and of Frascati from 1652. He was so absorbed by the collecting that formed the majority of his personal wealth that on his death in November 1661 the gallery displayed at least sixty-six paintings, twenty sculptures, and one hundred and five portraits of illustrious personages, apart from two of Bernardino himself by Guido Reni and Guercino.

All this was the fruit of a genuine passion shared by his brother Virgilio, who was also at the peak of an ecclesiastical career. He did not become a cardinal, but as Oratorian Father he excelled at secretly collecting funds for Pope Innocent X and Pope Alexander VII. He was also superintendent of the works on the fabric of St. Peter's.

Virgilio died in 1662, and it is certain that this palace would have had no further story to tell about its collection if these two Spada clerics had not named

their nephew Orazio (1613–1687) as their heir. He was a lawyer, married in 1636 to Maria Veralli, sole heiress of an illustrious Roman family, with whom he had twelve children. To her marriage into the Spada family, Maria brought a dowry of a rich patrimony of works of art which enlarged the gallery, as well as a number of properties, among which was the marquisate of Castelviscardo. Orazio dedicated himself to this fief in order to encourage its rebirth and development but did not neglect the palazzo in Rome, which he restored and maintained.

Naturally, more family crests bloomed in the building. The Spada escutcheon was enriched by that of the Veralli and immortalized in the Sala Grande and in the back courtyard. Orazio's firstborn, Bernardino (1638–1716), became involved in improving the building, mainly in the renewed decoration of the ceilings with garlands and festoons, going on to

211

A corner of the neo-classical room frescoed by Vincenzo Angeloni, Felice Baldi, and Agostino Tofanelli in 1808. On the wall, decorated with medallions, satyrs, and fruit, trompe l'oeil drapery opens onto a view of a harbor with a boat.

whitewash the outside walls. It was his brother Fabrizio (1643–1709), however, the second cardinal in the family, who increased the magnificence of the princely residence, following in the footsteps of his uncle Bernardino in the political commitments of a prestigious career.

Fabrizio served as the apostolic nuncio in Turin, where he was heavily engaged in the restoration of the Catholic religion in the valleys of the Tesino, and then in Paris, at the court of the Sun King. He was appointed cardinal by Clement X (1670–1676),

reaching the peak of his power under Innocent XI (1676–1689) whose secretary of state he was for seven years. It was an important period for the palazzo, custodian of the Curia's political secrets, silent witness to military plans, like the crusade against the Turks which allied all the Catholic nations in the defense of Europe, successfully defending Vienna in 1683, and liberating Buda in 1686. In these rooms the pope's secretary of state meditated the shape of a policy that would bring the Holy See back into the context of the great international powers, based on religion.

However, these were the final successes of a state which finished by counting ever less in front of the growing strength of the other nations who were committed no longer to holy alliances but to territorial conquest instead.

The statesman Spada did not forget his interest in art, and his passion for it was renewed, bringing him to restore structures and decorations in the gallery, even setting up in his own apartment near the library a small collection of forty paintings, among which were the *Histories of the Twelve Caesars* by Lazzaro Baldi.

With the son of Bernardino, Clement (1679–1759), the Roman branch of the Spada family died out for lack of a male heir, bringing a second, Romagna branch from Faenza into ownership of the palazzo, in the person of Giuseppe Spada (1752–1840). He preferred to live in Bologna, however, so the mansion was somewhat left to itself. The only positive note is the inventory of the art collection he provided, which did not save it from dispersal at the end of the eighteenth century in the period of Jacobin Rome and at the beginning of the nineteenth century with the reign of Napoleon. A real process of breaking up the collection took place which could not be halted even by the family's third cardinal, Alessandro (1787–1843), who bought a precious portrait of Cardinal Benedetto Naro by Vincenzo Camuccini.

Once papal power was restored in Rome and the palazzo was reopened, Giuseppe hastened to put things to rights, instituting after 1816 a deed of trust which allowed the gallery to be placed under guardianship in accordance with a law of Cardinal Pacca which was subsequently confirmed by the Italian state in 1883. This was the salvation of the gallery, and, in substance, of the palazzo itself, which kept its dignity despite the not too brilliant financial condition of its owners. This situation improved thanks to the marriage of the last of the Spada family, Maria (who died in 1902), to Prince Giovanni Potenziani Grabinski in 1875. Their son Ludovico thus began the Spada Veralli Potenziani branch of the family, of which he was the only and last representative, dying without heirs in 1971.

In the meantime, the palazzo was no longer Spada property. It had been bought by the Italian state in 1926 as the seat of the Consiglio di Stato (Council of State), with all the appropriate restoration and rebuilding. The gallery was opened to the public in 1927, but the collection had to be restored by reacquiring works through purchases from several places. It was only in 1951 that the gallery was brought back to its early splendor, with all its works again in place and the rooms fully restored. The Palazzo Spada, despite its new use, has only in recent years wholly reacquired the refined elegance that cardinals and diplomats had bestowed upon it in the past.

QUIRINAL PALACE

The Quirinal has stood for Rome, going all the way back to ancient times. It is often alluded to by the word *collis* (hill) alone—recognition of its excellence among the seven hills that identify the city of Rome. It was an urban area defined by the religious purpose of its buildings, starting from the temple dedicated to Romulus Quirinus, a mythical commemoration of the origins of Rome to which the hill is closely linked and on which its own prestige is based.

It was an affluent *quartiere*, a high-class area for rich patricians, which during the Renaissance became the residential quarter for cardinals, erasing the original pagan traces, witnessed only by the Dioscuri, of the Temple of Serapis soaring over the piazza on the hill, and confirming its characteristics of excellence in a new direction.

In this *quartiere* Cardinal Oliviero Carafa had his villa at the end of the fifteenth century, a vineyard and

vegetable garden on the slope of the hill toward Trevi, a green area conceived as a place of humanistic idleness, where scholars and friends could meet. It was bounded by a terrace with a panoramic view in front of the present Piazzale dei Dioscuri, where a small house stood at the corner with Strada Pia, balancing the large group of houses at the end. In 1545 the heirs of Carafa leased the villa to the Farnese, who remodeled the group of houses to make them more comfortable for the family pope, Paul III, who loved to spend the hottest days of the summer there, as a change from the Aracoeli where he had also built a tower.

When Paul III died in 1549, the Farnese family left the villa. From the following year on, it was leased to Cardinal Ippolito d'Este, son of Alfonso, duke of Ferrara, and the notorious Lucrezia Borgia. Deprived of his splendid villa in Tivoli and deeply enamored of the green countryside, the cardinal planned a second

The great internal courtyard of the Palazzo that extends between two long wings of the colonnade. At the end, the view of the sixteenth-century palazzetto with a double loggia built for Gregory XIII by Ottavio Mascherino.

Tivoli-style villa in Rome with Girolamo da Carpi. Italianate geometric gardens were planned, dotted with fountains and antique marbles, and various changes were made to the interiors of the two houses, with the addition of new rooms built toward Trevi. Another pope, Pius V of the Ghislieri family, was accommodated at the villa, and a chapel was built for him. Courtyards were created, alternating with gardens with arboreal pavilions, so that a great network of flower beds was created between pathways, all done in a style conforming to Renaissance taste.

The villa of the Carafa family, who are still its owners, became a splendid residence in which Cardinal Ippolito lived until his death in 1572, when his nephew Cardinal Luigi succeeded him there. In the summer months, Pope Gregory XIII came to stay there as guest of the cardinal, and the pope fell in love with the area. It was more central with respect to the Lateran and the Vatican itself, and enjoyed a natural luxuriant setting. Gregory liked it too much to consider it only a holiday place: the Quirinal was about to supplant the Vatican and become the Holy See all year round. He planned a great palace with his favorite architect, Mascarino; he might not see it completed, but in 1583 he made up his mind and authorized the work to begin.

The following year the edifice was completed. It was a kind of Torre dei Venti (Tower of the Winds), and it would remain a point of reference in the final

On the following pages:
View of the Sala Regia, now called Sala dei Corazzieri, with an impressive ceiling of carved polychrome wood lacunars, decorated at the ends with the insignia of Paul V and with the coat of arms of the house of Savoy, inserted in the center after 1870. The frieze on the walls is by Agostino Tassi, Giovanni Lanfranco, and Carlo Saraceni.

Palazzo del Quirinale overlooking the Piazza of the same name, dominated by the monumental complex of the obelisk and with the Dioscuri.

215

construction of the palazzo. Its façade and interior were also decorated.

Thus when Pope Gregory died in 1585, what he had been achieved might be seen as a caprice, more than anything else. In fact, a great deal of money had been spent on the undertaking—and yet it was as if the money had been thrown away since the owners of the villa were still the Carafa and the leaseholder was Cardinal Luigi d'Este, who owned the usufruct of the new building. However, the cardinal enjoyed it for barely a year, as he

the side of Via Pia as quarters for the Swiss Guard. The appearance of the complex was majestic, and it seemed immediately suitable for a court of many people and a Curia whose complex functions had recently been reorganized by a decree of Sixtus V.

When the pope died in 1590 the work was still incomplete, but the new Holy See was by then habitable. Clement VIII, from 1595, was the first pope to live for long periods at the Quirinal, in the wing overlooking the piazza. He gave new instructions for

died in 1586. The new pope Sixtus V then made an important decision: in the name of the Holy See, he bought the property from the Carafa family and started transformation work on the villa on a vast scale, determined to make it the new papal residence.

The plan drawn up by the architect Domenico Fontana was ambitious, as required by a seat of power, and included the remodeling of the whole complex starting with the building of a new edifice opposite the small palazzo built by Pope Gregory and joined to it by two long arcaded wings. The palazzo continued along

the gardens and had numerous fountains installed, fed by water from the Acqua Felice. Of these fountains, the most imposing was the Organo, with its sizable decorated niche and large-stepped stairway for the cascades of water, which could set musical instruments playing with particular sounds, accompanied by unexpected spurts of water that splashed the people standing nearby. This was an example of the theatrical aim that inspired the complex, even in the details of its furnishings, as a glorification of the powers who inhabited it.

In the Sala del Thorwaldsen, so called after a precious relief frieze carried out by the Danish sculptor, a marble fireplace is decorated with two figures of Dacian prisoners, copies of antique statues. The floor is enriched by a mosaic of the Roman period (opposite).

It was with Paul V (1605–1621), however, that the Quirinal became the official papal residence. This gave a definitive style to the palazzo, with exact details of the area included in the complex in accordance with the final plans by Flaminio Ponzio. Thus was erected the wing of the internal portico on the garden side, with a second storey above part of it, to house the Sala del Concistoro (Hall of the Consistory). An imposing double staircase of honor was built here and the palazzetto on Via Pia aligned with the main structure. Two chapels were also built, on the ground floor, the Chapel of the Nativity, intended for prelates who lived in the area, and on the first floor, the Chapel of the Annunciation, used privately by Paul V.

After the death of Ponzio, the direction of the work was taken over by Carlo Maderno, who continued until the death of Paul V. The façade on the piazza was defined with its great portal set between two columns and the architrave with the reclining statues of St. Peter and St. Paul and the long building converging on the façade of the palazzo that faces the present Via della Dataria took shape. It was a wing set diagonally to the complex, almost a building on its own, created

expressly for the papal family. Lengthened in the eighteenth century and raised in the nineteenth, it came to be called the *Panetteria* (Bakery) because of its proximity to the *Panetteria apostolica* where bread was distributed to the staff of the Papal Palace and, on occasion, to the poor.

The interiors were laid out sumptuously. Two areas, the Pauline Chapel, modeled on the Sistine Chapel in the Vatican, and the Sala Regia (Royal Room), now called Sala dei Corazzieri, were painted in a majestic manner thanks to a series of decorative works, from the frieze by Agostino Tassi to the frescoes on the walls, like the one representing a simulated loggia with balustrades covered with carpets and scenes from the Old Testament, and others with figures having Oriental features. It was an iconographic image of papal apotheosis which took its inspiration from strictly religious motifs but which nevertheless emphasized the glorification of the papacy of Paul V, in particular through the ubiquitous appearance of the Borghese heraldic crest.

Intercommunicating through great double doors, the two areas were the pivot of a suite of six reception rooms that all fit together in solemn but austere magnificence, and whose furnishings and decoration were not changed over the following centuries—the opposite of what usually happened in the private apartments of the popes at the Vatican. There were tapestries of crimson damask, enriched by gilded borders and a great profusion of chests and small stone tables of sober and solemn appearance so as to give the palazzo an air more of a monastery than a palace.

With Urban VIII and under the direction of Bernini, the exterior of the palazzo took on a more completely unified architectural style. A guard tower was built, which also functioned as the link to the oblique Palazzo della Panetteria, and on the façade was placed the so-called Benediction Loggia. Under Alexander VII (1655–1667) the first stretch of the so-called *Manica Lunga* (Long Sleeve) was built. This was the longest part of the structure which, as an extension of the palazzo, was continued for as much as 360 meters along Via Pia (now Via del Quirinale). Its construction, which went ahead under Innocent XIII in 1722, was completed by Clement XII in 1732 under the direction of Ferdinando Fuga, who also rebuilt the end building, which had been the residence of the Swiss Guard. This became the house of the secretary of the cipher.

The last pope to become involved in the layout of the papal residence was Benedict XIV (1740–1758), who had a "coffee house" built in the park, in the place where the Este family had once had a simple pavilion. It was a small masterpiece by Fuga, decorated on the inside with urban scenes by Pannini and landscapes by Batoni and Masucci—a last touch of elegance for the prestige of the gardens, which remain the most vivid decorative element of the entire complex.

After this came gloomy times for the palazzo, with Rome under Jacobin rule at the end of the eighteenth century and Pius VI a prisoner in France. The papal residence was sacked by the French, who, according to

contemporaries, "portarono via dal palazzo anche le porte" (even took away the doors from the palace).

It once again became the papal seat with the new pope, Pius VII (1800–1823) but the Quirinal could not be restored on account of the economic difficulties that confronted the Papal State, for as long as that existed. Napoleon, as emperor, abolished the Papal State, and in 1808, Rome was occupied. The Quirinal became a virtual prison for the pope, who stayed closed in the palace, without any power. It was from here, after a secret consistory, that he excommunicated Napoleon, instructing Catholic bishops not to recognize him as emperor.

The French governor, General Miollis, reacted by ordering the pope's arrest, which was carried out on 5 July 1808 in an extraordinary way. To gain entry to the rooms in the palace, a group of Roman "Imperialists" dramatically scaled the walls, thus profaning the papal powers. Pius VII was deported to Genoa and then to Fontainebleau; the palace was occupied by the French army. In 1811 Napoleon declared the Quirinal his "imperial palace" and planned the rebuilding of the papal residence in the context of an ambitious program of urban development in Rome, which was intended to be the second city of the empire.

The architect Raphael Stern carried out alterations and new decorations culminating in a series of frescoes and bas-reliefs representing emblematic figures of the Roman Empire—a specific glorification of the Napoleonic regime—in the small palazzo of Pope Gregory. The Gallery of Alexander VII was transformed into three rooms and the Throne Room was created, but Napoleon never entered Rome, nor did he sit on that throne.

Instead, Pius VII came back in 1814, and it was he who restored his residence, ensuring, among other things, that the decoration of the Pauline Chapel was renewed. It was then that the figures of the apostles were frescoed along the walls, almost as if they were being asked to take care of the pope's private chapel after its Napoleonic profanation.

These were the last papal touches to the palazzo, although further papal events were still to take place there. It was here that the last four conclaves of papal Rome were held: the Pauline Chapel was used for the voting, while the apartments of the participating cardinals were arranged in the Manica Lunga. The first conclave took place between 2 November and 28 November 1823, and Annibale Sermattei della Genga was elected; he took the name of Leo XII. After him came Francesco Saverio Castiglioni, with the name Pius VIII, elected after a conclave that lasted from 23 February to 31 March 1829. The third conclave was very long, lasting from 14 December 1830 until 2 February 1831; it finally resulted in the election of Bartolomeo Mauro Cappellari, with the name Gregory XVI. The fourth was very brief, 14 June through 16 June 1846, and brought Giovanni Maria Mastai Ferretti to the papal throne. This was Pope Pius IX who, from the loggia of the palazzo, bestowed his famous benediction on Italy which was accepted by the liberals as proof of the

pope's sympathies with the cause of national independence.

But this same Pius IX, in his address from the Quirinal on 29 April 1848, kept his distance from the war of independence and proclaimed the political neutrality of the Holy See. Again, this same Pius IX, six months later, on 18 November, left the Quirinal precipitously in order to take refuge at Gaeta, leaving an open field to the triumvirs of the Roman Republic, Mazzini, Saffi, and Armellini, who took possession in March of the following year. This was a brief Republican parenthesis which, however, did constitute effective advance notice on the future course of events since Pius IX, returning from Gaeta in 1850, did not return to his Quirinal Palace but took up permanent residence in the Vatican. From that time onward, no pope would set foot in the Quirinal.

Shut up in his Vatican Palace, Pius IX awaited the end of his state and the handing over of his city to the king of Italy, together with the Quirinal Palace. However, the taking of possession by General Lamarmora, the king's representative, on the evening of 8 November 1870, was like a second breach of Porta Pia: it took place by knocking the gates down because the secretary of state, Cardinal Antonelli, refused to hand over the keys.

The climate of enmity between victors and vanquished did not cool down, and the arrival of Vittorio Emanuele II in Rome on December 31 took place in a very muted fashion. When, on New Year's Eve, the king came out to greet the crowd waiting in the piazza, he did so from a window of the mezzanine, the third on the left of the keep—from the Benediction Loggia, in fact. It might have appeared to be a profane act.

Thus the Quirinal Palace became a royal residence. The official installation of the king of Italy took place in July 1871, after appropriate work had made the rooms suitable for the new court life. The little palazzo of the secretary of the cipher became the home of Vittorio Emanuele II, who did not like living at the Quirinal and preferred some of the rooms on the ground floor of the palazzo at the end of the courtyard, which were made over in accordance with the king's own taste and decorated with trophies of rifles. Fireplaces were built in the Manica Lunga to heat the building better, and a special heating plant was installed in the rooms of Prince Umberto and Princess Margherita. Furniture, tapestries, pictures, and porcelain were brought from the royal palace in Turin and from the estates of Colorno and Parma in order to furnish the palazzo.

It was the princes of Piedmont who gave the mansion its tone with great balls that were held every Wednesday. These alternated with literary-society gatherings on Thursdays, where the nobles of the anticlerical-party aristocracy participated together with the most well-known exponents of Roman culture. These took place in the former Sala del Concistoro which had been changed into a Salone delle Feste (Salon of Celebrations), a transformation achieved at the expense of the fresco by Tassi and Gentileschi on the vault.

The palazzo remained the venue of the most important official ceremonies, with famous personages as guests there, including Wilhelm II of Germany, who visited Rome in 1889, and Hitler, in 1938, for whom an apartment was prepared on the main floor of the small Gregorian palazzo. The marriage of Vittorio Emanuele III to Elena di Montenegro in 1896 and that of Umberto II to Maria José in 1930 were held there. Its society function grew gradually less frequent, however, because the Savoy family considered it an official residence and preferred to go and live in the Villa Potenziani outside Porta Salaria, renamed Villa Savoia in 1911.

And yet certain initiatives were not lacking. Some of them were curious, like those taken by Queen Elena, who used the Sala dei Corazzieri as a tennis court and for roller skating and had a canal dug in front of the stables so that boats could be used for games and sport. However, it is also true that the palazzo was open to humanitarian initiatives, as in 1915, when a military hospital was accommodated in its reception rooms. The ballrooms were transformed into wards with long rows of iron bedsteads for the sick and the dying.

Beginning in 1947 the palazzo became the official residence of the president of the Republic. The first president, Enrico De Nicola, did not live there, however; he preferred the Palazzo Giustiniani. But Luigi Einaudi did live there (1948–1955) and chose the house of the secretary of the cipher as his private living quarters. Of the subsequent presidents, Giovanni Gronchi (1955–1962) used the house only as a study, while Antonio Segni (1962–1964), Giuseppe Saragat (1964–1971), and Giovanni Leone (1971–1978) actually lived there. With Sandro Pertini (1978–1992) and Oscar Luigi Scalfaro, the Quirinal returned to its earlier use for official receptions only.

The gardens are one of the attractions of the Quirinal. At the back of the Palazzo, extending along the hill above Villa Colonna, they are composed of a sort of labyrinth with high espaliers of myrtle, numerous palm trees, and a series of fountains around the Coffee House (below), a pavilion for recreation and repose which Benedict XIV built in 1741. Opposite it is the Fontana di Caserta, which Umberto I of Savoy placed here with three statues of women on a group of rocks, which came from the park of the Palace of Caserta.

PALAZZO COLONNA

COLONNA

The interior façade of the Palazzo, where the famous Colonna Gallery, created by Cardinal Girolamo between 1654 and 1665, is housed. It was added to by Lorenzo Onofrio and Fabrizio Colonna and has been kept in all its splendor up to the present day.

This is a building of great historical importance because, for a long time, since its medieval origins in a tower structure, it has been one of the cornerstones of city life. It belonged to the counts of Tuscolo, masters of Rome around the year 1000, from whom the Colonna family descended and who in turn were protagonists for centuries in the baronial struggles which often placed them in opposition to the papacy. It was the theater of important events in the thirteenth century, especially in the period of Boniface VIII, who imposed on the quarter the power of his Caetani family; the pope withdrew into the nearby Torre delle Milizie (Military Tower) and finally ended up actually living there in defiance of its Ghibelline owners, whose property he had confiscated. The Colonna,

however, took power again in communal Rome during the so-called Babylonian Captivity of the popes in Avignon, thus bestowing again great prestige on their own house.

In 1341, the visit of Petrarch is recorded; he had been invited to lunch on Easter Day after his solemn crowning with laurels on the Campidoglio as guest of the venerable Stefano, senator of Rome and vicar to Roberto di Napoli, who wished to celebrate privately the apotheosis of the poet.

The tower was reestablished in 1424 with the Colonna Pope Martin V, who incorporated it with other houses in a single complex, turning it into his pontifical residence. So it was that the new structure of the palazzo took on particular prestige as the residence

The coat of arms of the Colonna family held by two sirens in a large shell, on the side wall of the Palazzo in Via IV Novembre. Detail of one of the frescoes in the Galleriola.

of a pope, alongside a church dedicated to Santi Apostoli which had also been restored. The palazzo was, however, still of modest size despite the strength of its long crenelated wall, and its extension into the surrounding area was blocked by other buildings.

At the end of the fifteenth century, a house on the other side of the church which had belonged to Cardinal Giovanni Bessarione was rebuilt by Cardinal Pietro Riario, nephew of Pope Sixtus IV. Another small building was built symmetrically, flanking it, in the space behind the Colonna house and in

continuation of the apse of the church, in a *viridarium* (garden) on the slopes of the Quirinal hill, by another of the pope's nephews, Cardinal Giuliano della Rovere. The extension of Palazzo Colonna seemed to be unavoidably blocked.

Unexpectedly in 1506, however, the expansion came about through a wedding gift from Giuliano, who had become pope with the name of Julius II, to his niece Lucrezia della Rovere, bride of Marcantonio Colonna. The two buildings were connected temporarily to the fifteenth-century palazzo of Martin V. The high turreted walls gave the buildings the appearance of a medieval fortress while waiting to be made into a single large complex.

In this period the palazzo housed the great military undertakings of the family soldiers, such as Prospero (1452–1523) and his cousin Fabrizio (1450–1520), and his descendants through his son Ascanio (1495–1555) to his grandson Marcantonio (1535–1584), the celebrated hero of the Battle of

Lepanto. This was a glorious military victory of considerable significance in the history of the kingdom of Naples, where six viceroys were from the Colonna family and where, from 1515, they held the hereditary post of grand constable. However, the building also reflects the echo of the passionate poems of the poet Vittoria for her husband Ferdinando d'Avalos, soldier in the service of Charles V, and of platonic love for Michelangelo, before she closed herself into the convent in Via della Mercede.

This was a palazzo that became fundamental to the urban topography of the noble *isole*, where the papal processions ended when processing outside the

protagonist was the Roman people. From the windows of the palazzo corresponding to the interior of the basilica, birds and tidbits were thrown to the crowd who rushed to catch them. From the roof a pig was lowered on a rope and people jumped up to get hold of it while from the windows of the palazzo showers of cold water were emptied over the people to the hilarious amusement of the nobles together with the ecclesiastics and the pope.

The residence continued to have separate buildings for the entire sixteenth century, and even the *viridarium* looked unkempt and wild. It was from here that the restoration work started: between 1611 and 1618, the

Detail of the Sala della Colonna Bellica, with busts placed in front of the painting Venus and Cupid by Michele di Ridolfo del Ghirlandaio.

Vatican. Thus when Clement VII in 1523 carried out his historic cavalcade after his coronation to take possession of the Lateran, he stopped at Palazzo Colonna and was welcomed by Cardinal Pompeo. The latter had made a substantial contribution to Clement's election as pope and for this reason was appointed vice chancellor of the Church, a high office that brought the palazzo with it.

Again, to celebrate the alliance of the pope with Charles V on 1 May 1524, Clement VII took part in the celebrations of the event at Palazzo Colonna with a sumptuous banquet, culminating in a curious spectacle, the "carnival of SS. Apostoli", in which the

Colonna systematized the garden area, creating a number of terraces divided by great boxwood hedges and borders amid flights of steps and fountains.

The idea of combining the various buildings into one large complex was projected in 1654 on the initiative of Lorenzo Onofrio Colonna and designed by Antonio Del Grande, with the construction of an arcaded façade (now closed) in the interior of the courtyard, making the buildings lead into a central body and connecting the gardens to the palazzo by a series of bridges on the present-day Via della Pilotta. The work proceeded slowly because some of the details were defined during the work itself and

required a considerable outlay of capital, such as the
famous gallery which was completed by Girolamo
Fontana and inaugurated with solemn pomp in 1703.

The vaults, richly decorated with frescoes, evoke
the glories of the Colonna family, especially those of
Marcantonio, victor over the Turks, and function as an
apotheosis of the noble house, from the Sala della
Colonna Bellica (Hall of the Warrior Colonna), with
its column of *rosso antico* (red marble), the historic
family emblem, to the Hall of Martin V, in a
glorification that radiates in masterpieces by great
painters of the sixteenth and seventeenth centuries,
including the works in the Throne Room (for visiting
popes) and the Sala di Maria Mancini, niece of
Cardinal Mazarin and bride of Lorenzo Onofrio.

The architectural arrangement of these rooms is
magnificent: they are divided by two great arcades
supported on huge columns of *giallo antico* (yellow
marble). Their great value is increased by huge painted
mirrors, Venetian lamps, and gilded plasterwork,
among which are exhibited antique statues and
hundreds of valuable paintings. This collection has
gradually grown over the centuries, and despite the
forced sale of some masterpieces in the Napoleonic
period, it has maintained its original splendor through
subsequent acquisitions.

The organization of the palazzo continued thanks
to Fabrizio Colonna, who in 1730 commissioned the
architect Niccolò Michetti to build the façade on
Piazza dei Santi Apostoli. It was thanks also to
Cardinal Girolamo that the completion of the side on
Via della Pilotta was carried out in 1760 by Paolo Posi.
In this way, the limits of the building area were
established as they can still be seen today: between the
piazza, the side of the church, Via della Pilotta, and the
present Via XXIV Maggio.

The palazzo grew up around a courtyard, where a
large column was centrally placed, surrounded by trees
and flower beds, while two low buildings overlooked
the piazza. At the corner of Via IV Novembre these
were surmounted by a pavilion which was originally a
"coffee house." The Museo delle Cere (Waxworks
Museum) is now located there, and on the second floor
is a special room with an octagonal vault frescoed in a
splendid *Story of Cupid and Psyche* by Francesco
Mancini. Despite the demolition and subsequent
rebuilding of the south façade in 1885 by Andrea
Busiri Vici on account of the opening of Via IV
Novembre, the layout of the whole residential complex
is very little changed.

The palazzo has indisputably kept its dignity, in
honor of the noble house that has succeeded in wisely
administering its inheritance. In 1816 the Colonna was
the first among all the great Roman families to give up
its claims to feudal territorial jurisdiction, while it
simultaneously kept alive all the traditions that have
characterized certain palace customs as aristocratic
and avoided the risk of seeming ridiculous. Thus, the
parties and banquets given by the Colonna have
remained famous, especially during carnival. Their
guests included princes, nobles, and cardinals who,
however, in obedience to an old tradition—and for

Detail of the Galleriola that links the courtyard to the prospect over the gardens that lead up to the Quirinal. On the walls are frescoed views of gardens and fountains connecting to the reality beyond the bridges joining the Palazzo to Villa Colonna.

practical reasons—were obliged, before entering the reception room, to urinate into elegant vases adorned with myrtle and orange branches. A vulgar rite, a typical eccentricity of the nobility, which the ambassador La Tour Maubourg tried in vain to have abolished; until 1870 religious and political personages deposited their souvenirs into the

magnificent vases. Another feature of the mansion was its trembling on June 28, the eve of the feast of Sts. Peter and Paul. According to popular superstition, the phenomenon occurred as a result of the pope's excommunication of the king of Naples in 1777. This was because the king had suspended the custom of donating to the pope on that date, as a sign of a vassal's homage, a white horse and 7,000 gold ducats through his constable, the prince of Colonna. The curse was lifted only in 1855 when Pius IX abolished the excommunication, giving up the homage. These tales hover between legend and truth, and still today help make up the legendary past of the palazzo.

The collapse of temporal dominion did not surprise the Colonna princes of Paliano, who had boasted the title of "assistants to the papal throne"

1904 and from 1914 to 1919, and always headed a moderate and pro-clerical administration. Between 1936 and 1939 Piero was governor of Rome.

After the war the Colonna remained strong in their secular wealth, which had been constantly reinforced by advantageous marriages, thus guaranteeing its ability to remain the faithful custodians of the long history of the palazzo and of the precious works of art in its legendary gallery.

since the seventeenth century (a title abolished by Pope Paul VI in 1970). They are at the head of the body of Roman nobility and the palazzo remains the symbol of this prestigious position. They were engaged in the political life of the Italian kingdom, and the young Prospero and Fabrizio were both appointed senators. Prospero was also twice mayor of Rome, from 1899 to

The Beaneater *by Annibale Carracci in the Sala dell'Apoteosi di Martino V.*

PALAZZO ODESCALCHI

Standing imposingly on three-quarters of the length of the Piazza dei Santi Apostoli, Palazzo Odescalchi almost seems to challenge the hegemony expressed on the other side by Palazzo Colonna. The latter stands up to the challenge, with the help of the basilica that gave the piazza its name. At the back it extends with its villa to the lower slopes of the Quirinal, while Palazzo

Odescalchi extends as far as the Via del Corso, which it overlooks at the back, a prestigious reference point for every princely family on the main artery of the city. The challenge grew over time with the gradual development of the building, and was opposed by the Colonna for as long as they themselves were the owners.

Palazzo Odescalchi originated, in part, in 1308 as a hospice for indigent Lombard women, thanks to Donna Antonia Benzoni, originally from Crema; it was built on an empty lot on Piazza dei Santi Apostoli. Bought in 1488 by the church of San Nicola de Tufis, it later passed to the Colonna family. The lot extended back toward Via Lata as property of the church of St. Catherine of Siena. It was purchased in the second half of the fifteenth century by the Mandosi, a family of Germanic origin who built their residence on it. There were two buildings then, separated by a corner garden between the far side of the piazza and the Via dei Santi

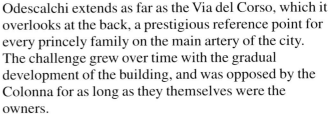

Apostoli, and the two buildings have two entirely different histories.

The Palazzo dei Mandosi on the Via del Corso was austere and did not boast a prestigious architectural design. It reflected the not very aristocratic spirit of the family that owned it. Among its members was Antonio, an apostolic protonotary in 1566, and various *conservatori* at the Campidoglio: Giovanni Battista in 1617, Ottavio in 1632, and Valeriano in 1661. The person endowed with the most prestige in the Mandosi family was Marcantonio, a famous lawyer, who was appointed bishop of Nicastro by Pope Urban VIII in 1637.

The princes of Gallicano, a branch of the Colonna family, owned the building facing the Santi Apostoli basilica. Their fief in the Roman countryside was originally autonomous but was joined to that of Palestrina in 1433 and to that of Zagarolo in 1523 through the marriage of Camillo to his cousin Vittoria, daughter of Pierfrancesco di Zagarolo, following a policy of territorial unification. This branch of the family had been involved, along with the main branch, in the civil wars that troubled Rome. We know that Clement VII was forced by the attacks of the Colonna

army to flee to Castel Sant'Angelo and that in revenge he sent his troops on a punitive expedition to Gallicano and Zagarolo, almost completely destroying them.

The two towns were rebuilt with much difficulty, and Marzio Colonna incurred numerous debts in order to restore his property there, neglecting his city home, which maintained its fortress-like medieval appearance. Soon mortgages were raised on the real estate, creating problems for his sons Camillo and Pierfrancesco, and they were forced to sell.

The palazzo in Rome was bought in 1622 by Cardinal Ludovico Ludovisi, who immediately set about its systematic restructuring. This important commission was taken on by Carlo Maderno, whose style is clearly recognizable in the ample rectangular courtyard with its arcade of pilasters and Doric columns. It so happened that Cardinal Ludovisi became vice chancellor of the Holy Roman Church in 1623 and, as such, had his residence in Palazzo della Cancelleria. He gave the palazzo in Piazza dei Santi Apostoli to his relatives, but the Ludovisi, not interested in living there since they already had a villa at Porta Pinciana, put the renovated building on the market.

Opposite:
Detail of the front elevation of the Palazzo giving onto Piazza Santi Apostoli, created by Bernini, with its portal with columns surmounted by a balcony and coat of arms. On the right, basin with eagle as represented in the Odescalchi coat of arms.

Detail of the arcaded courtyard, with Doric columns and pilasters, by Carlo Maderno.

243

In 1628 the Colonna princes of Gallicano bought it back, having weathered their financial problems and having evidently convinced themselves that they were now in a position to maintain a prestigious mansion. Their plan was to incorporate the building into the Colonna property on the other side of Piazza dei Santi Apostoli, thus making a single great complex. The renovation work at the foot of the Quirinal hill had already begun under Filippo I, but it seemed likely that this would take a long time and, above all, a great deal of money.

Thus, when in 1654 Lorenzo Onofrio Colonna began the work to restructure the buildings on the sides of the Santi Apostoli basilica, the prince of Gallicano changed his mind. Not only could he not afford the work, he could not even afford the maintenance. He did not have to think twice when, in January 1657, Mario Chigi, brother of Pope Alexander VII, asked to rent the building. He quickly came to a contractual agreement with him, especially since Chigi, in order to be able to use the building right away, rented for Colonna a building belonging to Donna Olimpia Maidalchini at the Trevi fountain.

The person who took care of all these expenses was, naturally, the pope, who also paid for the "beautification" of the palazzo in Piazza dei Santi Apostoli directed by the architect Felice Della Greca, "so that the said building might be brought to the form of a comfortable and decorous habitation" for his brother Mario and nephew Agostino, son of his dead brother Augusto. The result was nothing extraordinary because it was a temporary solution for the lay family of the reigning pope.

What brought about a definitive decision in this respect was the marriage of Agostino to Virginia Borghese, daughter of Paolo and Olimpia

Sala di Cibele on the piano nobile, so named because of the representation of tales of the goddess on the vault, with the coat of arms on a red background in the wall furnishings, and the portrait of a cardinal.

Aldobrandini on 18 July 1658. The celebrations were not extravagant. There was only a simple ceremony in the private chapel of the pope in the Quirinal and a lavish dinner for a few intimates in the palazzo in Piazza dei Santi Apostoli. And yet the rank of the two families could have aspired to more. The bride brought a dowry of 180,000 scudi toward the purchase of a princely fief by the young Agostino.

It seemed, however, that the Chigi were saving their capital for a more important investment. Don Mario Chigi and his son Agostino bought the Palazzo Aldobrandini on Piazza Colonna for 41,314 scudi in 1659. This became the splendid home of the Chigi family. Cardinal Flavio Chigi, son of Mario, who had been appointed cardinal two years before, went to live in the palazzo in Piazza dei Santi Apostoli.

It was this young cardinal who was mainly responsible for affirming the prestige of the palazzo because he wanted to make it his palace. Consequently, he did not want to rent but planned to make an outright purchase—and not only of the Palazzo Colonna. He wanted to enlarge his home onto the Via del Corso, and so he also bought the Palazzo dei Mandosi. The complete rebuilding was entrusted to a great architect, Gian Lorenzo Bernini, who finished the masterpiece between 1664 and 1667. On the side of Piazza Santi Apostoli he created a three-part façade on a central body with a colonnaded portal surmounted by a balcony with the coat of arms of the Chigi family. On account of its great sobriety and elegance of line it was destined to become an architectural ideal, famous throughout Europe. The two wings on the sides that fall back slightly from the central mass, inscribed in a geometric complex, are elegantly proportioned in the overall structure of the building. The rear part, however, develops a façade in line with those of the other buildings facing the Via del Corso, without any particular structures along the three floors that are cut by a balcony in the central one.

Inside, the rooms became luxurious and regal, starting from a room in the cardinal's alcove, described in a contemporary guide to the marvels of Rome as "admirable" and "so well harmonized that it induces wonder," with "a bed all of white satin painted with flowers, mostly by Brueghel, and with golden braiding, the portico with four gilded Corinthian columns, designed by Giovanni Paolo Schor," and "the painted mirrors by Stanchi," as well as the painted tondo of *Sleeping Endymion* by Baciccia.

With his rich prebends, Flavio Chigi was able to live as a great lord, and the building reflected this luxury, revealing his inclinations for society life and his predilection for the pleasures of the table and beautiful women. He was also a handsome man, tall, and with black curly hair that immediately made him stand out in a crowd. He had a collection of thirty-six portraits of the most beautiful women in Rome, among whom was Maria Mancini, at the time the wife of Prince Lorenzo Onofrio Colonna, living in the building opposite the cardinal's palazzo.

But the palazzo was also open to intellectuals because Flavio Chigi was a man of culture. The

Accademia degli Sfaccendati often met in his salon and held musical and theatrical performances. He had an extensive library: it contained not only 8,600 printed books, mostly rare editions, but also 2,655 handwritten manuscripts, mostly from the personal collections and papers of Pope Alexander VII. With him the palazzo finally took on a truly prestigious character.

It also became a den of political intrigue, where his colleagues, the other cardinals, would meet to discuss neutrality expressed in the group of cardinals called "the flying squadron." His salon gave rise to the directives of no fewer than seven conclaves, attesting to Flavio Chigi's extraordinary political skill.

With his death on 13 September 1693, the history of the Chigi family in the "large palazzo in front of the Santi Apostoli" also ended. His heir, Prince Agostino, was forced to reorganize the entire administration of his property and to give up his powerful cousin's monumental mansion, since he

Cybele Seated in a Coach Drawn by Two Lions, *painted in the center of the vault of the room named after her, probably the work of Girolamo Conti, also known as Dentone (1570–1632).*

the future of the pontifical state every time a pope died, in the maneuvering that took place behind the scenes of the various conclaves. In fact, upon the death of his uncle, Pope Alexander VII, Flavio Chigi became the head of the "creature"—as the cardinals nominated by the defunct pope were called in those days—and therefore the arbiter in the election of the new pope. He carried out this function, too, with skill and with the dignity of the Holy See in mind, under the banner of

already had a princely home in Piazza Colonna. He rented it to Livio Odescalchi for 1,600 scudi per year, emptying it first of the many precious furnishings which were to be used in his other palazzo. Thus, the marbles, tapestries, and furniture—and also the precious library—were carried away, as was the painting by Baciccia, which would be applied to the ceiling of the Salone d'Oro of the palazzo on Piazza Colonna.

For his part, Livio Odescalchi was the last representative of the illustrious family from Como, raised to the heights of the Roman aristocracy with Cardinal Benedetto, who became pope with the name of Innocent XI (1676–1689). He made use of his personal glory to ennoble his own residence. He was against nepotism and did not provide his nephew Livio with prebends. He wanted him to make his own way and indeed Livio obtained his fortune only from his military exploits in the service of Emperor Leopold I

he was not the owner, with paintings, sculptures, and tapestries that had belonged to Christina of Sweden and were put on sale at her death. Nevertheless, since he had no children, he did not consider buying the property.

On the other hand, he spared no expense in receptions and dinners, keeping up the tone of the palazzo, even if not with the atmosphere of intrigue and culture that Cardinal Flavio Chigi had brought to it. It did have a sudden rise in this sense when Livio

in the siege of Vienna and in the war against the Turks. He was nominated prince of the empire and general of the Holy Roman Church (though only at the death of Innocent XI), he was invested with the duchy of Sirmio in Hungary, and he was declared a grandee of Spain by Charles II; he also became duke of Bracciano, having bought the duchy from the Orsini family. All this gave him economic security, making it possible for him to enjoy furnishing his home, even if

Odescalchi received Maria Casimira Sobieski, the widow of King John III of Poland, in exile in Rome, as his guest. He reserved the residential wing facing the Via del Corso for her. With her was her aged father, the French Henri de la Grange d'Arquiem, who had received his cardinal's hat from Pope Innocent XI.

The queen, who would live there until 1702, moving on to the house of the Zuccari family at S. Trinità dei Monti, became an important figure in

Detail of the carved and gilded ceiling of the main salon of the piano nobile, with gilded rosettes and Odescalchi eagles.

Roman society. Her salon became a reference point in society life, with a touch of culture. Maria Casimira was accepted into the Accademia dell'Arcadia and organized poetry readings and literary salons in her home. She was determined to imitate the academic fortunes of Christina of Sweden and was thus the object of a famous pasquinata—a traditional form of satirical poem—which, among other things, spoke ironically about her birth from her French father, or "rooster": "Nacqui da un gallo semplice gallina/ vissi tra li pollastri e poi regina/ venni a Roma Cristiana e non Cristina" (Born of a rooster, as a simple hen/ I lived among the chickens and then as queen / I came to

Piazza dei Santi Apostoli could still be rented in their name.

But with so many titles and property, it became almost obligatory to own this aristocratic building. In 1745 Baldassarre Odescalchi took the big step. He bought the palazzo from the Chigi for 90,000 scudi and, taken by a taste for grandeur, had the front of the building overlooking the piazza enlarged, developing its imposing presence lengthwise.

The work was directed by the architects Nicola Salvi and Luigi Vanvitelli in 1750. In this way, the façade was lengthened, a portal added under a new balcony, and the right wing rebuilt as far as the corner

Representation of the Odescalchi castle in Bracciano in one of the overdoor decorations in the main salon of the piano nobile, decorated by Dentone.

On the following pages: The dining room on the piano nobile with rich rococo overdoor decorations, mirrors, and gilded frames in truly princely splendor.

Rome Christian and not Christina). Maria Casimira gave distinction to the palazzo in Piazza dei Santi Apostoli in other ways, if indirectly, on the occasion of the Jubilee of 1700. With her three sons, the princes James, Alexander, and Constantine, she was an honored guest at Christmas 1699 for the opening of the Holy Door in St. Peter's, which did much to increase her queenly status.

Livio Odescalchi died in 1713, and all his titles passed on to Baldassarre, son of his sister Lucrezia, of the noble Como family, Erba, with the obligation of taking his mother's last name. Thus the Odescalchi family continued the family line, and the palazzo in

of Vicolo dei Santi Apostoli. This construction altered Bernini's original design and also spoiled the garden. On the other hand, the change was all to the advantage of the grandeur of the building, over which the coat of arms of the Odescalchi could stand out prominently, finally able to vie with that of the Colonna in face-to-face confrontation.

From then on, the history of the palazzo has been identified with the history of the Odescalchi family and it has been referred to by their last name, since they are still the owners after two and a half centuries. During this time, those who have resided there have always managed to give luster to their family and their

Sala della Fontana, so named because of the water basin placed in the center, enriched by a precious polychrome marble fireplace. To complete the decoration are antique busts in ovals as overdoor decorations and a frieze with the Odescalchi coats of arms supported by putti in a series of variants, including one of Pope Innocent XI and the princely and ducal arms.

Detail of Sala della Fontana with a seventeenth-century tapestry and a splendid cupboard, with richly sculpted supports with putti and female allegorical figures.

home, often with cultural initiatives. Thus Baldassarre II, duke of Ceri (1748–1810), son of Vittoria Corsini and a Livio, wrote plays, poems, and a history of the Accademia dei Lincei and founded the Accademia degli Occulti. Pietro (1789–1856), son of Baldassarre III and Caterina Giustiniani, made himself known among neo-classical writers with his treatise on Comedy, his translated excerpts from Cicero's *Republic*, and his editorship of the *Giornale Arcadico*.

The person who did the most to mark an era in the palazzo in recent times was indisputably Baldassarre Ladislao (1844–1909), liberal patriot and author of numerous writings on art, history, and politics. After 20 September 1870 he was a member of the provisional government of Rome, and on 9 October of the same year, together with the duke of Sermoneta, he brought to King Vittore Emanuele II the results of the plebiscite of the Roman provinces that favored annexation to the kingdom of Italy.

In 1877 he was forced to look on powerlessly as a fire damaged the top floor of his palazzo and the entire façade on the Via del Corso. But Baldassarre Ladislao undertook to repair the damage. For the rooms, he limited himself to a simple restoration, but the façade on the Via del Corso needed to be completely rebuilt. He gave the project to Raffaello Ojetti but demanded

named Ladislao-polis after him—known today as Ladispoli.

Untiring in his initiatives, he even opened an outlet for the sale of Hungarian wine in a carriage house on the Via del Corso, with the name "Magnate of Hungary." This was considered highly eccentric, especially since Ladislao ran the business personally, among other things discrediting the nobility of his palazzo. For this he was the butt of a caustic

that it be an imitation of Palazzo Medici Riccardi in Florence, characterized by ashlar work that was completely out of keeping with the surrounding environment. It was a banal solution, on which it seems the influence of his Florentine wife, a Rucellai, had a certain weight, despite the prince's well-known intuition for building: in 1890, on the Odescalchi property on the coast between Rome and Civitavecchia he even had a small town built,

pasquinata in the form of a business card that was certainly not fitting for a prince: "Baldassarre Odescalchi," it said, "magnate e bevete d'Ungheria"—with the play on words on "magnate," which in Roman dialect also means "eat", hence "eat and drink of Hungary."

Detail of the frieze in Sala della Fontana with the Odescalchi coats of arms.

PALAZZO BORGHESE

POPE PAUL V

The façade of the Palazzo. Opposite, detail of the courtyard with the portico.

This is the famous *Cembalo* (harpsichord), a name that this princely residence has always had on account of its shape, which is comparable to that of a piano, with the end part facing the area that was once enlivened by the port of Ripetta and called "the keyboard." With this name it became part of the élite of the so-called "four

marvels" celebrated in Rome until the last century, in which were included the great *scalinone* of Palazzo Ruspoli, the Gate of the Sciarra Colonna, and the Palazzo Farnese.

The origin of the *Cembalo* dates back to the building by Monsignor Paolo del Giglio which gave onto the present-day Largo di Fontanella di Borghese: it was built in a late Mannerist style, designed probably by Vignola, with three floors and a courtyard. It was worked on between 1560 and 1578, the year of the owner's death, but was not finished. It was bought as it was, without a roof and with the courtyard only half completed, in 1585 by the Spanish cardinal Pedro Deza, and the work then continued under the direction of Martino Longhi the Elder until 1591, and subsequently under Flaminio Ponzio. The façade was delineated by a cornice, and two of the three wings planned to close off the courtyard were defined. After the death of Cardinal Deza in 1600, the palazzo was inhabited by Ambassador Raimondo della Torre and Cardinals d'Ascoli and Piatti until, in 1602, it was leased to Cardinal Camillo Borghese. He paid 1,000 scudi a year, without committing himself to continuing work on a building that was not his. He fell in love with that part of Rome stretching over the Tiber and thought about creating a great family residence, extending the building toward Ripetta and thus marking out the quarter into a whole "island" owned by his family.

In 1604 the cardinal bought the building, commiting himself to a bank loan of 40,000 scudi, sufficient to start a grandiose project which he entrusted to Flaminio Ponzio. It was a gamble for Camillo Borghese, but luck was on his side, because the following year he was elected pope. He took the name Paul V, and from then onward, needless to say, the matter of the debt simply became risible. Indeed, an additional 36,000 scudi were committed to completing all the building work. As pontiff, he could not live in the palazzo that was in any case still being built—because his official home had to be at the Quirinal—so he in turn had his brother Giovanni Battista live there.

Naturally, it was a somewhat risky residence with the work still going on, but it was the best way since at

least a Borghese could supervise the work directly. This proceeded with the completion of the left wing, the definition of the arcaded courtyard, the organization of the garden, and the erection of the long wing that faced onto Piazza Borghese and continued up to Ripetta, so that the building did effectively take on the irregular appearance of a harpsichord, with the "keyboard" facing the Tiber, in accordance with Carlo Maderno's invention.

The interior of the residence was sumptuous, starting with the wing facing the piazza. There, on the main floor, a suite of rooms culminated in the salon which soared two floors in height, where the walls bore mythical scenes of the Borghese family frescoed

by Cosimo Piazza, subsequently destroyed. On the ground floor the "long sleeve" wing was opened toward the Tiber with the backdrop of jets of water giving the theatrical illusion of disgorging from the opposite bank of the river.

It was a splendid home but so far uninhabited by the Borghese family, who moved there only in 1621 on the death of Paul V. The family members living there were Cardinal Scipione Caffarelli (1576–1633) and his cousin Marcantonio II (1601–1658), the very young designated heir to the family patrimony, whom the pope managed to have elected prince of Sulmona, named grandee of Spain by Philip II, and married to Camilla Orsini.

The Bath of Venus, *a vast nymphaeum with antique statues and three baroque water displays, between large niches supported by gigantic caryatids, against the boundary wall.*

With them the palazzo came to life, and the layout of the proprietary "island" or "block" in the context of the quarter was defined. These urban operations were directed by the cardinal, who went to live in the wing giving onto Ripetta, where he created his own rooms on the second floor, including a study and a chapel. The piazza was opened and at first was called a "dirt road" because it was not paved, but it finally took the name "piazza nuova di Borghese" (new piazza of the Borghese). It covered places where houses had once stood but which had been bought and demolished. On the opposite side was erected a building intended to lodge approximately one hundred serving staff. The piazza was then surrounded with columns and chains. The widening seemed to have been conceived as a sort

of external courtyard, a precise affirmation of
dominion over the quarter, of which the palace had
incorporated a part.

The palazzo had no peace because Prince
Borghese continually wanted to update its appearance
in accordance with architectural fashion: his princely
home must not seem less impressive than those of
other Roman nobles. Thus, Giovanni Battista
commissioned new improvements from Carlo Rainaldi
in 1671. The "long sleeve" with its severe and
impressive façade and the portal in the center of the
piazza were redone. The whole wing was closed on the
ground floor, and the backdrop was eliminated to make
a magnificent gallery. This was sumptuously decorated
with painted mirrors on the walls and frescoes on the
vaults and with plaster figures and busts of the twelve
Caesars, so that it became a genuine museum of
pictures and sculptures, the highest expression of art
and splendor in the palazzo.

On the main floor and on the second floor were
opened numerous rooms that were frescoed by Ciro
Ferri and Domenico Corvi, while on the two
mezzanines a summer residence for the princess was
created which constituted a particular refinement of
the building, rarely encountered in other noble homes
in Rome. The garden was transformed by Rainaldi into
a great nymphaeum known as the Bagno di Venere

260

(Bath of Venus): this consisted of three displays of water between large alcoves supported by gigantic caryatids in an exhuberant baroque burst of decoration, the work of Giovanni Paolo Schor. Even the "keyboard" was improved with two balconies: the first was covered by a gallery and supported by pillars and Doric columns between closed shutters; the second, built over it, was a terrace with a hanging garden. The ultimate in refinement, it had a view of the river port below, a unique panorama of the city.

Rebuilt in this way, the prince's mansion lived its season of splendor uninterrupted for two centuries, representing a point of reference for the Roman aristocracy, distinguishing itself in the restricted circle of weekly salons, open for receiving society, the so-called "*conversazioni*" every Friday in the year, which could not be missed even during Lent, and for which special papal concession was granted. It was always the Borghese princesses who gave these receptions their special character.

Those of the eighteenth century with its symbol of gallantry were the triumph of Donna Agnese, amiable and full of life, the organizer of great tables of card games of all sorts. In the nineteenth century it was the inimitable mistress of the house, Adele Rochefoucauld, wife of Prince Francesco, who, though widowed from 1839, was, even in the Rome of Pius IX, "the soul of the Borghese house," as reported by the diplomat Henry d'Ideville who was a resident in the city from 1862 to 1867. At the balls in the Borghese palace it was "easy to contemplate the Roman princesses in all the glory of their jewels and their diamonds, see the cardinals and bishops from nearby, and be presented to ambassadors."

The last great fancy-dress ball held in papal Rome was in fact the one given at Palazzo Borghese on 7 February 1866: "The fancy-dress ball at the Borghese palace," wrote Nicola Roncalli in his diary, "was magnificent. There were costumes of all centuries and all nations and two in particular were talked about: one was the costume of Princess Borghese who dressed as Mary Stuart, the other was Princess Rospigliosi who was dressed in the style of Maria Mancini, niece of Cardinal Mazarin, and she wore around her neck the very pearls that Louis XVI gave Maria Mancini when she married Prince Lorenzo Onofrio Colonna, having a value of seventy thousand scudi."

Perhaps the most famous Borghese princess of all remained outside the aristocratic and high society of the palazzo, that is, Paolina Bonaparte, wife of Prince Camillo (1775–1832), immortalized by Canova in his famous statue. In 1803 her personal apartments were furnished in imperial style on the fourth floor to the right of the entrance to the building, including a circular salon, a bedroom, and a small chapel. She did not like it; instead, she preferred to open the drawing rooms of the villa at Porta Pia, which was then called the Paolina.

Canova's marble statue of her in the role of Venus the Conqueror stayed for a while in the Ripetta palazzo, and her husband showed it to friends and guests with pleasure, together with the masterpieces in

the gallery—or at least those that remained after his brother-in-law Napoleon had appropriated some. Finally, however, he became jealous and had the statue moved to the lodge at Porta Pinciana where it was less visible.

The palazzo has inevitably followed the Borghese family through the crises that afflicted them, together with other noble papal families. Today it is occupied by the offices of the Spanish embassy, but the princes still reside in part of it, guaranteeing a care that will ensure the maintaining of prestige.

Furthermore, the Circolo della Caccia (Hunting Club) on the main floor ensures an aristocratic flavor, while in the "keyboard," the setting for exhibitions of antiques, can still be breathed the artistic air that was once that of the gallery, whose masterpieces were sold to the state in 1891 and are now housed in the Museo della Villa Borghese.

A drawing-room in the private apartment of the Borghese family, with splendid period furniture and lamps against the background of costly wall and door decoration, a room evoking parties and receptions which were famous in the aristocratic Rome of the gallant eighteenth and the romantic nineteenth century.

PALAZZO PALLAVICINI ROSPIGLIOSI

The garden at the back of the Palazzo overlooking the Casino dell'Aurora with the splendid nymphaeum called "Il Teatro", designed by Vasanzio and built in 1611–1612, with the statues of the rivers Po and Tiber by F. Landini and tritons by S. Sollaro.

On the slopes of the Quirinal, this palazzo does not look directly over the Via XXIV Maggio but rises majestically beyond a high wall that does not look like a bastion but rather is decorative and thus hides its practical purpose, which is to isolate the palazzo from its urban context. It is in the center of a vast green space that has surrounded it right from the beginning, when in 1605 Cardinal Scipione Borghese Caffarelli,

nephew of Pope Paul V, planned it as an alternative residence to the family home that his uncle in the same period was having built at Ripetta, but which the cardinal was uncertain that he would be able to live in.

The project envisioned a complete organization of the land along the slope of the hill along with a simultaneous construction of the palazzo. This was undertaken by Flaminio Ponzio, while Giovanni

ROSPIGLIOSI

264

Vasanzio superintended the preparation of the gardens, which were to slope down over three terraces, each with a lodge decorated with statues and frescoes.

On the first terrace, with a double staircase for access, was built the Casino dell'Aurora, a small building made of marble provided by the ruins of the ancient Baths of Constantine, which had been completely destroyed during the earth-moving work on the hill. Its name came from the famous *Aurora*, the fresco painted by Guido Reni on the ceiling of the main room, a work of art framed on the walls by the *Four Seasons* by Brill, and in the side rooms by other frescoes by Baglione and Cresti. It was a jewel in the midst of greenery, counterbalancing the Loggia delle Muse (Loggia of the Muses), frescoed by Tassi and Gentileschi, on the second terrace, in front of a large semicircular fountain called a "water theater" on account of its theatrical appearance. In 1876, however,

267

The gallery of Palazzo Pallavicini Rospigliosi, on the piano nobile, *boasts around five hundred paintings, drawings (Pietro da Cortona and Bernini), and sculptures (Pierre Puget and Giuseppe Mazzuoli). The rooms, decorated between 1622 and 1627, are resplendent with the overdoor decoration of frescoed landscapes and caisson ceilings.*

the third terrace with its lodge frescoed by Cardi with the myth of *Psyche* (now in the Museo di Palazzo Braschi) was destroyed to make room for the Via Nazionale.

The palazzo, worked on from 1613 by Carlo Maderno, was no less impressive than the lodges, despite the extreme simplicity of the façade and its Renaissance structure. It was its decorations that made it a magnificent palace, starting with the loggia frescoed with putti and landscapes by Reni and Brill.

Suddenly, however, in 1616 when the mansion had just been completed, Cardinal Borghese abandoned it

even though he had started living there. He went to live in the family mansion at Ripetta and decided to sell the other. It was bought by Giovanni Angelo Altemps, who also had a mansion in the Parione district which he was improving in various ways. He bought it because he had a lot of children, but then regretted it because the expense of continuing the work on the interior of the building was still substantial. Thus, he in turn sold the property only three years later to the wealthy Bentivoglio family of Bologna.

Cardinal Guido lived there, a private valet to the pope and supreme head of the Inquisition. To him is

owed the decoration in the immense rooms on the ground floor and the main floor carried out between 1622 and 1627 which formed a sumptuous framework for this representative of the tough papal policies of the Catholic Reformation. In these rooms the cardinal meditated on decisions that left their mark on the culture of the times, synonymous with the most bigoted conservatism: suffice to think that it was he who signed Galileo's death sentence in 1641.

In that year Cardinal Jules Mazarin came to live in the palazzo, and he bought it a year later for his sister Girolama, wife of Michele Lorenzo Mancini, while he

Camilla, the last of the Pallavicini, princes of Gallicano, and Giovanni Battista Rospigliosi, nephew of Pope Clement IX, prince of the Holy Roman Empire and duke of Zagarolo, continued the construction and expansion work with the building of a stable in the main courtyard, and, above all, in the establishment of the famous gallery, which was laid out in the private apartments. The nucleus of the collection was based on the numerous Emilian paintings bought by Cardinal Lazzaro Pallavicini, uncle of Maria Camilla, while he was in Bologna as papal legate, and inherited by his niece.

On the following pages: Some of the masterpieces of the Pallavicini collection, including, at the top, the Transfiguration with Sts. Jerome and Augustine *by Sandro Botticelli and, on the right,* Rissa Before the Spanish Ambassadors *by Diego Velázquez.*

The Room of the Tapestries and the Great Hall dedicated to portraits showing, among valuable furniture, silverware, porcelain vases, and carpets, the splendor of the prestigious families who succeeded each other in this palazzo, including the Borghese, the Bentivoglio, the Mancini, and the Pallavicini Rospigliosi.

On the death of Maria Camilla and Giovanni Battista, all their property was shared between their older son, Domenico Clemente Rospigliosi, and their younger, Niccolò Maria, who took the name of Pallavicini so that the house should not die out. The art collection grew during the next two centuries, remaining a point of reference of the Pallavicini Rospigliosi line, even though the two branches united and separated again several times. An impressive number of paintings acquired after marriages, with funds from the Colonna and the Lante della Rovere, and divided as property between the two families, still remained in the same palazzo.

In the early part of the twentieth century, however, the Rospigliosi encountered serious financial problems and had to sell the collection, which the Pallavicini tried in vain to buy. It ended up, together with part of the palazzo, in the hands of the

Federazione Italiana dei Consorzi Agrari. The Pallavicini collection of about 540 paintings and some sculptures remained with the Pallavicini family who still live in the palazzo. They are not the direct line, however, because in 1929 Giulio Pallavicini, having no male heir, adopted his nephew Guglielmo de Bernis, who inherited the name with the title of prince.

VILLA BORGHESE

This park of this splendid villa, which extends beyond Porta Pinciana for at least 85 hectares and is six kilometers in circumference, is one of Rome's public parks and is also the site of a richly endowed museum. It was created at the beginning of the seventeenth century by Cardinal Scipione Caffarelli Borghese, nephew of Pope Paul V, as a place of enjoyment rather than as a real residence, intended for parties, hunts, holidays, and art collections.

It was all developed on a vineyard owned by the Borghese family since 1580 in the district called Parioli and always marked as *Vigna Vecchia* (Old Vineyard), to which were added through purchases and gifts six further vineyards between 1606 and 1609. These constituted the basis of the plans designed by Flaminio Ponzio with the lodge and the gardens made in Italian style, with woods and shaped hedges. The palazzo was finished in 1613, the year in which its architect died, to be replaced by Vasanzio who took care of its decoration. The four façades, consequently, were almost completely covered by numerous sculptures which were for the most part antique, including 144 bas-reliefs, 70 busts, and 43 statues.

View of Villa Borghese in a 1636 watercolor by Johann Wilhelm Baur.

PALATII VILLAE BVRGHESIAE PROSPECTVS

Everywhere on the exterior of the mansion exuberant decorations embellished alcoves and ovals, harmonizing with the splendid double staircase which opened onto the piazza in front of it which was closed off by a balustrade; this too was rich with vases and statues that no longer exist. Behind the mansion was another piazza with a fountain and two Italianate gardens along the sides. It was in this house that the antique collections of Cardinal Scipione found an immediate home. In 1608 he had bought the statues of Palazzo Ceoli, now called Palazzo Sacchetti, and, a year later, the collection of G. B. Della Porta. At the same time, on the occasion of the works carried out on the façade of St. Peter's, his uncle gave him as a gift the sculptures found in the ancient basilica.

Between 1610 and 1620 the villa grew bigger by means of additional purchases and gifts. The land belonging to the brothers of Cardinal Scipione Borghese and his nephew Marcantonio which lay adjacent to the complex became part of it, and four more vineyards were also added to it, so that the complex finally had a perimeter of three miles.

The park was created over this ample terrain. Construction of its extensive and beautifully laid-out gardens and architecture was carried forward by Girolamo Rainaldi, who replaced Vasanzio (who had died in 1621), and the fountains were built by Giovanni Fontana. Three enclosures were also developed.

The first was organized in thirteen squares, as it still is today, stretching from Via Pinciana to the villa.

The main façade of the palazzo with its restored spectacular two-flight staircase. The impressive Borghese Gallery is housed there, previously owned by the Borghese family, and bought by the Italian State in 1900.

On the following pages: Venus Victrix (Venus the Conqueror) *the famous statue by Antonio Canova of Paolina Borghese, sister of Napoleon and wife of Prince Camillo Borghese, the symbol of the Gallery.*

A long avenue of elms led to the piazza-theater with the two *termini* sculpted by Pietro Bernini, while the Oval Fountain and the Round Fountain made a fresh and artistic accompaniment to the shrubs and pines that waved their branches between the hedges of boxwood and the support walls. It was a geometry of greenery divided up artificially by two systems of nets which were spread out to catch birds. This entire structure still exists, though it is now deteriorated, as the wine lodge testifies. Built in 1609, it was used by the princes as a natural refrigerator; open-air parties were held there and verses declaimed. Now abandoned, it is used as a public lavatory.

The second enclosure, to the east of the palazzo, was planted with laurels and divided into six squares with a row of cypress trees. The Secret Garden and the Pomegranate Garden gave onto the two adjacent sides of the building, while from the piazza at the back was developed the so-called *Prospettiva* with the Narcissus Fountain, which has since disappeared. Continuing on

In the second room of the Borghese Gallery is the dominating figure of David *by Gian Lorenzo Bernini, who made it for Cardinal Scipione Borghese in 1624. Along the walls is a series of antique sculptures, including, on the left, the sarcophagus with small columns, and the* Labors of Hercules, *sculpted in the year 160 A.D.*

On the following pages: View of the whole of the fourth room, dominated in the center by the group by Gian Lorenzo Bernini, Rape of Proserpine; *the room, used by Cardinal Scipione Borghese for parties and banquets, was modified by Antonio Asprucci in the eighteenth century with marbles, mosaics and stucco decorations, and the arrangement along the walls of busts of Roman emperors in porphyry and alabaster, together with two tables in porphyry made in 1773 by Luigi Valadier.*

279

The marvelous sculpture by
Gian Lorenzo Bernini, the Rape
of Proserpine, *executed in 1612
with extraordinary realism, as
is evident from the details,
including the tears pouring
from Proserpine's eyes, and
Pluto's fingers dug into the
woman's flesh.*

282

this side were the aviaries, for which copper wire was used which was brought specially from Venice, then the vast Deer Park which was home to deer and gazelles, as well as another semicircular piazza–theater, surrounded by boxwood, and finally the Great Forest, with its laurels and pines, statues, sarcophagi, and fountains.

The third enclosure, to the north of the palazzo, kept its natural appearance. It was a continuous vineyard set amid valleys, plains, and hills, where a large number of domestic and wild animals were kept, with the Casa del Gallinaro (Bird House), subsequently called the Fortezzuola, an enclosure for ostriches and peacocks, and even a menagerie of lions. Then came a large fishpond, surrounded by forty-two plane trees which are still growing in the valley toward the Zoological Gardens, and the Casino del Graziano, which already existed in a vineyard bought by the

Sleeping Hermaphrodite, a statue of the first century A.D., a Roman copy of an original sculpted by the Greek artist Polycles in the second century A.D., found in 1781 and restored by Vincenzo Pacetti. It is in the fifth room of the Gallery.

View of the sixth room of the Gallery, dominated in the center by the statuary group of Aeneas and Anchises, *carried out by Gian Lorenzo Bernini in 1620, in collaboration with his father, Pietro.*

The seventh room of the Gallery. A typical example of neo-classical taste, it was designed by Antonio Asprucci and inspired by ancient Egypt, as is revealed in the frieze with its papyruses and the large statue of the goddess Isis in black marble, sculpted in 150 A.D. In the center, Youth Riding on a Dolphin, *a Roman copy of the first century A.D. of a Greek original of the Lysippus school.*

Detail of the entrance hall designed in neo-classical style, with typical late-eighteenth-century decoration on the walls and a herma, one of the valuable archaeological finds of the Borghese Collection.

The marvelous statuary group by Bernini in 1624, Apollo and Daphne, *representing the moment in which the god is about to grasp the woman who is then transformed into a laurel bush. It is in the center of the third room. On the pedestal are carved the Latin lines composed by Cardinal Maffeo Barberini, later Pope Urban VIII: "Quisquis amans sequitur fugitivae gaudia forma/fronde manus implet baccas seu carpit amaras" (He who loves to follow the fleeting forms of pleasure/finally finds leaves and bitter berries in his hands).*

Borghese family in 1613, in which would be housed part of the prince's collection of sculptures and paintings. The external relief decorations are now gone, and no more than the dragon of the Borghese family crest remains.

This was the appearance of the villa up to halfway through the eighteenth century. It was continually cared for and the gardens were properly maintained, with the garden partially rebuilt between 1776 and 1793 under

extend the themes of the statues and groups placed in the rooms. In this way an Egyptian chamber was realized for the Egyptian works. The *Myth of Apollo* was frescoed in the same room where Bernini's *Apollo and Daphne* stood, and the *Myth of Hermaphroditus and Salmacis* was painted on the vault of the room where the *Sleeping Hermaphrodite* was placed. The outside was also transformed by the elimination of the double ramp and its replacement with the present simple flight of steps.

The Danaë *by Correggio, painted in Mantua in 1531, was donated by Federico Gonzaga to Charles V and bought by the Borghese family in 1827.*

Prince Marcantonio Borghese IV. This work was entrusted to Antonio Asprucci, assisted by his son Mario and by an army of painters engaged in decorating the interior of the house. The most radical work was the new arrangement of the rooms inside the palazzo, with Rococo preciosity in the cornices on the walls and neo-classical taste in the delicate cameos in plaster and in the polychrome marble floors. The decoration tended to

In the park, which was extended by the purchase of a vineyard and a cane thicket, Asprucci, with the collaboration of gardening expert Jacob Moore, took on the redesigning of the third enclosure, which in substance lost its wild nature. There the Temple of Faustina was placed, created in accordance with the prevailing taste for pseudo-antiquity, together with the Fontana dei Pupazzi (Fountain of Puppets) and

The Lady with a Unicorn *painted by Raphael in 1506, represents a noble woman with the mythological beast in her arms which, according to legend, could be tamed only by a virgin.*

the Fontana dei Cavalli Marini (Fountain of Sea Horses). The most significant contribution to this new image of the park, however, was made by the Giardin del Lago (Lake Garden), which became a sort of miniature park inside the park, featuring the Temple of Aesculapius on the little island, and the Piazza di Siena set up for Barbary horse races. Over and above this was the transformation of the Casa del Giardiniere (Gardener's House) into the Casino dell'Orologio (Clock Lodge), which took its name from the four-faced clock on the bell tower, and in which were placed archaeological objects brought there from the Borghese estate at Pantano. On the other side, the Casino dell'Alboretto dei Gelsi (Lodge of the Mulberry Wood) was restored with the creation of a chapel dedicated to the *Virgin*, and nearby was built the Tempietto di Diana, another classical remake, the prototype of the artistic passion for ruins prevailing at that time.

A bad period in the villa's existence began with the arrival of Napoleon, the brother-in-law of Prince Camillo, who was the husband of Napoleon's sister Paolina. In 1807 the emperor forced Camillo to give up

immortalized by Canova in the role of *Venus Victrix* (Venus the Conqueror) which was set to shine in the room dedicated to her alone, after having been displayed for some years in the entrance hall of the *Cembalo* at Ripetta.

Further consolation came to him in the extension of the villa with the purchase between 1820 and 1831

Boy with Basket of Fruit, painted by Caravaggio in 1594. It is in the eighth room of the Gallery, dedicated to the great painter, displaying five more important paintings, including the great Madonna of the Serpent.

the majority of the antiquities in the villa which then became the nucleus of the classical art collection of the Louvre. It was a straightforward theft, because only some of the works seem to have been purchased. As a result, all the statues and reliefs on the façade disappeared from the villa, as did numerous masterpieces that had decorated the rooms. Camillo could only console himself with his Paolina, as

of five more vineyards so that the park embraced the entire area flanking the Muro Torto and reached the Porta del Popolo. The works started again with the restoration of the park. Now it was designed to be a broad vision of both countryside and city, and it aimed to link the villa to a public street. A determining factor in realizing this project was the purchase of one more Bourbon vineyard in 1833. The work, entrusted to

Luigi Canina from 1825, was completed in 1834. Avenues and bridges were opened, Egyptian propylaea were reinvented, and the junctions with streets were concealed by the Fountain of Flame and the Arch of Septimus Severus, yet another recreation of the antique, until finally the grandiose avenue was built which led from the Fountain of

and confirmed on a wall panel behind the palazzo, "Va dove vuoi, chiedi ciò che vuoi, esci quando vuoi: più che per il proprietario, qui tutto è allestito per l'ospite …" (Go where you will, ask what you wish, leave when you want to; rather than for the owner, here everything is intended for the guest …). People went there for the October celebrations, when they danced,

Circe, *the legendary woman capable of changing men into animals. The painting is by Dosso Dossi, from 1525, with wild fantasy and spectacular colors.*

Aesculapius to Piazzale Flaminio, with a theatrical entrance.

It was then that the villa lived its most intense season, freed from the private character it had always had until then. The prince decided to place it at the disposal of the Roman citizens every day except Monday, bringing about in this way Cardinal Borghese's original idea when the villa was built,

sang, and gambled. The Clock Lodge, emptied of sculptures, was transformed into a tavern managed by Stefano Giovannini and, logically, became a meeting point for picnics. Piazza di Siena became an ideal place for crowds of people, meeting perhaps for celebrations or general merrymaking, or for a lottery like the one organized for orphans of the cholera epidemic in 1842. Then there was the tombola

Opposite:
Cumaean Sibyl, *painted by
Domenichino in 1617, in the
nineteenth room of the
Borghese Gallery, a room
entirely dedicated to paintings
of the seventeenth century.*

organized during the October celebrations, with a stage for the drawing of the numbers in the middle of the piazza and the crowd sitting on the steps, all assisted by military fanfares. Marcantonio Borghese V invented some cultural celebrations too with the aim of educating citydwellers in the joys of returning to rural life with a precise political and economic program.

The pleasure of some of these days out was temporarily suppressed by the cannonfire that in 1849 destroyed the Casino del Muro Torto, the Casa del Portinaio, and the bridge of the Acqua Felice, as well as

reliefs, statues, and even the ancient double flight of steps and the balustrade of the piazzale. The Italian state entered the discussions, and in 1900 the government decided to buy the villa to honor the memory of King Umberto I. It would be presented to the Roman municipal council so that they could turn it into a public park, with the reservation that it would be called Villa Umberto I. However, everyone continued to call it Villa Borghese. The state also purchased the entire Borghese art collection, and the palazzo became the site of a national museum.

Venus Blindfolding Cupid *by
Titian, painted in 1565,
accompanied by the famous
and fascinating* Sacred and
Profane Love, *also by Titian
(1514).*

damaging several stretches of road. Once the Republic was over, everything started up again as before, but these were the last bursts of fun. After 1879 the prince closed the gates, opening them only for a few hours and in the presence of guards until, on 12 May 1885, Marcantonio Borghese ordered them to be definitively closed. The local Council protested and the matter finished in court where the tribunal found for the citizenry, which thus obtained free access on Tuesdays, Thursdays, and Saturdays. Those who wanted to go into the Giardin del Lago had to pay twenty-five *centesimi*.

Gossip started up again and the idea of buying the villa was aired. The local council decided to do so, but a bank mortgage came to light. However, the Borghese were ready to sell because they had considerable financial problems. They had already sold sculptural

The history of the villa became officially one of the people as the property lost its private and noble character. A few cases remained of smaller houses scattered throughout the park. These became private dwellings, including the Fortezzuola of Pietro Canonica and the Palazzina Lubin. The public aspect was now the determining factor, hence the creation of a network of roads inside the park which facilitated the merging of the park's greenery with the city's asphalt and cement but created the risk of degrading the park. This public aspect is the reason for the connecting roads with the Pincio and for the new area of the Galoppatoio (riding track or gallop), for the building intended as an aqueduct near the Deer Park, and for the opening of the Zoological Gardens, designed as a kind of annex, almost as a commemoration of the

Opposite:
*Piazzale Scipione Borghese,
which opens onto the back of
the Palazzo, with the so-called
Garden of Venus with its
circular basin and the statue of
the goddess, a copy of the
Medici Venus. On the boundary
wall is a series of statues of
gods and heroes as well as
hermas with busts bearing
baskets of fruit, by the Bernini
school.*

*Diana the Huntress, with a
detail above, painted by
Domenichino in 1617 and
taken by Cardinal Scipione
Borghese by force. He
imprisoned the artist who did
not want to sell it to him, until
the artist let him have it in
order to regain his liberty.*

menagerie of wild animals that lived there in the past.
As a public park, it could not be more different, being
as it is, inside the city, open to everyone and
everything, and suffering from the inevitable negative
consequences caused by atmospheric pollution, theft
and vandalism.

In the 1980s, however, an incentive to return the
villa to its past beauty was provided by the restoration
of the palazzo, which continues as the millennium
approaches. The façades are being returned to their
original Roman marble, and in front of the main façade
the theatrical seventeenth-century double staircase is
being rebuilt. Radical renovation has been made to the
gallery, restoring the rooms to their former glory and
displaying the masterpieces there with the help of
modern installations.

The new expository principle of the gallery must
be seen within the perspective of the great project that
is creating a genuine Parco dei Musei (Park of
Museums) in the Villa Borghese gardens. The project,
completion of which is planned for the year 2000, will
include sculptures, fountains, and monuments
displayed in the open air, and display areas that will
enhance the Gallery.

Included in the Parco dei Musei will be the Museo
Canonica, the Casino delle Rose (intended for
contemporary exhibitions), the so-called House of
Raphael (to be the site of a specialized Museum of the
Villa Borghese), and the neighboring Etruscan
Museum at Villa Giulia and the Galleria Nazionale
d'Arte Moderna. Thus, the Villa Borghese park will
take on a new life in the name of art.

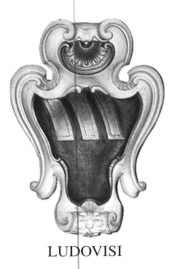

CASINO DELL'AURORA LUDOVISI

A *casino*, or lodge, is all that is left of the grandiose palazzo complex of the Ludovisi that once extended over the area of the ancient *horti Sallustiani* (gardens of Sallust). The family home was torn down and the land subsequently divided into lots between 1883 and 1885 in a historic example of real estate speculation from which arose the Ludovisi quarter, including the famous Via Veneto.

The villa was built between 1621 and 1622 with the purchase of the Del Monte and Capponi vineyards and Villa Orsini by Cardinal Ludovico Ludovisi

(1595–1632), who was a nephew of Pope Gregory XV and *camerlengo* of the Holy Roman Church. This amounted to nineteen hectares of land lying adjacent to the Aurelian walls between what is now Via di Porta Pinciana and Via Piemonte, and from Porta Pinciana to the convent of the Capuchins near Piazza Barberini.

The villa was a triumph of gardens and greenery by Domenichino, that combined various different types of terrain into a pleasing whole. It consisted of a succession of gardens, flower beds, and woods, run through with paths between the cypress trees and high

The Casino dell'Aurora is all that is left of the splendid Villa Boncompagni Ludovisi. The original sixteenth-century cruciform building was extended in 1858 by the architect Nicola Carnevali, with an avant-corps and arcade on each of the arms, as on the right.

hedges and decorated with fountains, ancient statues, and an obelisk from imperial Rome. There were three separate buildings in these gardens, the *palazzo grande* (principal palace) with an aviary, the Casino Capponi, containing art collections, and the Casino dell'Aurora, named after the painting by Guercino in the hall on the ground floor. This was the home of the first owner of the Del Monte vineyard, Francesco Del Nero, treasurer of Clement VII. It was bought in 1596 by Cardinal Francesco Del Monte and in 1621 became the property of Cardinal Ludovico Ludovisi.

This small palazzo already had a well-defined architectural structure, with its observation tower prominent in the center and a lantern above the three floors, and surrounded by what seemed to be an actual theater of ancient statues, which no longer exists. The cross-shaped central hall on the ground floor was very comfortable. The vault was decorated with grotesques, and there were four rooms leading off the four branches of the cross, one of which functioned as the entrance.

This plan was repeated on the main floor which was reached, as it still is, by a spiral staircase decorated with stucco niches, opening onto a small room that had been used as a scientific study by Cardinal Del Monte. On the vault, an "alchemy" scene painted by Caravaggio depicted the various stages of the transformation of lead into gold and showed

A putto carrying water, a rare archaeological find from the exceptional Boncompagni Ludovisi Collection. It is one of the precious ornaments of the villa, which was partly bought by the State and became the nucleus of the Museo Nazionale Romano at Palazzo Altemps.

One of the façades of the Casino dell'Aurora, now inside a garden which is very small compared to the luxuriant 30-hectare estate that once surrounded it, the only remains of it being, at left, the great palm tree.

Veduta del Giardino dell'Eccellentissimo Signor Principe Ludovisi a Porta Pinciana, *etching by G.B. Falda in 1683. The print shows the whole original complex of the villa, extending over the area of the ancient* horti Sallustiani, *which was, however, torn down between 1883 and 1885. Only the Casino dell'Aurora remains and can be seen in the middle of the print. At the front on the left is the Palazzo Grande enclosed by the Palazzo Margherita, the present seat of the embassy of the United States in Via Veneto.*

Jupiter, Neptune, and Pluto above the elements of the universe. The beauty of this pictorial jewel by Caravaggio stimulated Cardinal Ludovisi to have all the other rooms frescoed, and for this he engaged the services of the finest painters of the time, including Guercino, Tassi, Domenichino, and Brill.

One of the results was the *Chariot of Aurora*, painted by Guercino in 1621 on the vault of the main hall. The fresco shows the goddess on her golden chariot pulled by a pair of dappled horses. She is moving away from her elderly husband, Titus, strewing his path with petals while a cupid crowns her with a garland of flowers. Allegories of day and night were painted in the lunettes. The subject was chosen to glorify the Ludovisi family, in open conflict with the

Borghese princes, who only seven years before had commissioned another *Aurora* by Guido Reni for their residence on the Quirinal, later to become the Palazzo Pallavicini Rospigliosi. The inscriptions on the five doors exalting "Card. Ludovisus Camer." confirm this.

In the next room were a series of landscapes by G. B. Viola, Domenichino, Paul Brill, and again Guercino, who together with Agostino Tassi also decorated the vault with an aerial circle of dancing cupids. This feast of color continued into the salon on the *piano nobile*, where again Tassi and Guercino portrayed an allegory of Fame—which gave the room its name—Honor, and Virtue, all of which connected with the *Aurora* from a political point of view as a glorification of the Ludovisi family.

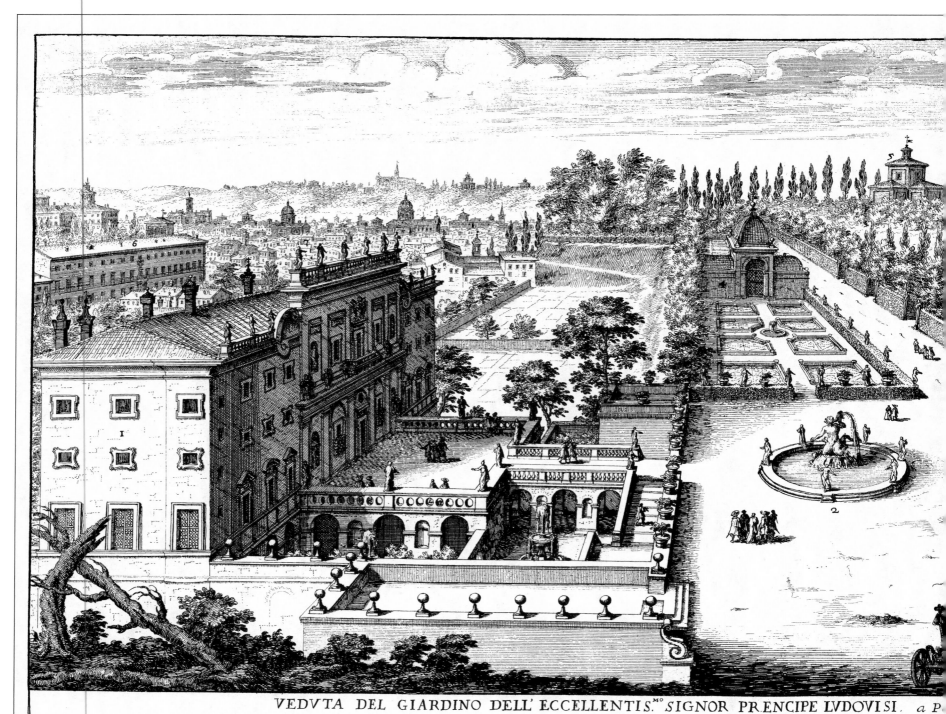

VEDVTA DEL GIARDINO DELL' ECCELLENTIS.^MO SIGNOR PR.ENCIPE LVDOVISI. a P

G. Bara Falda del' et in:

1. Palazzo Grande del Giardino.
2. Fontana del Tritone nella piazza auanti il Palazzo Grande.
3. Bosco del laberinto.
4. Vccelliera nel Giardino secreto adornato di statue.
5. Palazzetto detto delMonte adorn
6. Palazzo dell'Eccell.Sig.r Prencipe di P

The furnishings were exceptional. On the ground floor, for example, was a carved and gilded wardrobe, and in the room with the allegory of Fame was a precious bed, now lost, that Giovan Battista Pinaroli described in his *Trattato delle cose più memorabili di Roma (Treatise on the Most Memorable Objects of Rome)* in 1725 as "a bed of delights." It was "made of various oriental gems, which were estimated at a hundred thousand scudi. There were four columns of amethyst and oriental lapis lazuli with many other costly gems such as topaz, aquamarine, emeralds, and rubies. The headboard was decorated with ten oriental pearls the size of acorns, Apollo's chariot of gold with diamonds as the nails on its wheels, silver statues below, while above it was embellished with

balustrades in da Monte crystal. At the foot of the bed there were various large stones of jasper agate and flowered alabaster."

The decoration of the casino was continued up to Cardinal Ludovisi's death in 1632. The cardinal did not have much time to enjoy this masterpiece created within the context of the villa. It passed to his heirs, but they never showed much interest in it. In 1670 Giambattista Ludovisi sold it to the Rospigliosi family, but a few years later he bought it back for his daughter Ippolita by disposing of land in Zagarolo. It became the dowry for Ippolita, the youngest of the Ludovisi family, on her marriage to Gregorio Boncompagni (1624–1707), duke of Sora; this union was the origin of the house of Boncompagni Ludovisi, princes of Piombino, who from then on were the owners of the villa. In 1696, however, the Jesuits filed suit against the Boncompagni Ludovisi, claiming certain rights on the inheritance of Cardinal Ludovico, so that in 1697 they gained ownership of the villa with the Casino dell'Aurora. A long contentious procedure began until the two parties reached an agreement and the Boncompagni Ludovisi regained the property, but the splendid "bed of delights" went to the Jesuits, and they sold it a year later. From then on a veil of mystery covered the extraordinary treasure from the Casino dell'Aurora, and no trace has been seen of it since.

In any case, the villa was abandoned because the Boncompagni Ludovisi, who lived in the palazzo on Via del Babuino with its famous "talking statue," did not even use it for recreation or for taking walks in the woods and gardens. They had so little interest in the property that in 1734 they gave the obelisk to Pope Clement XII as a gift. The pope would have liked to have put it in front of the basilica of San Giovanni, but it was too small in proportion to the piazza. Abandoned next to the Scala Santa until Pius VI had the idea of raising it at Trinità dei Monti in 1789, the obelisk made a fine impression when it was finally erected on a suitable pedestal.

Then, at the beginning of the nineteenth century, the interest of the Boncompagni Ludovisi in the villa suddenly reawakened, and they finally went to live there. In 1825 Prince Luigi bought the neighboring property belonging to the Belloni family, between the present Via Piemonte and Via Lucania, and had the Casino dei Pranzi built. The halls were opened for receptions, but these were not very frequent and were reserved for an exclusive number of guests. The villa was frequented by nobles and illustrious persons, but only at the special invitation of the owners, who were reluctant to let their treasures, surrounded by their green gardens, be admired by outsiders. In 1827 Stendhal fell in love with the villa, and in particular with the Casino dell'Aurora. He would have liked to have owned it himself and wrote in his famous *Roman Walks*, "If I had the good fortune to own this fascinating place, no one would ever set foot in it in my presence. In my absence, though, I would charge two piasters to visit it, that would be passed on to poor artists."

In 1858 Antonio Boncompagni Ludovisi III bought another neighboring villa, the Borioni

ciana

7. Veduta di Roma.

del Giardino.

G. Iac. Rossi le stampa in Roma alla pace cō Priu: del S. Pont.

Opposite:
The vault of the Sala dell'Aurora, frescoed by Guercino, shows Aurora on her chariot drawn by two horses as she abandons the elderly Titon, who appears under a drape held up by a putto. A cupid is placing a crown on her head and another is following her with a basket of flowers.

The Sala dell'Aurora, on the short side on the right, with two doors with jambs and lintels in marble, where the inscription to Cardinal Ludovisi can be seen, surmounted by two marble busts in oval niches. The lunette, an appendix to the great fresco of the vault, represents an allegory of Night, showing the sleeping figure with two children at its side, one dead and the other asleep (because mythologically Night nourishes both sleep and death).

Santacroce, with a lodge nicknamed Torre di Belisario. This area lay between present-day Via Lucania and Porta Salaria, near Piazza Fiume. This was Villa Ludovisi's maximum extension—thirty hectares. Restoration works on the Casino dell'Aurora were well underway at this time. A porch was added at the entrance and a chapel created with the enlargement of the building.

The traditional attitude of the Boncompagni Ludovisi family as protective guardians of their property and the art masterpieces that gradually accumulated here did not disappear. The villa was accessible only to a select few, as were the works of art displayed in the building used as a museum. It continued to be visited only by the nobles admitted to the salon and a few writers as guests, such as Henry James, Nikolai Gogol, and Hippolyte Taine who pointed out its "*grâce*" and "*grandeur*." Louis Ehlert explained the difficulty of gaining access to the villa and its treasures as due to "the lack of hospitality that the prince of Piombino experienced on a trip to England where he wanted to visit private galleries, inducing him to open his famous collection one, and only one, day a week."

With the fall of papal Rome, the Boncompagni Ludovisi began to look at the villa and its buildings anew. They considered them unused capital and thus in 1872 decided to rent them out for a year. The tenant was none other than the king of Italy, Vittore Emanuel II, and the rent was 50,000 lire. The contract included the Casino dell'Aurora, the museum, and the Casino dei Pranzi, while the *palazzo grande* and the Casino Capponi were excluded. However, it was the pretty Rosina, the morganatic wife of the sovereign, who actually came to live here. The Casino dell'Aurora was practically reduced to a *garçonnière*.

On the death of Antonio Boncompagni Ludovisi III in 1833, his sons Rodolfo and Ignazio and their sisters decided to divide the villa into separate lots and sell them. In 1885 the demolition of the monumental entrance began, along with the trees and statues outside. All the buildings were torn down except the Casino dell'Aurora and the *palazzo grande*, which was incorporated into a new palazzo built by the Boncompagni Ludovisi on Via Veneto, later to become the embassy of the United States. Next to this, on the present Via Boncompagni, two smaller mansions and a house were built, where the archaeological masterpieces and art works were distributed. The collection of ancient statues from the Casino Capponi was given to the Museo Nazionale Romano.

The Casino dell'Aurora is the only structure remaining from the villa, and it is still the residence of the Boncompagni Ludovisi. Even though it now lacks the wonderful furnishings that once graced its floors, this building remains an extraordinary testimony to its former magnificence. The noble family keeps it as a treasure but, in accordance with the tradition begun in the nineteenth century, it allows visits only by appointment and only once a week.

Vault of the entrance hall of the Casino dell'Aurora, decorated with grotesques; in the center, the head of Janus in radial symmetry with four eyes representing the four seasons. At the corners of the ceiling are the coats of arms of the Ludovisi family and running along the sides are the repeated words "Franciscus Nero Secretarius Apostolicus," referring to the first owner of the building, Francesco Del Nero, treasurer of Clement VII.

PALAZZO BARBERINI

The bee, the Barberini heraldic symbol, in a decorative relief on the palazzo, which has been the property of the Italian State since 1949 and houses part of the Galleria Nazionale d'Arte Antica.

Severe in its solid and compact structure, the mansion's gigantic proportions dominate the piazza of the same name, where the Triton Fountain seems to pay homage with its stream of water to the regal presence of the palazzo. It was conceived from 1625 onward as a real palace for the family of the Barberini pope reigning at the time, Urban VIII, and this architectural image has been kept despite the reduction in the building's size.

This grandiose residence was built in an old vineyard which had belonged to the Sforza family, with a small mansion erected on the remains of ancient buildings, among which was the temple of the goddess Flora. The residence needed to express the pomp of a lineage with all the splendor of the Baroque, and this masterpiece succeeds in that aim. The work was started by Carlo Maderno, who was followed by Francesco Borromini, then by Gian Lorenzo Bernini, who completed the work in 1634 with Pietro da Cortona.

View of Palazzo Barberini on Via delle Quattro Fontane, with a garden and, on the street, an iron grille made by Francesco Azzurri in 1864.

It is an enormous structure, built as a central body and extended along two long parallel wings, harmoniously following the slopes of the Quirinal hill in the context of a park which once extended between Via Pia (now Via XX Settembre) and Via San Nicola da Tolentino, Piazza Barberini, and Via delle Quattro Fontane. The work was brought to its conclusion under the vigilant eye of Cardinal Francesco Barberini but with assistance on the financing from his uncle the pope, who did not hesitate to increase taxes on a regular basis in order to raise enough money to continue the project. For this reason he was nicknamed "Pope Tax." While only partly fancy, the traditional belief was that the Barberini had violated the Colosseum and the Pantheon for building materials, giving rise to the slanderous epigram "Quod non fecerunt barbari, fecerunt Barberini" (What the barbarians didn't do, the Barberini did).

And so the work proceeded without stopping, starting from the impressive architectural decisions of Borromini with the designs of the windows, the helicoidal staircase, and the back façade, and going on to the designs of Bernini in the great staircase with a square well in the left wing and the main façade extended in the three classical architectural styles—Doric, Ionic, and Corinthian—along Via delle Quattro Fontane. It is here that the main entrance to the complex is now located, through the nineteenth-century iron gates, through eight pilasters with baskets and telamons, constructed by Francesco Azzurri in

The large number of antique statues in the Barberini Collection decorate the palazzo, its gardens, atrium, and stairs, like this Apollo with His Lyre *at the top of a semicircular nymphaeum.*

The coat of arms of the
Barberini family with the three
bees on the gable above the
entrance to the salon on the
piano nobile.

The atrium of the palazzo,
designed by Maderno on the
lines of a nymphaeum with a
series of niches decorated with
antique statues, such as Ceres
and Apollo, below.
Opposite, the helicoidal stair
by Borromini.

Portrait of Urban VIII, *by Gian Lorenzo Bernini, c. 1625.*

Opposite:
The Triump of Divine Providence, *frescoed on the vault of the salon on the* piano nobile, *a masterpiece by Pietro da Cortona, who painted it between 1633 and 1639.*

1864. The stables were here, along the present-day Via San Nicola da Tolentino, in front of the portal built by Pietro da Cortona on the piazza, and the theater on the Via Bernini side, with, before it, the Cortile della Cavallerizza. From there the road began that passed under the mansion and ended in the garden behind it.

These are all places on the left side of the present Piazza Barberini which no longer exist: they were destroyed for the most part when Via Barberini was created, but they provided the setting, with the great palazzo and the luxuriant park, for the sumptuous life of the Barberini and the recipients of their patronage.

In fact this regal residence always had a particular cultural reputation as a meeting place for famous personalities of the seventeenth century, including the poets Gabriello Chiabrera, who recited his classicizing odes, Giovanni Ciampoli, welcomed for his sacred poems, and Francesco Bracciolini, who was appreciated in that climate of the Catholic Reformation for his comic-heroic poem *Lo scherno degli dei (Mockery of the Gods).*

In addition, there was the scientist Benedetto Castelli, the historian Gabriele Nardé, and, of course,

Gian Lorenzo Bernini, who showed his talents also as scene painter in the private theater.

Theatrical activities were inaugurated on 23 February 1634 with the melodrama *Sant'Alessio* with music by Giulio Rospigliosi, followed by a regular program of musical comedies interrupted by dances and celebrations at carnival time or wedding parties, like that held for Maffeo Barberini and Olimpia Giustiniani in 1656.

All this was in the service of patronage, a question of pride for the Barberini who saw pomp as itself a glorification of the family. This was reflected too in the decorative style of the mansion, especially in the left wing. Between 1633 and 1639 Pietro da Cortona frescoed its splendid salons with allegorical scenes, including the *Triumph of Divine Providence* on the immense vault of the central salon on the first floor, a Baroque glorification of the Barberini family as shown by the papal tiara and keys of Urban VIII, and the bees of the family crest.

Painted on the vault of another large room on the piano nobile is still another fresco that glorifies the Barberini family, this one by Andrea Sacchi. His *Triumph of Divine Wisdom* not only alludes to the various merits of the Barberini but also testifies to the triumph of divine knowledge over scientific knowledge.

The right wing of the building is no less sumptuous, as can be seen in the monumental Sala dei Marmi (Hall of the Marble Statues), so called on account of the splendid examples of classical sculpture that the Barberini family collected. It is one of the most

attractive halls in the palazzo, the family's greatest pride in the eyes of Roman high society, but now reduced to only a few examples, such as *La Velata (The Veiled Lady)* by Antonio Corradini. However, the salon, given its central position in the mansion and its imposing structure, was long known as the place for banquets. Before the theater was built, it was used for performances with temporary fittings of stage and benches so that up to two hundred people could be seated.

The salon was always considered a place of prestige, indirectly the boast too of Roman high society, so much so that it was often made available by the Barberini for ceremonies and special occasions of all the nobility.

Of particular fame is one sumptuous banquet offered on 27 November 1867 by the noblewomen

A further source of pride for this palazzo was the establishment here of tapestry production. This lasted from 1627 to 1683 and introduced into Roman baroque salons the type of decorative hangings that were Flemish in origin. They were produced under the guidance of the artist Jacobo della Riviera, whom Francesco Barberini brought from Flanders for the purpose. Pietro da Cortona also made important contributions to the industry through his drawings and cartoons that were used as designs for the tapestries.

On the top floor of the palazzo Cardinal Francesco installed his great library, which contained 60,000 books and 10,000 manuscripts. This remained a great cultural resource throughout the first half of the seventeenth century, highlighting the intellectual qualities of this cardinal.

Judith with the Head of Holofernes, *an impressive masterpiece by the mature Caravaggio (1599–1600).*

of Rome to the officers of the papal and French armies in honor of their victory at Mentana; the celebration was immortalized in a watercolor by the painter Carlo Santarelli which now hangs in the Museo di Roma.

The other cardinal nephew of the pope, Antonio, who also lived in the same palazzo, was restless and ambitious. His behavior was worldly, and he involved artists and eminent cultural personalities of his circle in great scandals. Another nephew, Taddeo, brother of

La Fornarina, *a famous painting by Raphael which traditionally portrayed the woman he loved. Raphael's signature is on the bracelet. Recent scholarship suggests that his pupil Giulio Romano participated in the work.*

the other two, created prince of Palestrina, prefect of Rome and general of the papal troops, rivalled his brother Antonio in dubious behavior and fraudulent dealings. He concentrated in himself all the questionable dealings that had brought the Barberini family great wealth, and it was he who inherited the patrimony, being in fact the one to continue the family line.

In 1645, however, a year after the death of Urban VIII, the three nephews were apprehensive when an investigation initiated by the new pope Innocent X brought up a proven accusation of embezzlement. They fled to France for a few years, and their mansion was confiscated. But once the storm had passed, through

prestigious residence. Among the unavoidable reconstruction projects was the maintenance of the garden, which was done mainly by Giovanni Mazzoni, who became gardener to the Barberini family in 1867 and who created the nursery and the greenhouses. In the same period, Francesco Azzurri built a fountain in the garden in front of the mansion on the side toward Via delle Quattro Fontane. Erected on an octagonal basin with four masks and three bees that encircle the water spout, it was certainly the last element of pomp that the Barberini allowed themselves.

They began to sell works of art, both paintings and sculptures. In 1900 the all famous library of Cardinal

Picus Transformed into a Woodpecker *by Benvenuto Tisi, called Garofalo, (c. 1480–1559).*

the good offices of the French prime minister, Cardinal Mazarin, in 1653 they were able to return to Rome and receive back their property, including the palazzo.

The dynasty did not survive for long. It ended in 1728 with Cornelia Costanza, wife of Giulio Cesare Colonna Sciarra, and it was from this union that the Barberini Colonna branch was born. This line too died out, in 1893, with the marriage of Maria to Luigi Sacchetti, from which originated the present dynasty of Sacchetti Barberini Colonna.

The mansion's history parallels the good and bad fortunes of its owners, who often had to sacrifice works of art in order to subsidize the upkeep of their

Francesco was sold to the Vatican with all the original shelving made by Bernini. The floor it had previously occupied became the headquarters of the Istituto Italiano di Numismatica (Italian Numismatic Institute). Then the part of the park backing onto the outside wall toward Via XX Settembre was divided up into plots, and the ball court built there for games was demolished. Large ministerial buildings were then erected there, giving a bourgeois tone to the area which had earlier been aristocratic because of its proximity to the countryside, surrounded only by vineyards.

This was the sign of a crisis that would oblige the Barberini family to get rid of the mansion. In 1935 the

maritime company Finmare bought the part that had been the old Sforza wing and restructured it completely. In 1949 the whole complex was bought by the State, and three years later the Barberini family sold all the paintings and *objets d'art*. It was the end of a glorious age. The left wing of the mansion became the headquarters of the Galleria Nazionale d'Arte Antica (National Gallery of Ancient Art), thus taking care of the artistic value of the works and structures; the right wing was made over to the Armed Forces who—unsuitably—set up their officers' club there.

The dinners and ceremonies organized by the officers' club certainly do nothing to recall the pomp of earlier times, and only a decision to use the mansion as a museum would constitute a guaranteed protection of the architectural and artistic structures. This is something that could be achieved if the officers' club were to be transferred to other premises. Then, though with difficulty, all the buildings of this estate could return to the dignity they once had.

The Fates *by Giovanni Antonio Bazzi, known as Sodoma, c. 1535.*

313

PALAZZO ALTIERI

North façade of the courtyard of the palazzo, surmounted by a balustrade with antique marble statues.

The Altieri, an ancient Roman family, dominated the Pigna quarter right from the beginning of the fourteenth century, extending its own houses into a broad block of ownership around the present-day Piazza del Gesù. Previously the piazza took its name from the Altieri. Their surname could also mean *altèri* (haughty) and a family motto ran "Tant'alto quanto si puote" (As high as you can). They were evidently proud of the responsibilities they had as local leaders of the quarter and masters of the streets, as well as of their kinship with numerous patrician Roman families, notable from the family crests painted on the façades of their houses: Alberini, Astalli, Capizucchi, Capodiferro, Cavalieri, Frangipane, Massimo....

In 1509 Marcantonio Altieri, the humanist of the family, celebrated the aristocratic world of Rome in the pages of his book *Li Nuptiali (The Nuptials)*, and then demonstrated his diplomatic talents as the maker of harmony among the barons with the *pax romana* desired by Julius II.

During the sixteenth century the Altieri family sold the part of the block where the Gesù and Palazzo Petroni (subsequently Palazzo Cenci Bolognetti) stood. They kept only the area contained within Via degli Astalli, Via di Santo Stefano del Cacco, Via and Piazza del Gesù, and Via del Plebiscito, making an area whose perimeter measured more than four hundred meters. This was the basis of the palazzo.

At the beginning of the seventeenth century the houses in this quarter were registered as the property of Lorenzo Altieri and Monsignor Mario Altieri, canon of the Vatican, and subsequently of the brothers Orazio and Lorenzo. It was a row of medieval houses all gathered within a compact wall except for one modest habitation, the property of a city woman called Berta, whose insertion into the superb residence of the Altieri no one could explain. The Altieri wanted to knock down the whole district in order to build a great house there.

Apotheosis of Romulus, *a fresco by Domenico Maria Canuli (1676) on the vault of the antechamber salon of the* piano nobile. *Left, detail of the perspective* quadratura *with the Altieri coat of arms, the work of Heinrich Haffner.*

Lorenzo began to enlarge his property, building a *casa nova* (new house) on Via del Gesù: this was only the beginning. Substantial financial investment was needed which was guaranteed a little later on by Giambattista, son of Lorenzo, when in 1644 he took the cardinal's hat. He guaranteed the initial investment for the undertaking in which his brothers Girolamo and Marzio were involved.

Thus began the project signed by Giovanni Antonio De Rossi and Mattia De Rossi. The first part of the fabric rose between 1650 and 1655. This was the part overlooking Piazza del Gesù, easily recognizable because it constituted the wing that was lower than the rest of the palazzo. At this point, construction work stopped: problems had arisen of expropriation and more money was needed. This arrived with the new cardinal of the Altieri house, Emilio, who was elected pope in 1670 with the name of Clement X. At this point, not a simple, but a more ostentatious, cardinal's residence was conceived, a monumental palace full of dignity, suitable also as the court of a pontifical household family.

The body of the fabric was defined in its entirety. The remaining houses were knocked down, but Berta would not give way to any offer; she was determined not to sell her four walls, so that they could be seen encircled by the sumptuous palace. Her door with its little window can still be seen on the façade of Piazza del Gesù, beyond the band of ashlar masonry, as if it wanted to compete in prestige with the majestic papal escutcheon over the balcony and the imposing portal.

And just in these years the Altieri risked extinction and the palazzo seemed fated not to have a master. However, the pope conferred on Gaspare Paluzzi Albertoni, husband of his niece, the right to continue the family line, with the use even of the name. This lasted until recent times: the male line died out only in 1955 with Ludovico Altieri, prince of Oriolo, Viano, and duke of Monterano.

It was an illustrious dynasty of cardinals and high municipal rank, including Paluzzo, husband of Princess Marianne of Saxony, who was senator of Rome (1819–1834). It was a dynasty that was a guarantee for the palazzo itself, which was constantly reshaped and redimensioned from one century to the next, and which was constantly embellished inside.

Illustrious architects followed each other on the fabric after the De Rossi, from Alessandro Speroni to Clemente Orlandi and Giuseppe Barberi, each time renewing and extending its structure, from the arcaded courtyard to the great staircase adorned with antique statues, including the *Barbarian Prisoner*, found at the Theater of Pompey, to the second courtyard with the overhanging gallery that once contained a library and is now the family archive, with a bust of Clement X, the work of Gian Lorenzo Bernini.

The *piano nobile* is a suite of luxurious apartments which lead to the Salone delle Udienze or della Clemenza (Hall of Audience or Clemency), with the same splendid decorations of the vault by Carlo Maratti. They are apartments whose rooms evoke mythical names, seasons, and colors immortalized in

Nude figure in the decoration on the vault of the antechamber on the piano nobile *and the landing of the staircase of honor, with the portal decorated with the Altieri arms, of which the star is also highlighted on the floor.*

Landing of the main staircase, adorned by an antique statue and a huge finger, the curious fragment of a colossal Roman statue.

317

Decorative detail of the valuable furnishings, and, opposite, of the coffered ceiling, painted and gilded with star and rosette heraldic symbols of the Altieri family in a room on the piano nobile.

Central square of the vault in the summer bedroom, Paris and Helen by Felice Giani, who decorated several rooms of the apartment of Prince Paluzzo Altieri between 1787 and 1794.

the vaults and the lunettes decorated by painters like Salvator Rosa, Unterberger, and Francesco Cozza: the Sala Verde or dell'Inverno (Green or Winter Hall), the Sala Rossa or dell'Amore (Red Hall or Hall of Love), and the Sala degli Specchi (Hall of Mirrors) are all found together, dating from the end of the eighteenth century, in the apartment of Prince Paluzzo Altieri. A further five rooms include the summer and the winter bedrooms, the oval office, and the main office with its floor made of an antique mosaic found in 1783 at Ostia, and a splendid Pompeii Room.

Plasterwork, mirrors, friezes, and mantels provide a backdrop for the precious furnishings, witnesses to a past of celebration and culture, immortalized in the poetry of Giacomo Leopardi, and honored also by the presence of Cardinal Angelo Mai, by the Accademia dei Quiriti, which organized annual art exhibitions,

The Hall of Mirrors, frescoed by numerous artists in different periods: Fabrizio Chiari in 1675 with the Chariot of the Sun *on the vault and other figures, Giuseppe Barbieri and Francesco di Capua with landscapes, between 1794 and 1795, then Giuseppe Cades with his frescoes of months of the year, and Salvator Rosa with several paintings.*

One of the antique statues adorning the Hall of Mirrors, restored in 1758 by Ponseler.

Putti in the marble frieze that runs around the high wainscoting of the Cabinet *by Vincenzo Paccetti (1788). Below, detail of the grotesques by Felice Giani and the four altars designed by Giuseppe Barbieri and executed by Ponseler.*

Opposite:
The Cabinet of the apartment of Prince Paluzzo Altieri, also called the Sala del Mosaico (Hall of Mosaics) because of the floor mosaics, representing the mythical meeting between Mars and Rea Silvia. On the vault is a large oil painting on canvas by Stefano Tofanelli, the Apotheosis of Romulus *and, above the doors, scenes from the* Rape of the Sabine Woman *by Antonio Cavallucci, Giuseppe Cades, Francesco Manno, and Anton von Maron.*

and by the Accademia Filarmonica which in 1863 gave performances of operas such as *Beatrice di Tenda* and *Semiramis* by fellow academician Rossini, cultural events that have indelibly left their mark on the twentieth century.

On the roof-terrace, with its entrance on Via degli Astalli, the actress Anna Magnani lived for more than twenty years, until September 1974 when she died at the age of sixty-four. The evenings spent in her drawing-room are famous for their concentration on literature and cinema, a message deeply cultural.

The palazzo, which is still the property of the Altieri heirs, has continued to keep its image of great dignity, with its rich original furnishings, despite the use to which the headquarters of the Associazione Bancaria Italiana (Italian Banking Association) has inevitably had to put it.

Opposite:
The portal between the Cabinet and the Hall of Mirrors, an indented panel in alabaster flanked by columns in porphyry and surmounted by a frieze with medallions and the Altieri coat of arms.

The library, a large area carved out of the upper part of the Palazzo and now housing the important Altieri family archive. Above the bookcases is the great bust of Pope Clement X, the work of Gian Lorenzo Bernini, placed here in 1677.

PALAZZO DORIA PAMPHILI

This splendid building, which occupies the vast block extending between Via del Corso, Vicolo Doria, Via del Plebiscito, Via della Gatta, Piazza del Collegio Romano, and Via Lata, is the largest building complex of Roman patrician society. Built over the course of four centuries, it is an architectural masterpiece of the Baroque. It is the residence of the princes of Doria Pamphili who are still its owners and who continue to live there.

Its history started in 1505 when Cardinal Giovanni Fazio Santoro bought part of the land where the whole complex stands today from the monastic chapter of Santa Maria in Via Lata and planned the construction of an imposing residence. The palazzo developed

View of the palazzo on Via del Corso and a portrait of Innocent X, sculpted by Alessandro Algardi.

around a large rectangular colonnaded courtyard—still in existence—that was probably the work of Bramante, with two gardens at the back. Before the work was completed, it was already obvious that this would be a remarkable palazzo, justly boasted about by the cardinal who was proud to have invested his money in it. When Pope Julius II was invited to inspect it, however, he was so struck with admiration that he obliged the cardinal to give the mansion to his nephew Francesco Maria della Rovere, duke of Urbino. Santoro could not refuse: he gave over the property and withdrew to his palace at San Lorenzo in Lucina where he died of grief a few months later.

The della Rovere family continued the work and acquired other houses at the edges of the property in order to demolish them and extend the area around the palazzo. An arcade was built, which in the eighteenth century was transformed into stables, with two rows of columns that closed off the western side of the Giardino dei Melangoli (garden of the Seville oranges). The salons of the main floor were then properly furnished and decorated so that they could be opened to the pomp of a ducal court, which

immediately made the residence famous. Ceremonies were conducted there in great splendor and luxury, such as the wedding of the young Francesco Maria I, appointed prefect of Rome and captain general of the Church, to Eleonora Gonzaga, the investiture into the same posts of their son Guidobaldo II, and the festive gatherings of Cardinal Giulio, who busied himself more than the other members of his family with the continuation of the construction work.

In 1601 the palazzo was bought by Cardinal Pietro Aldobrandini, and it remained Aldobrandini property until 1647. In order to enlarge the property, other acquisitions of new houses in the area took place, including the purchase of the "*stufa di San Marco*" (St. Mark's stove), a famous public bath of the period.

The quadrangular courtyard with two rows of arcades. The first dates back to the beginning of the sixteenth century, the second, with rococo closed window arcades, is eighteenth-century and by Valvassori.

A roof-terrace was built over the Giardino dei
Melangoli, which had become a courtyard. Prominent
in its decorative scheme was the Aldobrandini heraldic
escutcheon with its eight-pointed star. Annibale
Carracci was commissioned to paint biblical scenes
in the six lunettes of the family chapel (these
magnificent landscape–narrative scenes were moved
to the Galleria Doria Pamphili after the chapel was
demolished).

The palazzo became a prince's palace with
Giovanni Giorgio Aldobrandini, prince of Rossano,
but it was especially the cardinals in the family, such
as the nephews of Pope Clement VIII, who made the
mansion most famous: Pietro, Cinzio, Silvestro, and
Ippolito all contributed to embellishing and adding
value to its interior, though, strange to say, they
neglected the façade on the Via del Corso, which
stayed rough and was embellished only by a trabeated
portal. This is its appearance in a painting by Agostino
Tassi of 1631, which shows the procession of the
ceremony of investiture of Taddeo Barberini as
prefect of Rome, an appointment celebrated thirty
years earlier in this same residence for the della
Rovere.

*View of the Salone degli
Specchi (Hall of Mirrors) with
gilt-framed mirrors alternating
with precious antique statues,
almost all restored in the
eighteenth century. Above, a
detail of the decoration in the
lunettes above the windows,
with cupids holding up the dove
of the Pamphili family.*

*On the preceding pages:
Two rooms in the Galleria
Doria Pamphili: the Salone del
Poussin with the paintings by
Gaspard Dughet, called
Poussin, or Pussino, because of
his kinship with the more
famous Nicolas, and the second
arm, the Salone degli Specchi
(Hall of Mirrors), frescoed on
the vault by Aureliano Milani
with the* Labors of Hercules.

However, the prince's palace boasted no male line. The only heir of the Aldobrandini di Rossano family was a woman, Olimpia, who in 1647 married Camillo Pamphili, nephew of Pope Innocent X, bringing ownership of the palace with her as her dowry. So ownership changed again. The Pamphili moved into the palazzo in 1651.

From that date forward were written the most noble pages of the building's history. Festive celebrations were even more magnificent. It was the princess of Rossano who immediately raised its tone during the carnival of that year: she opened her drawing room daily to all the festivities and even had the rough façade on Via del Corso improved by constructing a porticoed wooden loggia richly decorated with artificial ornaments, from which one could view the processions of floats and masqueraders; she also had a merry-go-round installed under the loggia. This was the beginning of an uncontrolled desire manifested by the Pamphili family to enjoy the palazzo to the fullest extent. In addition, the edifice now assumed the appearance of a palace, on

Detail of the Salone Aldobrandini, with its wealth of statues and antique reliefs dating from ancient times to late Imperial, deriving mainly from the gardens of Villa Doria Pamphili, like the great sarcophagus with its bas-relief representing Apollo and the Muses.

account of the further substantial acquisition of property that led to its expansion onto the slope of the Piazza del Collegio Romano.

The building project was carried out by Antonio Del Grande in 1652 with the erection of two façades at the corner of the piazza, and a panoramic vestibule and staircase on Via della Gatta. Attention was then directed toward the decoration of the interior rooms, work which continued under the sons of the princess of Rossano, Prince Giovanni Battista and Cardinal Benedetto, patron and cultivator of the arts. With the cardinal, the palazzo also took on the aspect of a cultural centre, with meetings of writers, musicians, and painters. From the latter the cardinal bought additional works for his art collection, which became part of the important gallery started by his father. To direct the work, a series of famous architects were engaged, including Giovanni Pietro Moraldi and Carlo Fontana; it was Fontana who supervised the construction of the great family chapel on the side behind the church of Santa Maria in Via Lata.

The time eventually came to deal with the façade on Via del Corso; it was Prince Camillo the younger, son of Giovanni Battista, who took care of it. He commissioned Gabriele Valvassori, who carried out the work between 1731 and 1734, creating a splendid vision, a masterpiece of late Roman Baroque. It was

Bust of Olimpia Maidalchini Pamphili *by Alessandro Algardi and, below, the small dining room in the private apartments of the Palazzo.*

not appreciated by his contemporaries, who termed it in a public notice "extravagant and unpleasing architecture." At the same time, the part surrounding the courtyard was rebuilt, reducing the arcades of the first-floor loggia to windows so as to create a four-sided gallery. In this way, the different parts of the building were linked to each other. This gave birth then, on one of the wings of the gallery overlooking the Via del Corso, to the Hall of Mirrors, with its vault decorated by Aureliano Milani.

Two masterpieces by Caravaggio, Penitent Magdalene *and, opposite,* Rest on the Flight to Egypt.

Prince Camillo junior was effectively a second founder of the palazzo because he extended the complex even further. He bought a series of houses and cottages that faced onto Via del Plebiscito and had them demolished in order to build another set of apartments that were to be incorporated into the palazzo with a new façade. Paolo Ameli carried out the work in 1744, and in 1749 he also built the main staircase of the building facing Via del Corso, on the instructions of Girolamo, brother of Camillo junior.

This was the last work carried out on commission of the Pamphili family, who risked extinction, having no male heirs. Redemption came, however, in Princess Anna, sister of Cardinal Benedetto Pamphili, who married the Genoese nobleman Giovanni Andrea Doria III in 1671. Her son Giovanni Andrea Doria Pamphili IV (1747–1820) moved to Rome in 1760. With him began a new phase in the residence that could now be called a royal palace. The new owner was a prince of the Holy Roman Empire and married Leopoldina of Savoy-Carignano. For him, in 1769, the architect Francesco Nicoletti transformed the courtyard on the Via del Corso into a splendid ballroom for a celebration given in honor of Archduke Peter Leopold I of Austria, Grand Duke of Tuscany and brother of Emperor Joseph II, a sign of the high prestige to which the palazzo had now risen. The presence of kings became customary here, as in June 1781 for the baptism of the son of Prince Andrea, whose godfather was King Charles III of Spain, represented on that occasion by his ambassador, Duke Girolamo Grimani.

A parenthesis in the history of the palazzo and its magnificence is the residence within these walls, between 1808 and 1810, of the French general Miollis in his role as governor of Napoleonic Rome. He relegated the Doria Pamphili family to a private apartment while he lived in the rest of the building

with a "royal" court and gave splendid banquets, musical soirées, and dances. These were parties organized by an upstart who had no refinement; they were rather vulgar and organized entirely for political propaganda. There was a tendency to mix middle classes and nobility, as happened in the carnival party in 1810. According to the memoirs by Silvagni, the masques gave "an entry to ladies of the lower middle classes to show off their *toilettes* and beauty in such a magnificent and princely apartment, when they had never set foot in the salons of Roman high society." And yet Miollis recounts that "giving his arm to 'la Doria' (the Doria princess) he opened the buffet; it was a real dinner, with copious libations of champagne, a wine not unknown in Rome, but little used even in the great houses because it is very expensive."

It was not a dignified moment in the history of the palazzo, despite the magnificence which always distinguished it, but fortunately the period was of short duration. The air of aristocracy soon returned and the work on the building continued apace: between 1848 and 1890 Princes Filippo Andrea V and Giovanni Andrea commissioned new construction, and the architect Andrea Busiri Vici carried it out. A covered riding school was built, later transformed into the headquarters of the Banca Commerciale, as well as the stables and the façades on Via della Gatta and Piazza Grazioli, the latter with a staircase. The Doria

Pamphili drawing room was a point of reference for the Roman nobility. In the time of Pius IX it was open every Friday, and it was a pleasure to show to the guests the artistic masterpieces displayed in the gallery: paintings by Raphael, Titian, Tintoretto, Guercino, Rubens, and Velázquez and pictures by Sebastiano del Piombo and Bronzino as well as splendid tapestries, new acquisitions by the Doria, which enriched the collection, along with specimens from excavations. The high point of a "usual Friday society evening," as Agostino Chigi wrote in his diary on 8 February 1850, was a centaur "of *rosso antico* (deep red marble), a beautiful sculpture of the same size as those of the Campidoglio, found by the prince in a fortuitous excavation in his villa at Albani."

This gallery remained a legend of the palace, together with the magnificent reception rooms of the private apartment, which the Doria Pamphili managed to keep intact even after the fall of the papal state, up to the present day. The spirit of royalty was so strong that it embarrassed even Emperor Wilhelm of Germany when he attended the twenty-fifth wedding anniversary reception of King Umberto and Queen Margherita in 1883, affirming that he himself would not be in a position to offer such hospitality in his own palaces. It is now a treasure accessible to all, since the gallery is open to the public as a museum; the legend of nobility has adapted to changing times.

PALAZZO PAMPHILI

The splendid Baroque façade of Palazzo Pamphili overlooking Piazza Navona.

This palazzo brings to mind one of the most intriguing characters of Baroque Rome, Donna Olimpia Maidalchini (1592–1657), who was wife of Marquis Pamphilio Pamphili and sister-in-law of Pope Innocent X. Not only was she responsible for the most ostentatious period in the history of the building, but it was thanks to her that the mansion was built in the first place.

The original structure of the palazzo dates back to a simple house facing Piazza Pasquino, bought in 1470 by the first member of the Pamphili family, who came from his native Gubbio to live in Rome as fiscal procurator of the Apostolic Chamber. Other houses facing Piazza Navona were later bought by his son Angelo, clerk of the Curia, and by his nephew Pamphilio, who was several times a Conservatore at the Campidoglio. Thus by the middle of the sixteenth century the Pamphili family owned a series of homes next to one another and behind a single façade giving onto Piazza Navona. These constituted a small mansion, albeit a rather modest one, with an unimpressive façade and squashed between Palazzo Orsini, which loomed over it, the house of the Teofili, on which it was built, and those adjacent to it along the piazza.

Here lived Girolamo, appointed cardinal by Clement VIII, his brother Camillo, scholar and judge of the Rota, and his wife Flaminia del Bufalo Cancellieri, with their seven children. Although this was a patriarchal family, it had limited economic resources, as revealed by the fact that two of Camillo's daughters were forced to become nuns and by the modest middle-class marriages of the other two. At the beginning of the seventeenth century, the only residents were Marquis Pamphilio, Capitoline magistrate and bachelor, and his brother Giovanni Battista, a priest, judge of the Rota, and consistorial lawyer, with whom for various reasons the family line seemed destined to die out.

In 1615, however, Donna Olimpia Maidalchini arrived on the scene as the young wife of the fifty-year-old Pamphilio. Matured by widowhood after a brief marriage and the loss of a child, she brought into that sad, poverty-stricken household her youth, her considerable dowry—and her ambition to rise socially in a city dominated by noble families. Olimpia realized that she could not expect much from her husband, who was placid and without ambition beyond that of being a good husband and father. They had two daughters, Maria and Costanza, and a son, Camillo. While Olimpia was ready to make her inheritance available, Pamphilio was not.

Her brother-in-law Giovanni Battista, however, shared her social ambitions and desire for enormous wealth. He told her in confidence about the intrigues of the pontifical court where he worked. This was a world that could easily be corrupted in order to advance his career and consequently improve the social and economic level of the family—as well as, naturally, the appearance of the palazzo itself.

A tacit agreement grew up between the two whereby Giovanni Battista's advancement up the ladder of ecclesiastical power would be accompanied by Donna Olimpia's gradual acquisition of prestige. The first step to this common end would be the nunciature in Naples, for which they would have to determine just how much was necessary to corrupt the secretary of the cardinal viceroy. The position of nuncio, the step before being appointed cardinal, cost more than they possessed, however, so Olimpia sacrificed all her silver, which simply disappeared from the Pamphili household. After all, she was sure that one day it would come back transformed into gold.

The Pamphili family all moved to Naples in 1621—the nuncio, his sister-in-law, her husband, and their first daughter. The small mansion in Piazza Navona was abandoned for five years, the darkest period in its history. It came alive again, however, in 1626 when the Barberini pope, Urban VIII, called Giovanni Battista back from Naples for other diplomatic missions. The Pamphili family returned with the addition of the son, Camillo, who was destined to carry on the family line.

The mansion was opened up again, and Donna Olimpia began to reap the fruits of her sacrifice. She was invited to the parties given by the Barberini family, and she became at home in the Spanish embassy due to the fact that Giovanni Battista had become the apostolic nuncio in Madrid. He returned from Spain in 1630 and was appointed cardinal, but his taking the cardinal's hat was due in large part to his sister-in-law Olimpia.

With her own money and that sent to her by her brother-in-law during his advantageous nunciature in Spain, she restored and furnished the palazzo on Piazza Navona, where, thanks to her, Giovanni Battista could live in the sumptuous style befitting a cardinal. He found plans already prepared for the acquisition of the adjacent houses in order to enlarge the residence.

The central section of the palazzo with its superb portal under the long balcony of the piano nobile, the coat of arms inserted in an arch, and the airy roof garden.
On the following pages, The Flooding of Piazza Navona for the August Festivities, *an etching by Giuseppe Vasi from the second book of* Delle Magnificenze di Roma Antica e Moderna, *printed in 1752. The "lake" was a device of the Pamphili family for the enjoyment of the nobles of Piazza Navona, who considered the piazza their drawing room.*

Piazza Navona allagata

1. Obelisco e Fontana. 2. Altre Fontane. 3. Chiesa di S. Agnese, e

G. Vasi dis. e scul.

farsi nelle Feste di Agosto.
o Pamfilj. 4. Chiesa ed Ospitale di S. Giacomo degli Spagnuoli.

The renovation took place between 1634 and 1635 with the construction of a simple but elegant façade and the decoration of some rooms on the piano nobile by Agostino Tassi, including a frieze with seascapes in octagons and landscapes with idyllic scenes between roundels above laurel garlands held up by putti and masks.

The bare walls came to life as the palazzetto was transformed into a palazzo, a mansion suited to the rank of Giovanni Battista, who had never stopped advancing his career. He became prefect of the Congregation of Ecclesiastical Immunity and secretary to the Holy Office.

before, with the same interests and accounts, the only concession to widowhood being her black clothes—which in any case were quite becoming to her. By now she had a single goal in mind, that her brother-in-law become pope and she his first lady. This finally took place in 1644: Giovanni Battista became Innocent X and Olimpia the mistress of the Vatican—which is to say, of Rome itself, thanks to her ability to subjugate her brother-in-law, who gave her anything she wanted. She was the one who controlled the Vatican bursar, supervising the concession of favors, pensions, dispensations for marriage, and the collection of indulgences, all this with endless bribes. Anyone who

At the same time, the building reflected Olimpia's climb in the wake of her brother-in-law as she began to reap the fruits of the money she had sown, dedicating herself to the work of "milking" others that was part of her plans. The building effectively became a bank, with Olimpia buying, selling, and lending money. At the same time, she began to hold a salon, opened the ballroom, and set up gaming tables, all with the express purpose of amassing wealth, the key to power.

For this social climber *par excellence*, the death of her husband Pamphilio in 1639 was of marginal importance. She continued to run the mansion as

wanted a favor had first to go to her and knock on the door of her mansion, a mansion that Innocent X would take care to renovate, this time obtaining the services of an architect of standing, Girolamo Rainaldi, but always following the wishes of his sister-in-law.

Palazzo Cibo and Palazzo Millini were incorporated into the new building, extending it and turning it into an imposing structure with façades along Via dell'Anima and the piazza, where a central body emerged with a wide balcony over the doorway. On the sides were two symmetrical doorways, one of which led to a harmoniously designed courtyard.

One of the rooms in the palazzo on the side of Via Santa Maria dell'Anima, intended as a residence for the Pamphili family. Since 1960 it has been the property of Brazil and the seat of its embassy.

The gallery, which transverses the Palazzo, facing Piazza Navona and Via Santa Maria dell'Anima, with two elegant Serlian windows with three lights, with exquisite gilded stucco by Borromini, culminating in the winged coat of arms of the Pamphili family, with a motto inscribed in the cornice which also alludes to them: "Sub umbra alarum tuarum" (In the shadow of your wings). Along the long walls are rectangular niches, like the two above, crowned with ovals containing busts of the Caesars and imitations of antiques. On the vault are frescoes of Aeneas by Pietro da Cortona.

Twenty-three rooms opened onto it, all splendidly decorated by Poussin, Allegrini, Gimignani, and Camassei. Those of the *piano nobile* converged onto a masterpiece by Borromini and Pietro da Cortona, the superb portico extending for the entire depth of the building, which was the pride of the lady of the house, and which in fact was later to be called the Portico of Donna Olimpia.

The palazzo was finished in 1650 after only six years of work supervised by Donna Olimpia. She dictated changes to the designs, gave orders to the artists, and reveled in seeing hundreds of workmen toiling to obey her. In this sense, the mansion was an image of Donna Olimpia herself: she found almost a sense of supremacy and eternity in the stone that made up the building, a mirror of her taste for power.

After the mansion, the piazza now required work. This had the function of a garden, as gardens were

conceived in those days, around an architectural stage set with sculptures and nymphaeums, fountains, and theatrical water displays. Thus in the course of a brief pontificate, the piazza was cleaned up, clearing away the junk dealers, booksellers, and vegetable stands. Then Bernini's splendid fountain was built, and the little church of Sant'Agnese was demolished in order to erect a new one in line with the mansion, which Olimpia would not live to see finished. In that garden of stone, people would promenade, ride in carriages, or watch the shows put on between ephemeral constructions staged by Bernini. The "lake" was created on 12 June 1652, raising high sprays of water to the delight of the nobles, who in this discovered a new pastime.

It also became a setting for theatrical productions, Donna Olimpia's other great passion, one that gave her the same thrill as the gaming tables, with a backdrop

Detail of the frescoes of Aeneas opposite the entrance, with the representation of the wrathful Neptune, armed with his trident, signalling to the winds from his golden chariot to calm the storm so that the Trojan ships can continue their voyage.

Lintel over the door between the atrium of the piano nobile and the salon of the palazzo with the coat of arms of the Pamphili pope, Innocent X, a dove surmounted by three lilies, with an olive branch in its beak.

that supported her ambition to be noticed and to dominate. Even the Lent sermons of the Jesuit Father Oliva were theatrical events, given from the portico of the mansion to an aristocratic audience, but also to the prostitutes, Donna Olimpia's latest enthusiasm: she took them under her protection, naturally with a percentage for herself, while elevating them socially to the level of Renaissance courtesans.

This mixing of the sacred and the profane in Olimpia's mansion became the symbol of both its fame and its notoriety. The Roman people detested Olimpia, seeing in her greed the cause of every misfortune. The lady of the house appeared to them like the character in a Baroque comedy, Pimpa— despotic, unscrupulous, and domineering. Donna Olimpia became known as the "Pimpaccia" of Piazza Navona and the object of many satirical poems which were hung on the nearby Pasquino, one of the "talking statues" of Rome.

Olimpia's party in the mansion, however, ended with the death of Innocent X. She was seen grabbing what she could in the papal apartments right up to the pope's dying moments. The new pope, Alexander VII, ordered her to leave Rome and to retire to effective exile in San Martino al Cimino, the fief given to her by her brother-in-law. A case was brought against her for misappropriation of state funds, and she was ordered to give back her illicit gains. This she would not live to

do. She succumbed to the plague in 1657, leaving what was an enormous estate for those times to her relatives, two million scudi.

With her, the festive times at the Palazzo Pamphili on Piazza Navona also ended. Her son Camillo, married in 1647 to Olimpia Aldobrandini, had already been living in the new house on Via del Corso since 1651, even though it was still under construction. He used his mother's mansion only occasionally, though he found it hard to leave the stone courtyard that was an integral part of the building. A constant appeal remained, however, at least in the first years, in the annual creation of the artificial lake in Piazza Navona which was carried out by the Pamphili family every Saturday and Sunday in August, at least until that amusement of the nobility was taken over by the Roman people.

The palazzo took on a role as a residence for cardinals and other illustrious persons who were accommodated there, maintaining the prestige of the family, which would eventually come to an end with the Doria. Among its eminent guests was the poet Vincenzo Monti, who came to live there in 1778 before he moved on to the service of the Braschi as secretary. It was here that he found inspiration for the poem *La bellezza dell'universo* (The Beauty of the Universe), giving the mansion a literary dignity that it had never had before.

But the Pamphili family's interest in the mansion diminished in proportion to their interest in the princely dwelling on Via del Corso, and its rooms were thus rented out soon after the first half of the nineteenth century. The main floor was occupied by the Accademia Filarmonica Romana (Roman Philharmonic Academy) and later by the Società Musicale Romana (Roman Musical Society). The entry salon was then restored and dedicated to Pier Luigi da Palestrina, whose bust is located opposite one of Innocent X. In 1920 it became the Brazilian embassy as the "Casa do Brasil." Finally, in 1961, the Pamphili family broke off their relationship with the building, and it became the property of the Brazilian nation.

PALAZZO DI MONTE GIORDANO

Roman sarcophagus of the third century A.D., used as a fountain in the courtyard of the palazzo which belonged to the Orsini family of Monterotondo.

This complex of buildings is a virtual fortress. It stands on Monte Giordano, an artificial hill formed from the accumulation of archaeological debris and rubbish from the nearby river port dating from the Roman period, near Tor di Nona. Built halfway through the twelfth century as a fortress belonging to Giovanni Roncione, lord of Riano, it became known after 1286 as the Mons Ursinorum (Orsini Hill), the settlement of the Orsini family, an ancient Roman line.

As always, the interests of the house were linked to those of the Holy See, thus ensuring wealth and power, but its leap in status occurred with Matteo Rosso, lord of Monterotondo and senator of Rome in 1241, and with his son Giovanni Gaetano, who became pope with the name of Nicholas III (1277–1280). To the latter the family owed its enrichment, often illicit, since the pope helped himself to goods and money from the very treasury of St. Peter's. Dante relegated Nicholas accordingly to a place alongside the simoniacs in his *Inferno*.

This settlement on Monte Giordano immediately become a determining factor in the life of the city through the control of commercial traffic on the Tiber from this strategic position. The complex, comprised of a group of towers enclosed between high walls, housed a large number of members of the clan who were soldiers, thus ensuring the military defense of the hill from possible attacks by other families. These were baronial struggles, in which the Orsini were defined as Guelphs in opposition to the Colonna family, their eternal Ghibelline rivals in the fight for prestige in the city of Rome and the surrounding countryside.

Their military force confirmed the ownership of the hill, which took its name from a member of the Orsini family, Giordano, nephew of Nicholas III and patriarch of the Monte Giordano branch. The power of the family grew in the fourteenth century. They amassed fiefs in central Italy and survived the long Rome crisis of the fourteenth century that was linked to the exodus to Avignon and the Great Schism of the West. Giordano was senator in 1341 and led an expedition against Giovanni di Vico, prefect of Rome and tyrant of Viterbo.

The family, however, won new fiefs in southern Italy in compensation for assistance against the rebellious lords that was given to Egidio Albornoz for restoring Church territory to papal government and for defending it against the king of Naples, Ladislas of Durazzo. The counts of Nola were created, then the princes of Taranto, counts of Lecce, princes of Salerno, and dukes of Amalfi; the counts of Tagliacozzo, princes of Aquila and of Piombino, and marquises of Rocca Antica, Populonia, and Trevignano. It was from this branch that the dukes of Bracciano were born, who are the only ones who still exist today.

Monte Giordano remained the mother house for them all. The building was transformed between the fifteenth and sixteenth centuries into a complex of noble palazzi divided among the branches of the family that gravitated toward life in the city: the dukes of Bracciano, the counts of Pitigliano, and the lords of Monterotondo. The walls were maintained and even strengthened, and the so-called *turris maior* (principal tower) was kept in good repair within a courtyard.

The elegant fountain of the Acqua Paola, a picturesque background to the entrance arch to the Palazzo di Monte Giordano. Designed by Felice Antonio Casoni in 1618, it was modified in the eighteenth century by the Gabrielli family to its present appearance, with a quadruple basin within an exedra of laurels.

On the following pages: Ceremonial staircase leading to the piano nobile *of the palazzo, by Francesco Rusi. Opposite, the Salone degli Arazzi (Tapestry Hall) with its Baroque ceiling decorated with gilded carving and rich furnishings.*

The sixteenth-century façades were built over the medieval structures, possibly following a design by Baldassarre Peruzzi. The severe outward appearance of the complex did not fundamentally change. One entered through a great arch that opened onto a large courtyard containing an elegant fountain of the Acqua Paola, designed in 1618 by Felice Antonio Casoni. On the right stood the palazzo of the dukes of Bracciano, flanking the older buildings grouped on the smaller courtyard, and on the left was the palazzo of the counts of Pitigliano, with an internal courtyard. These two palazzi had been built as separate residences, but when, at the beginning of the seventeenth century, the counts of Pitigliano moved to Tuscany and the palazzo was acquired by the dukes of Bracciano, the latter unified the buildings with a bridge. Beyond, the palazzo of Monterotondo faced a third courtyard.

The external aspect did not in practice betray its origin. It maintained a dark intimidating appearance toward anyone who entered, while the interior developed into elegantly furnished salons with marvelous frescoes, of which there is now no trace. The frescoes are known from written descriptions such as that of a "bellissima sala istoriata con buone figure" (beautiful room decorated with excellent figures), seen by Giovanni Rucellai in 1450. Vasari wrote that this was "una sala piena di uomini famosi" (a room full of [painted] famous men). Recorded too are works by Girolamo Muziano, Cingoli, and Masolino, by whom an entire room was frescoed, according to Vasari.

The Orsini, busy with their military undertakings, lived only occasionally at Monte Giordano, in part because there was a gradual diminution in civil war and thus less need for defense of the fort, so they preferred living in their castles and palaces outside the gates of the city. In the end the residence was kept to accommodate important guests, cardinals, and ambassadors, who brought a different sort of history to the building, at times enhancing its cultural level too. Cardinal Gonzaga lived there, who entertained Uberto Strozzi, with his Accademia dei Vignaiuoli, and Cardinal Ippolito d'Este II, who invited Torquato Tasso there on many occasions.

In residence there from 1623 to 1637 was Cardinal Maurizio of Savoy, ambassador of his father, Duke Carlo Emanuele I, and appointed by the king of France as protector of the French crown at the Holy See. An able diplomat, he held splendid court in this residence, open to intrigue and espionage in favor of the major European powers. The cardinal succeeded in making an alliance between Duke Vittorio Amedeo I, his brother, and the Habsburgs, in order to create a counterweight to the powerful French hegemony. At the Holy See he assumed the office of protector of the Habsburgs of Austria and Spain.

With the death of Vittorio Amedeo I and the regency of his wife Marie-Christine of France, Maurizio organized a plot from this palazzo with his other brother, Tommaso Francesco, to take over Savoy. There was civil war, but everything finished diplomatically. The cardinal gave up the ecclesiastical life and married.

In 1688 Flavio Orsini, the last duke of Bracciano, burdened with debt, was obliged to sell the Monte. Thus ended an ownership that had lasted more than four hundred years and had witnessed the most tormented events of Roman baronial history. The new owners, the Gabrielli, while of ancient Roman nobility, could not be compared to the Orsini. They were marquises of Prossedi and Roccasecca, princes from 1762. Prince

Pietro married Camilla Riario Sforza, and their son Mario took as wife Carlotta, daughter of Lucien Bonaparte; in turn, their son Placido married his cousin Augusta Bonaparte. They were, certainly, the best nobility of modern times, without counting Cardinal Lucien Bonaparte who came to reside there (he died in 1895), thus linking the Monte degli Orsini to the Roman branch of the Napoleonic family, the Canino princes.

The splendid furnishings of the Taverna Gallarati Scotti apartment, with gilded door handles, frescoes for the Gabrielli family by Bonaventura Lamberti, and a series of seventeenth-century Flemish pictures of hunting scenes.

However, the architectural context did not suit this family, who tended to personalize the residence, aiming first of all to unify the different buildings. A new arm was built at the end of the courtyard to provide a better link between the Bracciano and

Pitigliano palazzi, and the group of houses around the Monte that the Orsini had kept separate was incorporated into the complex. The interiors were newly frescoed by Bonaventura Lamberti between 1688 and 1690, and by Liborio Coccetti between 1812 and 1816. In this way, the Orsini stories that had once decorated the walls were lost, although they had probably been ruined for a long time on account of poor maintenance and inadequate restoration. In sum, the past history of the palazzo was cancelled, and Prince Placido's construction in 1880 of a medieval-type tower with battlements in the courtyard of the Pitigliano palazzo, called Augusta in honor of his wife, was really a wasted effort.

The Gabrielli family lived here for two hundred years until their line ended in 1888 and the complex was taken over by the counts of Taverna of Milan, who still own it. Further restoration has been carried out in imitation of what remains of its old style, and the interior has been enriched even more with extraordinary tapestries and paintings by Sebastiano Ricci and Giovan Battista Pittoni. The palazzo has ended by taking the name of Taverna, its past thus completely obliterated.

MESSAPVS

PALAZZO CORSINI

CORSINI

The area of Trastevere where this eighteenth-century building stands kept its semi-rural character for a long time. The slope between the Tiber and the Gianiculum Hill was cultivated with vineyards and gardens, and the surroundings were well suited to the construction of farmhouses and villas. Thus in 1482 Cardinal Raffaele Riario (1461–1521), already the owner of a palazzo in Parione later called the Palazzo della Cancelleria, bought the land behind Porta Settimiana, which stretched as far as the top of the Gianiculum, and built a villa there. The building consisted of three floors around a large courtyard with stables on the side, next to which was an enormous park ending in a wood which grew along the hillside, with holly oaks, magnolias, laurels, and, at the foot of the hill, rows of vines.

The cardinal was not able to enjoy his twenty-hectare villa for long, involved as he was in the plot against Pope Leo X. He was condemned to death, and although he was pardoned, morally he was a broken man and left Rome in 1517. The villa was inherited by Francesco Riario Sforza, who in turn gave it to his brother Galeazzo in 1518 on condition that he did not sell it. In the end, Galeazzo rented it out to numerous illustrious people.

In 1587 Mario Sforza, count of Santa Fiora, lived there; in 1593 Cardinal Paolo Emilio Sfondrati, and in 1611 Pompeo Targone, an architect and engineer in the service of Alexander VII. Finally, in 1669, it was taken over as a residence by Christina of Sweden, the queen who had converted to Catholicism, given up her throne, and moved to Rome. She was received in Rome on 20 September 1655 with great honor and lived in Palazzo Farnese for a year. Then she traveled extensively through Europe looking in vain for a kingdom, returning every so often to Rome, until she finally settled there in 1668, in Villa Riario, until her death in 1689.

The villa had its period of greatest splendor while she resided there. Christina had terraces and fountains built and statues set in the surrounding park. She had an extraordinary number of orange and lemon trees as well as jasmine bushes planted in the flower beds and arbors.

The palazzo was furnished like a royal palace, with works of art and precious ornaments reminiscent of the aristocratic taste typical of Baroque palazzi. The ground floor was decorated with a succession of statues and busts, even in the bathroom, which had two marble bathtubs and a bed. The Sala delle Colonne (Hall of Columns) was resplendent with statues of

Apollo and the Muses and a gilded chair under a canopy with a golden fringe, where Christina received in solemn splendor. Friezes and hangings abounded, in a profusion of green, red, and lilac.

The throne room was on the first floor, richly decorated with golden accessories, a canopy, and beautiful tapestries by Aubusson. A long gallery followed, with paintings by Caravaggio, Titian, Leonardo, Raphael, Dürer, and Michelangelo, then a study with a collection of medals, cameos, and jewels, and a library that occupied three rooms. Wherever possible, Christina's crest, a phoenix looking at the sun without fear of burning up, was painted in silver and gold. Her private apartments also contained a chapel. The walls were frescoed, and the room furnishings were massive pieces upholstered with damask and velvet, reflecting the luxury of court life at its most costly and extravagant.

Her court was made up of a host of squires, attendants, and secretaries of noble rank: the marquis del Monte, the queen's factotum; the duke of Poli, the queen's steward, and his wife, the first lady-in-waiting; the duke of Northumberland, Charles Dudley, also

count of Warwick; count d'Alibert, director of the theater Tor di Nona owned by the queen; the marquis di Malaspina and marquis Cincinnati, renowned for his good looks. This cosmopolitan court was augmented, even if for short periods, with aristocrats in Christina's service. Together they made this palazzo into a royal palace equal to any other in Europe.

Concerts and theatrical performances were given on the second floor where a theater was built with a stage that could hold up to one hundred and fifty musicians. Salons were held where art and science, politics and literature were discussed. Christina even founded what she called a "royal academy" with the purpose of defending the Italian language from "the modern taste for hyperbole and exaggeration." The academy of Arcadia continued its work. There was also an alchemy laboratory where Christina passed many long hours with Cardinal Decio Azzolini and the marquis of Palombara before the burner, with alembics and powders of lead and mercury, in the vain search for the philosopher's stone, gold, and the elixir of life.

At Christina's death, her great art collection and most of the furnishings were looted by her courtiers.

*On the preceding pages:
The Gallery also possesses
antique sculpture and valuable
archaeological items such as
the Coppa Corsini, dating from
the end of the first century A.D.,
and the Corsini throne, placed
in the center of the room, from
the same time.*

*The Room of the Painted Doors,
named after the doors
decorated by the Roman painter
Domenico Roberti
(1642–1707), with
reproductions of antique
buildings, including triumphal
arches and temples.*

However, such great luxury only made sense when the queen herself was there. The building's later residents, such as Cardinal Vincenzo Grimani and Abbot Ridolfi could at most play the role of courtiers, but certainly not that of a sovereign.

In 1736 Count Riario Sforza sold the villa to Cardinal Neri Corsini and his brother Prince Bartolommeo III, viceroy of Sicily. The Corsini, princes of Sismano, were an old noble family of Tuscan origin, who until then had resided in a building on Piazza Navona. They bought this other palazzo because they needed a larger residence where they could install the great library founded by Cardinal Lorenzo Corsini (1653–1740), now Pope Clement XII, as well as the considerable family art collection. Rather than tearing it down, they renovated the building, enlarging it and making it more functional. Francesco Fuga was in charge of the renovations that brought the complex to its present form.

The modified palazzo had three floors, with three rows of windows on the austere façade overlooking Via della Lungara. There were three balconies on the *piano nobile* and a central block with a large three-part passage that crossed through the building all the way to the park behind. Clement XII had the library placed on the *piano nobile* in accordance with his precise instructions.

The books were divided over five rooms according to subject: history, philology and literature, philosophy and science, religion, and law. Clement also introduced some modern innovations into this library. For example, he allowed even heretical and forbidden books to be kept there, but with the threat of excommunication "for anyone daring to take even one of them away." He also made the provision that if the building was sold, the family was obliged to have "a suitable place built in order to store and preserve said Library . . . in the neighborhood of Trastevere or Regola or Borgo or Via Giulia, areas that are all distant from other public Libraries." The library was opened to the public in 1754, alternating its hours with those of others in Rome.

Tommaso Corsini the Elder (1767–1856) added two further rooms for the classics and for manuscripts, as well as seven more rooms with periodicals and books in English and French. The library was enriched with other important endowments, like the Chiti musical collection in 1759, and purchases such as Abbot Nicola Rossi's library, bought in 1786 by Bartolommeo Corsini. With the advent of Jacobin Rome and the later Napoleonic dominion, the Corsini family was forced to make the building available to the authorities. In 1797 Joseph Bonaparte resided there as ambassador of the Directory and occupied the vast apartments on the first and second floors. However, this period in the history of the building was saddened by a fatal accident involving General Leonard Duphot, who was in the ambassador's train. He was killed in a riot that broke out in the stretch of Via della Lungara between Porta Settimiana and the palazzo.

Later, from 1801 to 1808, Princess Marianne of Austria lived there. When she left, Abbot Lucantonio

The splendid vault of the room called Sala dell'Alcova (Hall of the Alcove) or Sala della Regina Cristina di Svezia (Hall of Queen Christina of Sweden), which has kept its original form from the earlier Palazzo Riario, the work of the Zuccari school. Right, a refined cupid in classical style.

On the following pages: Some of the seven rooms of the Library, all with decorated ceilings. The bookshelves are walnut and each has a frieze with medallions in leather representing theological writers, in particular Protestants and non-Catholics, chosen in the name of toleration and cultural open-mindedness. The door of each room is flanked by columns in antique yellow giallo antico (with a lintel) where a gilded cartouche carries an inscription of the subjects in the bookcases.

Benedetto informs us in his diary, transcribed by David Silvagni, that all she gave Prince Corsini in payment was a snuffbox with her portrait on it "as a sign of gratitude for having accommodated her as a guest." Moreover, she left Rome with a debt of 40,000 scudi.

Cardinal Giuseppe Fesh, however, paid his rent when he lived there with his step-sister Letizia, Napoleon's mother. Throughout this time, the palazzo maintained its lavish decoration, and the library and art collection were preserved intact.

Prince Andrea Corsini (1804–1868), politically involved as minister of foreign affairs for the grand duke of Tuscany from 1849 to 1856, was the last member of the Roman family to live in the mansion on Via della Lungara, which he was able to do only because he had managed to hold onto his property. His wife, Luisa Scotti, possessed the most famous diamonds in Rome. According to the diplomat Henry d'Ideville, "she regretted bitterly that she had lost her son because their titles and possessions would pass to their 'terrible nephews,' the Corsini of Florence."

And so it was. The heir, Tommaso Corsini, sold the palazzo to the Italian state in 1883, and it became the

headquarters of the Accademia dei Lincei, which had its official address in the nearby Farnesina. The City of Rome bought part of the wood which later became the Botanical Gardens and the Passeggiata del Gianicolo. The garden surrounding the palazzo was fenced in to separate it from the city property.

The library and the art collection, each of inestimable value, were donated to the Accademia dei Lincei, thus essentially respecting the will of Clement XII, who wanted the library to remain intact. It had increased significantly over time through numerous endowments, such as that of Leonardo Caetani, who donated an Oriental collection in 1924 and that of Levi Civita, who donated another of mathematics in 1946.

The art collection became the Galleria Nazionale d'Arte Antica (National Gallery of Old Masters) in 1895 with the addition of numerous donations, including that of Duke Giovanni Torlonia in 1892, the Chigi in 1918, the Barberini in 1952, and Cervinara in 1962. In this way, the building has maintained its high dignity in line with the cultural commitments of its past.

The Orto Botanico (Botanical Garden), which has its entrance on Largo Cristina di Svezia (opposite, above) is entered by a stepped fountain (opposite, below). Indigenous and exotic plants can be found there, grouped according to habitat and evolutionary adaptation. In the central avenue are beautiful palm trees and the remains of the ancient forest that once covered the whole of the Gianiculum.

371

PALAZZO CHIGI

CHIGI DELLA ROVERE

Piazza Colonna, an etching by Giuseppe Vasi from the second book of Delle Magnificenze di Roma Antica e Moderna, *published in Rome in 1752. On the extreme right is Palazzo Chigi, the work of Felice della Greca and Giovanni Battista Contini.*

This palazzo has been a center of power ever since the Italian state bought it in 1917. First, the Colonial Ministry was housed there, followed by the Ministry of Foreign Affairs, then finally the Premiership of the Council of Ministers. In this way, the State made the monumentality and magnificence that had originally been the pride of the Chigi family its own. The Chigi had been owners of the building since 1659, and the building is still today remembered with their name.

The original structure of the building on the corner of Largo Chigi and Piazza Colonna dates back to a simple house that overlooked Via del Corso in the sixteenth century and was owned by the notary Adriano Tedallini, who died in 1575. Three years later it was bought by the Consistory lawyer Pietro Aldobrandini, son of Silvestro, who had been exiled from Florence for political reasons. He decided to enlarge the house, even though he was not independently wealthy and had to rely on his income

G. Vasi dis. inc.

Piazza Colonna

1. Colonna Antonina, 2. Palazzo Ghigi, 3. Curia Innocenziana, 4. Residenza di Monsigr. Vicegerente, 5. Ch. della nazione de Bergamaschi

The courtyard of the palazzo seen from the entrance hall, with its fountain and open arcade. It is surmounted by a Doric frieze, decorated on the metopes with trophies and surmounted by a false colonnade on the first floor with gabled windows in the closed arches, rich with decoration which is repeated on the upper storeys.

to pay for the work. He bought several of the neighboring houses, owned by the physician Girolamo Agapeto of Spoleto. These all faced onto Via Montecitorio, the present Piazza Colonna. They were conjoined to form a single building with two façades in the middle of the block. The façades were not connected externally, since they were separated by the corner houses owned by Angeletti and Vannuzzi, but the interiors were joined by a series of restructuring projects begun in 1585 by the architect Matteo Bartolini of Città di Castello.

In 1587, however, Pietro Aldobrandini died, and his wife Flaminia, with her two young children Pietro and Olimpia, could not afford to live in the house, far less continue construction. She was forced to sell. Fabrizio Fossano bought the house as it was, half-finished. He was of Milanese origin and the prior of the Roman *caporioni*, or local leaders. He lived there with his wife Clarice and two servants and was determined to continue construction although he too was not wealthy and had to proceed a little at a time. When he died in 1615 the building was almost the same as when he had bought it, not finished in any detail. Again it was the widow who sold the house. Strangely enough, it was bought back by an Aldobrandini, in 1616. The buyer was a cardinal, Pietro, son of the same Flaminia who had sold it to Fossano. The new owner was determined to finish the

Opposite:
The courtyard fountain with its mask framed by the Della Rovere oakleaves and surmounted by the Chigi mountains and star.

The mountains and the star of the Chigi family arms, raised in 1659 on the façade overlooking Via del Corso and now in the entrance hall of the palazzo at the foot of the monumental staircase.

building, but this time the design would include the corner as well. Cardinal Aldobrandini bought the houses between the two buildings in 1618, incorporating into a single palazzo the row that extended along two-thirds of both façades on the block.

Pietro Aldobrandini was wealthy, and it seemed that he would finally be able to bring the family to the level of magnificence that his uncle, Pope Clement VIII (1592–1605), had wished for his relatives. The lucrative posts Pietro occupied brought him even more money. The building of a splendid villa in Frascati and the acquisition of the fief of Rossano, complete with the title of princess for his sister Olimpia, tell us something of the extent of his wealth. But the owners of the building on Piazza Colonna and its renovation seemed to be doomed. In 1621 Cardinal Pietro Aldobrandini, like his father and Fabrizio

Everything seemed to be going well when two tragic events took place in 1623. Giovan Giorgio's son, who would have been the only male heir in the family and thus would have inherited everything, died just a few months after birth. And Gregory XV, the Ludovisi pope who had been a protector of the family, died and was succeeded by none other than Urban VIII, of the Barberini family, always at loggerheads with the Ludovisi and the Aldrobrandini. Olimpia was in difficulties.

What should she do with the mansion that began to look like a scaled-down version of the never-ending building-yard at St. Peter's, seemingly destined never to be finished? She was struck with the brilliant idea of ceding it without charge to a distant relative, Cardinal Giovan Battista Deti, for the duration of his lifetime on the condition that he continue construction. The

The second-floor Sala delle Marine (Room of the Seascapes), after the frescoes by Adrien Manglard, set in heavy architecture with scrolls, festoons and overdoor decorations.

Fossano before him, died without ever seeing the work completed.

His sister Olimpia, widow of a distant relative, Gian Francesco Aldobrandini, inherited the estate and naturally also the building under construction. The idea of owning an elegant home was extremely tempting, considering her many children, among whom were a cardinal, Ippolito, and Giovan Giorgio, who married Ippolita Ludovisi, niece of Pope Gregory XV—which gave her a second princedom of Meldola and Sarsina in Romagna. Olimpia therefore ordered that the work continue but she did not go to live there herself.

cardinal accepted and lived there from 1624, with twenty-eight people in his service. He was enthusiastic about his new home, which continued to grow and become more beautiful until it was finally worthy of his rank as bishop of Albano.

The crucial step was the construction of the corner building between Via del Corso and the piazza, corresponding on the inside to the first-floor portico, with its frescoes that are still intact to this day and the cardinal's coat of arms. The balcony–verandah appeared over the corner, and above it the coat of arms of Pope Clement VIII, posthumous homage to the source of the Aldrobrandini family's fortune. Above it all, as a sign of nobility, a covered roof-terrace was boldly displayed on the side of Via del Corso.

The rooms were finally opened in the mansion, but not for parties and music. The cardinal had a weakness for card games and his home soon became a gambling den, with many tables where guests played for high stakes and where many nobles lost fortunes. The cardinal himself degenerated, and his excesses reduced him to a pitiful physical condition. He died at the age of fifty-one, in 1630.

The mansion naturally returned to Donna Olimpia Aldobrandini, but the princess was canny and continued to rent it out, so other cardinals came there to live, Girolamo Vidoni, for only two years—because he also died there at the age of fifty-one in 1632—Egidio Camillo Albornoz in 1633, Gian Domenico Spinola in 1634, and Albornoz again from 1635 to 1649 as head of the Spanish delegation. His time of residence there was the most significant for the building's history, not only on account of his personal prestige—he was a grandee of Spain—but also because he oversaw completion of the enlargement of the wing on the piazza side of the building according to the drawings by Giovanni Pietro Moraldi.

Olimpia Aldobrandini died in 1637 during Albornoz's period of residence there, and the property passed to her son Ippolito, also a cardinal. He lasted there only a year before he died, still young. The property was then inherited by Ippolito's niece, another Olimpia, princess of Rossano, married at the time to Paolo Borghese and later to Camillo Pamphili. The new owner did not change the management of the building but continued renting it out for another twenty years or so. The building had a rather uninteresting history in this period, first with Cardinal Teodoro Trivuzio and later with some members of the Brancaccio family.

In 1659 it was bought by the Chigi family, who could count on the support of Pope Alexander VII, a member of the same family who wanted to see his family's splendor restored to that of their ancestor Agostino in the magnificent Villa Farnesina, which they had had to sell sixty years earlier. They lived in the mansion in Piazza Santi Apostoli which would later belong to the Odescalchi. It was too small for them, and only the cardinal, Flavio, remained there. Don Mario Chigi, the brother of the pope, and his son Agostino, newly married to Virginia Borghese, the daughter of Olimpia who had sold them the house, would go to live in Villa Aldobrandini.

The arrival of the Chigi family marked a new page in the history of the mansion. It was a period of unprecedented ostentation. The new owners planned to double the size of the building so that it would cover the entire block delimited by Via del Corso, Via dell'Impero, Via dello Sdrucciolo, and Piazza Colonna. This plan called for the purchase of the assortment of houses clustered over the entire area—a total of twenty-four buildings—which between 1661 and 1664 were torn down or incorporated according to the instructions of architect Felice della Greca, who directed work until 1676 and was followed by Giovanni Battista Contini.

Based on the structure of the old building, a new and much larger building was built on a rectangular plan, with a series of monumental innovations, from the ostentatious grand staircase to the grandiose entrance hall, from the colonnaded courtyard to the new prestigious covered roof-terrace, higher than the

Corner view of the Sala delle Marine with the eighteenth-century overdoor decoration.

existing one and built to compete in height and prestige with the Palazzo di Montecitorio owned by the Ludovisi family directly opposite.

There were two main doors with the addition of a new one on the piazza, the latter not yet quite as prestigious as the other on Via del Corso, almost merging as it did with the doors to the various premises used as carriage houses. This was because the Chigi family still considered the façade facing the piazza a back entrance. As a coping over the walls of the building, a distinctive and elegant balustrade was built which unfortunately was later eliminated with the creation of an attic storey in the last years of the

The Salone d'Oro (Salon of Gold), decorated between 1765 and 1767 for the occasion of the marriage between Sigismondo Chigi and Maria Flaminia Odescalchi by painters, sculptors, and silversmiths under the direction of Stern: Tommaso Righi (stucco), Giovanni Angeloni and Nicola La Piccola (pictorial decoration), Lorenzo Cardelli (marble carving), Giovan Battista Stazi (gilding), and Luigi Valadier (metallic decoration).

seventeenth century. As construction proceeded slowly, the interior was decorated with equal care, from the courtyard façade, embellished with stucco, to its floor, paved with marble brought all the way from the rectory of San Giovanni in Laterano and the great rooms adorned with paintings from various sources and with Flemish tapestries.

To this "royal palace" came a prince of the Holy Roman Empire as well as of Farnese and Campagnano, with other titles too, including that of duke of Ariccia and Formello and marquis of Magliano Pecoreccio, along with his impressive court of more than one hundred people. The life of the palazzo was one of pomp and well-being, as dictated by the Spanish-style customs of the time, with parties requiring the rooms to be specially decorated for each occasion.

But it was not only the society life that attracted nobles and prelates to Palazzo Chigi. There was also a cultural side, represented by the frequent meetings of the Accademia degli Sfaccendati, taking place under the auspices of Prince Sigismondo, with concerts and poetry readings.

The palazzo acquired the hallmark of an even higher level of culture after the death of Cardinal Flavio Chigi in 1693. Then, not only the precious collections of art, furniture, and marble were transferred here from his palazzo at Piazza Santi Apostoli, but also a library of more than 8,600 printed books and 2,655 handwritten volumes and codices. All this was organized in a library with superb bookshelves by Contini, run by well-known scholars as librarians. It was open to the public and destined to be an important place of reference for scholars of history and archaeology.

Another novelty in the history of the palazzo was the renovation of the façade on Piazza Colonna between 1738 and 1739. This included the elimination of the carriage houses and mezzanines and the creation of new windows in their place, and the introduction of the magnificent door with the small loggia above it, resembling the other one on Via del Corso. From this portal led a passage to the courtyard, where a beautiful mask fountain was built, which gave the mansion a new relationship with the piazza turning it effectively into a great triumphal entry.

This was apparent every time the prince left by this doorway and was honored as Marshall of the Holy Roman Church and Custodian of the Conclave, a position held by Agostino Chigi since 1712 and the death of the last of the Savelli family, to whom the position had belonged since the fifteenth century. A regiment of papal troops arrayed in front of the doorway would come to attention and unfurl the white flag displaying the Chigi coat of arms with the papal banner flying above it. It was a ceremony of great prestige that gave a certain tone to the piazza as well. The column of Marcus Aurelius, where the soldiers were arrayed, seemed itself to become a symbol of homage to the Chigi family.

The splendor of the palazzo increased inside the building. In 1748 the so-called Camera delle Marine

Opposite:
Sleeping Endymion by Baciccia
(1639–1709) in the center of
the ceiling in the Salone d'Oro.
This was transferred here from
Palazzo Chigi, subsequently
Odescalchi, in Piazza Santi
Apostoli, for which it had been
created by the artist.

(Room of the Seascapes) was embellished with
frescoes by Adrien Manflard in *trompe l'œil*
architecture with scrolls, festoons, and fanlights, and
the adjacent Camera dei Paesi (Room of the
Landscapes) with woodland scenes. But the greatest
marvel was the Salone d'Oro (Salon of Gold),
decorated between 1765 and 1767 especially for the
wedding of Sigismondo Chigi and Maria Flaminia
Odescalchi, the product of an entire team of
decorators, silversmiths, and sculptors under the
direction of Stern. It was an exceptional feat of

his mansion a place where theorists of the new liberal
ideals could meet.

In the secrecy of his home he wrote a *pasquinata*
(satirical poem) in the form of a play, *Il conclave di
Clemente XIV da recitarsi nel carnevale dell'anno
1775 (Clement XIV's Conclave to be Performed
during Carnival in the Year 1775)*. This work caused
a scandal, and although it was anonymous, Don
Sigismondo was fingered as its author, to the
chagrin of the nobility, especially considering his
position as Marshall of the Holy Roman Church

Overdoor decoration in the
Salone d'Oro with a seascape
in an oval by the Fleming Jan
de Momper between female
figures by Tommaso Righi.

ornamentation in which Baciccia's *Sleeping
Endymion*, transferred here from the palazzo at Santi
Apostoli found an appropriately opulent setting.

The history of the mansion took a new turn with
Don Sigismondo Chigi, the prince who had been
master of the house since the death of his father
Agostino in 1769. A man of culture and friend to
artists and men of letters, he opened his salon to
famous writers such as Metastasio, Monti, and Alfieri,
and took on the archaeologist Ennio Quirino Visconti
as librarian. A luminary of the Enlightenment and a
freemason, his revolutionary behavior and ideas made

and Custodian of the Conclave, two posts which he
lost as a result.

The prince was undaunted, giving parties and
organizing theatrical productions that could exalt his
palazzo. The ball in honor of Archduke Maximillian of
Austria on 27 July 1775 is still famous. Piazza
Colonna was transformed into a great theater with a
colossal firework display depicting Vulcan's anvil. The
following year the prince had the opportunity of
showing off the splendid carriages he had ordered
expressly from Paris, on the occasion of the
celebrations held for his second wedding, to the

Neapolitan Giovanna Medici. But this marriage provoked such an avalanche of gossip about the bride that she was forced to seek a legal separation from her husband soon after.

Other sad events were on their way for the prince, in any case, a consequence of his extravagant and libertarian behavior. In 1790 he was openly accused of being the leader of a sect called the Illuminati and his mansion was depicted as a den of spies and conspirators. At the same time he was pronounced guilty of the attempted poisoning of Cardinal Carandini, prefect of the Santa Congregazione del Buon Governo (Holy Congregation of Good Government). Don Sigismondo was considered a revolutionary and conspirator. He escaped from Rome in September 1790, leaving his property to his son Agostino. He died in Padua three years later.

The palazzo kept its dignity and decorum intact with Prince Agostino V (1771–1855), despite the unchanging aura of libertarianism and cultural spirit that surrounded its salon. It was always open on Thursdays and Sundays for literary gatherings. The prince played the Jacobin with the coming of the Republic but was not believed and ended up in prison. When he was finally released, he became somewhat reclusive. With the coming of the Napoleonic era, however, he openly showed homage to the emperor and was nominated count of the empire. Palazzo Chigi again became one of the favorite salons of the philo-Neapolitan aristocracy of Rome. Here, again, balls were held and the gaming tables were opened, and the game of faro triumphed.

Even nobles who remained faithful to the pope frequented the Chigi salon because the prince was cautious. Careful not to break off relations with pontifical circles, he avoided excommunication. A dramatic episode that took place in this salon on an evening in June 1809, however, did create a sensation. The protagonist was Donna Anna Maria Borghese, mother of Prince Camillo and mother-in-law of Paolina Bonaparte. She was a Jacobin, naturally, and in the midst of a reception she boldly and loudly declared her contempt for Pope Pius VII's recent declaration of excommunication for those who collaborated with the French. That same evening Princess Borghese was struck dead, falling to the ground, probably from a heart attack, in the middle of the Chigi salon.

This episode affected the image of the Palazzo Chigi, whereby the prince was increasingly involved in public positions in the Napoleonic regime but did not alienate the trust of the pope. At his restoration, the salon opened its doors again in the literary spirit inspired by the Accademia dell'Arcadia. The poetic "academies" repelled any political idea that went against the power of the papacy. This is evident in the honor bestowed upon the Chigi family by Pope Leo XII when on August 11 he listened from their mansion to the public sermon of the "Mission" held in Piazza Colonna in preparation for the Holy Year.

Finally, the palazzo took on a rather staid existence, detached from the various liberal movements that often made themselves felt in Piazza Colonna. Diplomacy reigned, especially since the first floor began to be rented out, for financial reasons, to foreign diplomatic representatives. Thus between 1840 and 1842 the embassy of Belgium was installed there with Count Émile d'Oultremont of Warfusé, and between 1845 and 1846 the embassy of Sardinia was there with Count Federico Broglia of Mombello.

Those were hard times for the palazzo, which had a moment of splendor only in 1857, on the occasion of the marriage of Don Mario Chigi, son of Prince Sigismondo, to Donna Antonietta, daughter of Prince Ludwig of Sayn-Wittgenstein, when the salons were reopened. The coat of arms of the Germanic princes remain to testify to this event in the vestibule outside the present hall of the Council of Ministers, next to the emblems of the Chigi. The decoration of the so-called Sala delle Quattro Stagioni (Room of the Four Seasons) was the last in the palazzo.

With the end of papal rule nearing, the economic situation became critical, and renting out the first floor became the rule. From 1862 to 1871 the attaché to the British legation, Odo William Russell, and from 1871 to 1878 the young Russian prince Peter Wolkonsky both resided there. From 1878 the ambassador of Austria and Hungary moved in and stayed until 1915. By this time, there was little of the Chigi family left in Palazzo Chigi, reduced as the palace was to a rented piece of real estate. From 1881 even part of the third floor was rented out to a succession of tenants, and on Via del Corso a wool shop appeared.

The closing of the Austrian embassy with the First World War gave the Chigi family the opportunity to get the building off their hands. In 1917 it was bought by the Italian state as an official building and immediately became the headquarters of the Colonial Ministry and later, in 1923, the Ministry of Foreign Affairs, the minister being Benito Mussolini. In these circumstances, many works of art that were stored in national galleries as part of the nation's artistic heritage were distributed for the decoration of bureaucratic headquarters. The library was donated entirely to Pope Pius IX and installed in the Vatican.

Thus the history of the palazzo took on an entirely political slant, with speeches delivered from the balcony by Mussolini before his move in 1927 to Palazzo Venezia. The building was then abandoned and began to deteriorate, until it was decided to make it the headquarters of the president of the Council of Ministers, and it was carefully restored for this purpose. Its image is now identified with the governments that make up the history of the Italy of our time.

KNIGHTS OF MALTA

Church of Santa Maria del Priorato near the Villa of the Knights of Malta on the Aventine Hill. The façade is decorated with the heraldic insignia of the Rezzonico family, as ordered by the Grand Prior Giovan Battista Rezzonico, nephew of Clement XIII, who had the church rebuilt in 1765 over the ancient church of San Basilio.

The Villa of the Knights of Malta sits on the top of the Aventine, one of the legendary seven hills of Rome. It was here that the plebeians withdrew when they broke away to promote their political and civic claims. And it was here that Albericus II, "princeps atque omnium Romanorum senator" (prince and senator of all the Romans), had his palazzo when, in 932, the city declared itself a republic, ridding itself of the temporal power of the popes. But in 939 the senator relinquished his residence to the great Abbot Odo of Cluny, the monastic reformer. Thus the turreted castle became a Benedictine monastery, with a church dedicated to St. Basil. This famous monastery was one of the city's twenty abbeys—there were so many because the abbots traditionally assisted the popes in their solemn ceremonies.

Toward the end of the twelfth century, the property passed to the Knights Templar, the militant religious

defenders of the Holy Land against the threat of Islam. More than ever, the monastery retained its turreted appearance, even if the rule of the Templars in places far from the Holy Land required a conventual life that was not dissimilar to that of the Benedictines.

When, in 1312, Clement V suppressed the Templars, the monastery was given to the Knights of Rhodes, who already owned their own house, on the edge of the Forum of Augustus. The Knights of Rhodes maintained their priory here for 154 years, until 1466, when, under Cardinal Marco Barbo, the nephew of Pope Paul II, they returned for a few years to their house at the Forum of Augustus so that restoration work could be carried out on the Aventine.

From the end of the fifteenth century, the priorate had its seat here, at the same time as its change of name from the Knights of Rhodes to the Sovereign Military Order of Malta. Further rebuilding took place in 1547 under the prior Celidonio Boscos and between 1568 and 1598, under the prior Michele Bonelli. It was no longer a monastery surrounded by green fields and trees; it had become a villa with a residential mansion—that still had the appearance of a fortress—and a church. The natural element played an increasingly important part in the ambience, from the vegetable gardens and the Italianate gardens that encircled a fountain to the well-head that was part of the original monastic structure. The air breathed here was no longer limited to clerics; an underlying secular

The imposing complex of the Villa of the Knights of Malta on the Aventine, with the flag of the Order on the tower. It is a palace-castle, the fruit of the architectural imagination of Giovan Battista Piranesi.

presence could also be felt, one that was completely intellectual.

This became evident in the second half of the seventeenth century, when Cardinal Benedetto Pamphili was prior of the Order (1653–1730). Heavily engaged as librarian of the Holy Roman Church and dean of Santa Maria Maggiore, and subsequently of San Giovanni in Laterano, he took refuge in these gardens whenever he could and even had a "coffee house" built there. Here "he loved to spend in scholarly discussion the few hours of leisure allowed him by his numerous and heavy Curia duties." It was an arcadian time, revealing of the serenely intellectual, though deeply Christian, spirit which animated the Order of Knights.

The new image of the complex was implemented in 1765 when Grand Prior Giovan Battista Rezzonico, nephew of Clement XIII, had the small medieval church of St. Basil completely rebuilt and the mansion and gardens radically transformed by the Venetian architect Giambattista Piranesi, so that the villa took on the appearance that it has today.

Beginning from the monumental entrance set in the perimeter wall of the little piazza in front, the entrance wall contains the door with the famous keyhole through which it is possible to see, in a magical perspective view, the dome of St. Peter's framed by the hedges of the park. Two pilasters, framing the portal under a gable, boast trophies showing the glorious deeds of the Knights of Malta and heraldic symbols of the Rezzonico family, including crown, tower, cross, and eagle on two large panels. On the enclosure wall is a series of buildings with figures relating to the Order, flanked by obelisks and a high memorial stone set up to glorify the cross, in a marvelous unity of sculpture and architecture.

Once inside the walls, the greenery builds up between geometric borders in a luxuriant wealth of plants and flowers, with majestic palms brought here from the East and planted in the early nineteenth century by Ludwig I of Bavaria. The buildings seem to have been set between them in a harmonious whole circling the church, which was rebaptized Santa Maria del Priorato and had its main façade facing the Tiber. Within the building, the succession of the Grand Masters of the Order is shown in the gallery of portraits going from Geraldo (1113–1120) to the present day. Here too are the rooms of the prelate, a living witness to the continuing religious spirit of the Knights of Malta.

The church is still the most interesting part of the complex, from its splendid façade, divided by four fluted pilasters, with panels containing swords and capitals decorated with the heraldic undertakings of the Rezzonico family, to the magnificent interior, conceived as an immortal celebration of the Knights over and beyond death. The series of tombs on the sides makes it feel like an immense mausoleum, from the sarcophagus of the fifteenth-century humanist Baldassarre Spinelli, declaiming poetry, to the

cenotaph of Piranesi, buried here as architect of the architectural beautification, the sepulchers of the Grand Master G. of Thun and Hohenstein, who died in 1931, and of Bartolommeo Carafa, a prior of Hungary who died in 1405, who in 1400 uncovered a plot by the Colonna family against Pope Boniface IX. On the other side, it starts from the sarcophagus of the Grand Master Riccardo Caracciolo and goes on to the sepulchers of Cardinal G. F. Portocarrero, who died in 1760 and was viceroy of Sicily and friar of the Order, and Giorgio Seripando, who died in 1465, and was admiral of the Knights of Malta.

All the elements flow together toward the high altar in the raised presbytery, with the sarcophagus of St. Basil set in a great globe surrounded by putti among the clouds of the saint's glory, evocatively set against the light.

The true commemoration of the long history of the Sovereign Military Order of Malta is here, and it seems to find in the testimony of death the glorification which is still alive today in the apostolic spirit which guides the Order of St. John of Jerusalem, as noted earlier in the discussion of the House of the Knights of Rhodes.

Opposite:
In the rooms on the piano nobile of the palazzo is the seat of the Priorate. On the walls are portraits of the Grand Masters of the Sovereign Military Order of Malta and paintings showing the original homes of the Order of Jerusalem, the islands of Rhodes and Malta.

On the following pages:
The dome of St. Peter's as it appears, almost unrealistically, from the famous keyhole in the door in the wall of the Piazzetta in front of the villa. Below, a panoramic view of the gardens, with geometric borders in a luxuriant growth of plants and flowers.

INDEX

A

Academie de France 165, 167
Accademia Archeologica Cristiana 181
    degli Occulti 254
    degli Sfaccendati 152, 246, 378
    dei Lincei 108, 181, 254, 370
    dei Quiriti 321
    dei Vignaiuoli 354
    dell' Arcadia 195, 248, 360, 382
    di Napoli 107
    d'Italia 108
Accademia Filarmonica 325
    Romana 349
Acetti, Palazzo 19
Ackerman 13
Acqua Felice (acqueduct) 24, 81, 220
    bridge of 292
Acqua Paola (acqueduct) 24
    fountain of 354
Acqua Vergine (acqueduct) 24
    fountain of 23, 171
Aesculapius, Fountain of 291
    Temple of 289
Agapeto, Girolamo 375
Albani, Alessandro 91
    Francesco 131
    Villa 26, 32, 33, 38, 40
Albano 206
Albericus II 384
Alberini (coat of arms) 46, 48
Alberti, Cherubino 28
    Giovanni 28, 74
    Leon Battista 20
Albertoni, (coat of arms) 46
Alboretto dei Gelsi, Casino dell' 289
Albornoz, Egidio Camillo 350, 377
Albule, Acque 113
Aldobrandini, Cinzio 331
    family 46
    Gian Francesco 82, 376
    Giovanni Giorgio 331, 376
    Ippolito 331, 376, 377
    Olimpia 245, 332
    348, 375, 376, 377
    Palazzo 245, 377
    Paolo 244
    Pietro 327, 331, 372, 375, 376
    Silvestro 331, 372
Alessandro, Cardinal (later Pope Paul III) 10
Alexander III Borgia 46
Alexander VI 61, 67, 70, 95, 112
Alexander VII 172, 206, 222, 224, 244, 246,
    358, 377
Alexander the Great 28
Alfieri, Vittorio 380
Algardi, Alessandro 21, 27, 38, 47
Alle citta d'Italia, Palazzo 42
Allegrini 344

Alli (coat of arms) 46
Altemps, Annibale 70
    family 46
    Giovanni Angelo 268
    Giuseppe 180
    Lucrezia 180
    Marco Sittico 174, 176
    Palazzo 18, 34, 36, 174-185
Altieri, Emilio 316
    Famiglia 46, 48
    Giambattista 316
    Girolamo 316
    Lorenzo 315, 316
    Ludovico 316
    Marcantonio 315
    Mario 315
    Marzio 316
    Orazio 315
    Palazzo 17, 20, 32, 36, 40, 314–325
    Paluzzo 321
Amayden, Teodoro 48
Ambasciatori, Sala degli 34
Ameli, Paolo 334
Amici, Palazzo 42
Ammannati, Bartolomeo 156, 169, 171, 186
Anastasius I 93
Anesi, Paolo 194
Angelico, Beato 67
Angelis, Giulio De 42
Anguillara (coat of arms) 46, 48
Aniceto, Pope 177
Anima, Via dell' 343
Annibaldi (coat of arms) 46
Annunciation, Chapel of the 34, 222
Antici, Carlo Teodoro, 126, 131
    Giambattista 131
Apollo 26
    Sala di 32
Apostolic Chamber 338
Apostolica, Panetteria 222
Apostolico Vaticano, Palazzo (Vatican Palace)
    66–75
Apostolico, Palazzo (Papal Palace) 67, 68, 70,
    71, 72, 73, 74, 172, 214, 226
Aquilone, Fontana dell' (Fountain of the Great
    Eagle) 72
Aracoeli, 214
Aragona, Alfonso of, duke of Bisceglie 70
    Ottavio Acquaviva d' 146
Arazzi, Sala degli 74
Archinto 166
Arpino, Cavalier d' 82
Arquiem, Henri de la Grange d' 248
Asprucci, Antonio 288
    Mario 288
Associazione Bancaria Italiana (Italian Banking
    Association) 325
Astalli (coat of arms) 46

Via degli 64, 315, 325
Ateneo Leoniano 181
Aubusson 359
Augusta (tower) 356
Augustus, Forum of 53, 54, 385
Aurelian walls 296
Aurora, Casino dell' 267, 297, 299, 300, 303
Austria, Joseph II of 64
    Madama Margaret of 148, 150, 152
    Marie-Christine of 166
    Marianne of 365
    Maximillian of 380
    Peter Leopold I of 195, 336
Avalos, Ferdinando d' 234
Aventine (hills) 47, 53, 54, 93, 384
Avignon 46, 67, 77
Avila, Francesco Guzman de 204
Azetta (coat of arms) 48
Azzolini, Decio 360
Azzurri, Francesco 305, 312

B

Babuino, Via del 299
Baccio Bigio, Nanni di 138, 156, 186
Baciccia 245, 246, 380
Baglione 14, 26, 267
Bagnoli, Antonio 196
Baldi, Lazzaro 213
Baltard 167
Balthus 167
Banca Commerciale 336
    Palazzo della 43
Banca d'Italia 42
Banca Romana 41
Banco di Santo Spirito, Via del 17
Bandiere, Sala delle 86
Bandinelli, Baccio 148
Bandini, Marquis 180
Barberi, Giuseppe 195, 316
Barberini, Antonio 310
    Carlo 82
    Cornelia Costanza 312
    family 30
    Francesco 305, 310
    Maffeo 47, 308
    Palazzo 17, 20, 27, 30, 34, 36, 38, 40, 47,
    304–313
    Piazza 296, 305
    Taddeo 310, 331
    Urban VIII 47, 206, 222, 304, 308, 312, 339,
    376
Barbo, Appartamento 28
    Marco, Cardinal 54, 56, 385
    Pietro 58
Barcaccia, Fontana della 47
Bargellini, Giulio 43
Bari, count of 121
Baronino, Bartolommeo 202

Bartolini, Matteo 375
Basile, Ernesto 43
Bavaria, Ludwig I of 387
Bazzani, Cesare 43
Beaufort, Pierre Roger de 46
Beauharnais, Ortensia, 196
Belisario, Torre di 300
Bellavista, Girolamo 59
Belle Arti, Viale dell 173
Bellori 34
Belrespiro, Casino del 21
Beltrami, Luca 43
Belvedere 70, 71
Benaglia 21
Benedetto, Lucantonio 366
Benedict XIII 64
Benedict XIV 82, 146, 222
Benedict XV 73
Benediction Loggia 222, 226
Benzoni, Antonia 242
Bergès, Maurice 152
Berliès, Louis-Hector 167
Bernini, Gian Lorenzo 20, 27, 38, 40, 47, 165,
    245, 248, 288, 304, 305, 308, 312, 316
    Pietro 279
Bernis, Guglielmo de 272
Beroaldo, Count 189
Bessarione, Giovanni 233
Bethune, comte de 204
Boccacci (coat of arms) 48
Boito, Camillo 41
Bologna 71, 146, 206, 213
Bonaparte, Augusta Amelia 355
    Carlotta 355
    Giuseppe 366
    Lucien 355
    Louis 196
    Napoleon 55, 64, 72, 166, 224, 290
    Napoleon III 196
    Palazzo 40
    Paolina 261, 382
Boncompagni Ludovisi, Antonio III 299, 303
    Casino 32, 38, 297
    family 46
    Luigi 299
    Palazzo 41
    Villa, dell' Aurora 296–303
Bonelli, Michele 385
Bonfigli, Benedetto 67
Boniface VIII 230
Boniface IX 67, 79, 387
Bonsignori (coat of arms) 48
Bonzi, Pietro Paolo 30
Borghese, Anna Maria 382
    Camillo 256
    Cembalo 186
    family 20, 46
    Giovanni Battista 256, 260
    Marcantonio II 259
    Marcantonio IV 288
    Marcantonio V 292
    Palazzo 17, 18, 20, 23, 26, 27, 34, 36, 38, 40,
        47, 256–263
    Paolo 377
    Scipione, Cardinal 27, 30, 146
    Villa 19, 20, 26, 30, 33, 34, 38, 41, 168, 263,
        274–295
    Virginia 244, 377
Borgia, Cesare 69
    Gaspare 189
    Lucrezia 214
Borioni Santacroce, Villa 298, 299
Borromeo, Ortensia 70
Borromini, Francesco 18, 36, 47, 204, 304, 305,
    344
Boscos, Celidonio 385
Botanical Gardens 370
Bouguereau 176
Bourbon family 107, 119, 120, 121, 152
    Ferdinand 120, 166

Philip 107
    Maria Teresa Isabella 120
Bourbon (vineyard) 290
Bracciano, Palazzo di 356
Braccio Nuovo 87
Bracciolini, Francesco 308
Bramante 40, 47, 70, 136, 326
Brancaccio, Palazzo 42
Braschi (coat of arms) 46
    Palazzo 40
Breccioli, Bartolommeo 189
Brescia, Arnaldo da 77
Brill, Matthijs 74
    Paul 267, 268, 298
Broglia, Federico 382
Brosses, Charles de 10, 11, 24, 26, 27, 34, 36,
    38
Brueghel 245
Bulgamini (coat of arms) 48
Buonarroti, Michelangelo 10, 36, 38, 40, 47, 76,
    79, 81, 112, 171
Burba, Garibaldi 43
Burchard, Giovanni 68
Busiri Vici, Andrea 238, 336
Butij (coat of arms) 48

C
Caccia, Circolo della 263
Caelia (hills) 10, 11
    Villa on 131
Caetani, Filippo II 189
    Francesco IV 189
    Gaetano Francesco 194
    Leonardo 370
    Luigi 189
    Palazzo 36
    Ruggero III 194
    Via 128
Caffarelli Borghese, Scipione 259, 264, 274,
    275
Caffarelli, Palazzo 87
Caffarelli Vidoni, Palazzo 19, 20, 36
Calabresi, Palazzo 41
Calderon, Pedro 69
Callixtus III 46
Camassei 344
Cambarano, Giuseppe 196
Camerini 115, 121
Camillo VII 48
Camillo Carlo Alberto, Prince 98
Campidoglio (Capitoline) 13, 17, 40, 64, 76, 79,
    81, 86, 87, 98, 99
    Palazzi 76–91
Campo Carleo, Via di 56
Campo dei Fiori 13, 112
Campo Formio, treaty of 64
Campo Marzio 186
Cancelleria, Palazzo della 19, 20, 22, 28, 34, 36,
    174, 243, 358
Cancellieri, Flaminia del Bufalo 338
Candelabro, Sala del 74
Canevari, Raffaele 43
Canonica, Museo 294
Canonica, Pietro 292
Canova, Antonio 47, 64, 261, 290
Capitani, Sala dei 82
Capitolina, Gallery 146
Capocci (coat of arms) 46
Capodiferro, Girolamo 202, 204
    Palazzo 200
Cappello, Bianca 164
    Pietro 64
Capponi, Casino 297, 303
    vineyard 296
Capranica (coat of arms) 46
Caprarola 110
Carafa, Bartolommeo 387
    Oliviero 214
Caraffa, Cardinal 14
Caravaggio 36, 297, 359

Caravaggio, Giovanni Mangone di 98
Caravaggio, Giulio Merisi da 202
Caravaggio, Polidoro di 21, 174
Cariatidi, Sala delle 56
Carignano, Leopoldina of Savoy 336
Carimini, Luca 42
Carnevale, Pietro 42
Carpegna (coat of arms) 46
    Palazzo 20, 27
Carpi, Girolamo da 215
Carracci, Agostino 10, 30
    Annibale 10, 30, 34, 331
    frescoes 115, 119, 121
    Ludovico 10
Caso do Brasil 349
Casa Madre dei Mutilati 43
Caserta, count of 121
    Reggia di 120
Casoni, Felice Antonio 354
Castagno, Andrea del 67
Castel Fusano 146
Castellani (coat of arms) 46
Castelli, Benedetto 308
Castello, Piazza 42
Castel San Pietro, count of 134
Castel Sant'Angelo 12, 28, 34, 67, 165, 243
Castelviscardo, marquisate of 211
Castiglioni, Francesco Saverio 224
Castro, dukes of 28
Castro, war of 115
Castro, Ripalda Salvador Bermudez de 108
Catania 55
Cattanei, Vannozza de 67
Cavalieri (coat of arms) 46, 48, 49
    Piazza dei 47
Cavalieri di Malta, see Malta
Cavalieri di Rodi, see Rhodes
Cavallerizza, Cortile della 308
Cavalli Marini, Fontana dei 289
Cavallo, Monte 14, 36, 38
Cefalo, Vicolo del 146
Celerus, architect 12
Celestine III 66
Cellini, Giuseppe 42
Cembalo Borghese, Palazzo, 110, 256, 290
Cenci, Beatrice 40
    (coat of arms) 46
Cenci Bolognetti, Palazzo 20
Centini, Palazzetto 21
Cento Giorni, Sala dei 28
Centro Italiano di Studi Americani 135
Ceoli, Palazzo 275
    Tiberio 138
Cere, Museo delle 238
Cerruti, Michelangelo 194
Cerveteri 196
Cesarini (coat of arms) 46
Cesi, Federico, duke of Aquasparta 177
    Maria 177
    Palazzo, in Borgo 20, 152
Charles II 247
Charles III 336
Charles V 54, 112, 148, 152, 234
Charles VIII of France 61
Chaulnes, duke of 115
Chiabrera, Gabriello 308
Chiari, Fabrizio 32
Chigi, Agostino 29, 36, 102, 105, 108, 244, 337,
    377, 378, 380
    Agostino V 382
    Flavio 245, 246, 247, 378
    Largo 372
    Mario 244, 245, 377, 382
    Palazzo 372–383
    Sigismondo 34, 380, 382
    Villa 11
Chigi Odescalchi, Palazzo 17, 20, 34, 36, 38, 40
Chiovenda, Palazzo 19
Ciampelli, Agostino 146
Ciampoli, Giovanni 308

Cibo, Apartment 60, 64
    Lorenzo 60, 61
Cignoni, Mario 48
Cicero 36
Ciceroni (coat of arms) 48
Ciceruacchio 86
Ciocchi del Monte, Giovanni (Pope Julius III)
    168
Cipolla 121
Civilta Italiana, Palazzo della 43
Civita, Levi 370
Claderini, Guglielmo 42
Clement I 28
Clement III 66
Clement V 385
Clement VII 34, 46, 72, 148, 150, 186, 234,
    243, 297
Clement VIII 26, 64, 72, 81, 177,
    187, 220, 331, 376
Clement IX 269
Clement X 212, 316
Clement XII 15, 98, 222, 299, 365, 370
Clement XIII 64, 131, 386
Clement XIV 166
Clementina, Sala 28, 74
Cluny, Odo of 384
Coccetti, Liborio 33, 356
Cola di Rienzo 77, 86
Coli, Giovanni 32
Collegio Romano, Piazza del 326, 333
Colonna, Ascanio 233
    Fabrizio 233, 238, 241
    Lorenzo Onofrio 234, 244, 245, 261
    Marcantonio 82, 233
    Martin V 230
    Marzio 243
    Palazzo 26, 32, 33, 36, 38, 230–241, 245
    Piazza, 245, 246, 372, 375, 376, 377, 378,
        380, 382
    Piero 241
    Prospero 233, 241
Colonna Bellica, Sala della 238
Colonne, Sala delle 358
Colonna Sciarra, Giulio Cesare 312
Colosseum 10, 12, 22
Colucci 104
Concistoro, Sala del 59, 74, 222, 226
Conservatori, Palazzo dei 13, 20, 22, 28, 29, 40,
    77, 81, 87
Consiglio di Stato 213
Constantine (Costantino), emperor 22, 28
    Sala di 71, 72
    statue 82
Consulta, Palazzo della 21, 23, 40, 47
Conti (coat of arms) 46
    Giuseppe Lotario 47
Contini, Giovanni Battista 195, 377
Coppedè, Gino 43
Corazzieri, Sala dei 222, 226
Corner, Cardinal 47
Corradini, Antonio 310
Correr, Pietro 64
Corsini, Andrea 366
    Bartolommeo III 365
    Lorenzo 365
    Palazzo 17, 20, 40, 108, 358–371
    Tommaso 365, 366
    Vittoria 254
Corso, Via del 21, 196, 326, 372, 377, 378
Cortona, Pietro da 30, 32, 34, 36, 47, 131, 146,
    304, 308, 310, 312
Corvi, Domenico 260
Cosciari, Marcantonio 54
Cosimo the Great, Duke 47
Costaguti, Palazzo 32, 40
Cozza, Alfonso 173
Cozza, Francesco 321
Cremona, Gerolamo da 28
Créquy, duke of 115
Crescenzi (coat of arms) 48, 48

Marcello 156
Cresti 267
Crivelli, Palazzo 21
Cusani, Agostino 204
Cyprus 53

D

Damasceni (coat of arms) 48
D'Annunzio, Gabriele 26, 180
Dante 33
Dataria, Via della 222
Davy du Perron, Jacques 187
Dea Flora, Tempio della (Temple of the
    Goddess Flora) 304
De Angelis d'Ossat 42
Deer Park 284, 292
Del Grande, Antonio 234, 333
Della Greca, Felice 244, 377
    Vincenzo 204
Della Porta, Giacomo 81, 113
    Giambattista (G. B.) 275
Del Monte, Francesco, 297
    vineyard 296
Del Nero, Francesco 297
De Nicola, Enrico 226
De Parente, Palazzo 42
De Rossi, Giovanni Antonio 316
    Mattia 316
Dentice, Carlo 152
Deti, Giovan Battista 376
Deza, Pedro 256
Diana, Tempietto di 290
Diocletian, emperor 12
Dioscuri 13, 14
    Piazzale dei 214
Directory 365
Discoteca di Stato 135
Dominicans, general house of the 56
Domenichino 32, 40, 131, 296, 298
Domitian, Odeon of 16
Domus Aurea 10, 11, 12, 72
Doria, Carlo 196
    Vicolo 326
Doria Pamphili, Filippo Andrea V 336
    Galleria 331
    Giovanni Andrea 336
    Giovanni Andrea III 336
    Giovanni Andrea IV 336
    Girolamo 334
    Palazzo 17, 18, 20, 21, 27, 33, 34, 38, 40,
        326–337
    Villa 21, 26
Ducale, Sala 72
Duclos, Charles 38
Dudley, Charles 359
Duodo, Niccolo 64
Duphot, Leonard 365
Durazzo, Ladislao di 350
Durer, Albrecht 359

E

Ecclesiastical Immunity, Congregation of 343
Egizia, Sala 33
Ehlert, Louis 300
Einaudi, Luigi 226
Eliodoro, Stanza di 71
Erizzo, Niccolò 64
Esedra, piazza 41
Esposizioni, Palazzo delle 41, 42
Esquiline (hills) 10, 11
Este, Alfonso d' 68, 244
    Ippolito d' 26, 214
    Ippolito II d' 354
Eugene III 66
Eugene IV 28, 58
Evangelisti, Sala degli 74

F

Falconieri, Palazzo 18, 40
Falda, Giovanni Battista 18, 24

Fame 299
Farnese, Alessandro 12, 24, 82, 110, 114
    Dado 186
    Elisabetta 107, 119
    family 110, 112, 113, 118, 119
    Giulia 67, 68
    Ottavio 152
    Palazzo 10, 13, 16, 17, 19, 22, 28, 30, 33, 34,
        36, 40, 47, 107, 110–125, 136, 152, 256,
        358
    Paul III 64, 110
    Pier Luigi 112
    Ranuccio, 114, 115, 121
Farnesina, Villa 13, 28, 29, 102–109, 377
Fasti Romulei 204
Faustina, Temple of 288
Fazio Santoro, Giovanni, Cardinal 326, 327
Federazione Italiana dei Consorzi Agrari 272
Ferretti, Giovanni Maria Mastai 224
Ferri, Ciro 260
Fesh, Giuseppe 366
Filippini, Convento dei 20
Finmare 313
Fiorentini (Florentine), quarter 136
    San Giovanni dei 146
Firenze, Maturino di 21, 174
Fiumi, Fontana dei 47
Flaminia, Via 168, 169, 172, 173
Flaminio, Borghetto 168
    piazzale 291
Fontaine, Pierre-François Léonard 24
Fontainebleau 224
Fontana, Carlo 34, 47, 64, 333
    Domenico 14, 47, 72, 220
    Girolamo 238
    Prospero 29, 171
Fontanella Borghese, Via della 186, 189, 196
    Largo di 256
Fossano, Fabrizio 375, 376
Fountain of Flame 291
France, Marie-Christine 354
Francesca, Piero della 67
Francis I 71
Francis II 107, 121
Frangipani (coat of arms) 46, 48
Fuga, Francesco 20, 21, 23, 47, 82, 222,
    365
Führich, Joseph 33
Funari, Via 128
Furlano, Nicolò 95

G

Gabinetto Nazionale dei Disegni e delle Stampe
    (National Cabinet of Drawings and Prints)
    108
Gabriele Orsini di Mugnano, Mario 49
Gabrielli della Regola (coat of arms) 48
Gabrielli, Mario 355
    Pietro 355
    Placido 355
Galatea, Sala di 104
Galilei, Galileo 269
Gallarati Scotti, Carlotta 135
Galleria Nazionale d'Arte Antica 313, 370
Galleria Nazionale d'Arte Moderna 294
Gallese, duke of 176
    Giovan Angelo 176, 177
Gallicano (civil war) 243
Gallinaro, Casa del 284
Gandi-Niccolini, Palazzo 17
Ganganelli, Gian Vincenzo, 166
Gaspare, Ulderico di 49
Gatta, Via della 326, 333, 336
Gendarme, Sala del 74
Gentileschi, Orazio 226, 267
Gerardo (monk) 52
Germany, Wilhelm of 337
    Wilhelm II of 226
Gesù, Piazza del 314, 315, 316
Gherardi, Filippo 32

Gianiculum (hill) 358
  Passeggiata del, 370
Giardin del Lago (Lake Garden) 289, 292
Giardiniere, Casa del (Gardener's House)
  289
Gibbon, Edward 38
Giglio, Paolo del 256
Gimignani 344
Giovannini, Stefano 291
Giovannozzi, Ezio 43
  Ugo 43
Giove, dukes of 128
Giraud Torlonia, Palazzo 20, 36, 40
Girolamo, Cardinal 238
Giulia, Via 107, 113, 114, 136, 146, 152, 156,
  204, 365
Giulia, Villa 17, 23, 29, 38, 168–173, 294
Giustiniani, Caterina 254
  Olimpia 308
  Palazzo 20, 36, 38, 40, 226
Giustiniani-Massimo, Casino 33
Giustizia, Palazzo di 41, 42
Goethe, Johann Wolfgang 24, 38, 152, 196
Goldoni, Carlo 181
Goldoni, Largo 186
Gomo, Girolamo da 24
Gonzaga, Costanza 128
  Eleonora 327
  Ferdinando 165, 204
Gran Consiglio del Fascismo (Great Fascist
  Council) 64
Graziano, Casino del 284
Grazioli, Piazza 336
Great Forest 284
Gregorovius, Ferdinand 41, 148
Gregory IX 67
Gregory XI 46
Gregory XIII 14, 72, 159, 215, 220
Gregory XV 177, 296, 376
Gregory XVI 224
Grillo, Piazza del 54, 55
Grimani, Domenico 64
  Girolamo 336
  Vincenzo 365
Gronchi, Giovanni 226
Guardie Nobili, Sala delle (Hall of the Noble
  Guards) 74
Guarini, Giovan Battista 152
Guercino 32, 33, 38, 206, 298
Guidetti, Guido 81

H
Hadrian, Villa 165
Hadrian I 72
Hapsburg, Maximilion of 195
Hardouin, Jules 180, 181
Henri II 204
Henri IV, 187
Hohenems, Wolfgang 174
Holy See 53, 64
Holy Sepulcher 52, 53

I
Iacobilli, Bernardino 186
  Francesco 186
Ideville, Henry d' 261, 366
Illuminati (sect) 382
Impero, Via dell' 377
Incendio di Borgo, Sala dell' 71
Infessura, Stefano 68
Inghirami 104
Ingres, Jean-Auguste Dominique 167
Innocent III 66
Innocent VIII 67
Innocent X 165, 206, 312, 332, 338, 343, 349
Innocent XI 212, 247
Innocent XII 14
Innocent XIII 222
Isis, Temple of 99
Istituto delle Neofite delle Domenicane 55

Istituto Italiano di Numismatica (Italian
  Numismatic Institute) 312
Istituto Nazionale delle Assicurazioni, Palazzo
  dell' 43
Istituto Storico Italiano per l'Età Moderna e
  Contemporanea (Italian Historical Institute
  for Modern and Contemporary History)
  135

J
Jacovacci (coat of arms) 46, 48
James, Henry 21, 26, 300
Jerusalem 53, 56, 71
Jesuits, Order of 166
John Paul II 74
John III, King of Poland 247
John XXIII 74
José, Maria 226
Joseph II 336
Joyeuse, François de 189
Julius Caesar 86, 87
Julius II 70, 71, 102, 315, 326
Julius III 138, 168, 172, 202, 204
Jupiter Optimus Maximus (temple) 76
Juvarra, Filippo 47

K
Knights Templar 384, 385
Koch, Gaetano 41, 42
  Joseph Anton 33

L
Lamberti, Bonaventura 356
Ladislao, Baldassarre 254, 255
Ladislao-polis (Ladispoli) 255
Lamarmora, General 226
Lancellotti ai Coronari, Palazzo, 32
Lancellotti, Arturo 73
Lancellotti Ginetti, Ottavio 99
Lanfranco, Giovanni 30, 34, 131
Larderel, Arturo 43
Lata, Via 59, 242, 326
Lateran 215, 234
Lavaggi Pacelli, Palazzo 41
Lavardin, marquis of 115
Lehnert, Pascalina 74
Leni (coat of arms) 48
Leonardo da Vinci 38, 40, 359
Leoncino, Via del, 186, 195
Leone, Giovanni 226
Leo III 71
Leo IV 72
Leo X 28, 46, 71, 72, 106, 148, 186, 358
Leo XI 46, 165
Leo XII 173, 224
Leo XIII 72
Leoni, Ottavio 177
Leopardi, Giacomo 126, 128, 134, 135, 321
Lepanto, Battle of 233, 234
Letarouilly 24
Lezzani, Natalia 180
Liberation of Saint Peter 39
Ligorio, Pirro 21, 72
Lippi, Annibale 165
  Giovanni 20
Loggetta, Sala della 56
Loggia, Sala della 114
Longhi, Martino, the Younger 27, 189
Longhi, Martino, the Elder 20, 47, 81, 174, 256
Lopodinec, Giuseppe 196
Lorenzetto 19
Lorrain, Claude 39
Lorraine, Joseph, Archduke 166
  Leopoldo I, Grand Duke 166
Louis XIII 206, 269
Louis XIV 167
Louis XV 180
Louis XVI 261
Lourdes, Grotto of 72
Louvre 290

Lubin, Palazzina 292
Lucania, Via 299
Luccherini, Francesca 98
Lucina, piazza in 186
Lucullus 156, 164
Ludovisi, Giambattista 299
  Ippolita 299, 376
  Ludovico 177, 243, 296, 297
  Villa 40, 41
Lungara, Via della 102, 110, 366
Lupa, Sala della 82

M
Macaroni (coat of arms) 48
Macarozzi de Lioni (coat of arms) 48
Macerata 48
Machiavelli, Niccolò 40
Madama, Palazzo 187
  Villa 29, 36, 40, 148–155
Maderno, Carlo 27, 128, 222, 243, 258, 304
Madonna, Sala della 74
Madonna della Guardia (chapel) 73
Madruzzi, Margherita 177
Maffei (family) 20
Maggi, Donato 27
Magliana 148
Magnani, Anna 325
Magni, Giulio 43
Mai, Angelo, Cardinal 321
Maidalchini, Olimpia, *see* Pamphili Maidalchini
  Olimpia
Maini 21
Malta 54, 55
  Cross of 56
  grand master of S.M.O. of 55
  Order of Knights of 386
  patron cardinal of S.M.O. of 55
  Sovereign Military Order of 52, 54, 56, 385,
    387
  Villa of the Knights of 21, 384–389
Mancini, Francesco, 238
  Maria 245
  Michele Lorenzo 269
  Palazzo 20, 167
Mandosi, Antonio 243
  Giovanni Battista 243
  Marcantonio 243
  Ottavio 243
  Palazzo dei 243
  Valeriano 243
Manflard, Adrien 380
Manica Lunga 222, 226
Mappamundi, Sala dei 28, 138
Mappamundo, Sala del 28, 29, 59, 60, 64
Maraini, Antonio 43
Maratta, Carlo 47
Maratti, Carlo 316
Marcus Aurelius 13, 77, 79, 91
  column of 378
Marforio 91
Margani (coat of arms) 46, 48
Marignoli on the Corso, Palazzo 42
Marine, Camera delle 378
Marino, Roberto 43
Mario, Monte 72, 148, 152
Marmi, Sala dei (Hall of the Marble Statues)
  308
Martin V 79, 202
  Sala di 238
Maruscelli, Paolo 204
Mascarino 215
Mascherino, Ottaviano 14, 27, 72
Mass at Bolsena 39
Massimi, Piazza dei 92
Massimo, alle Colonne, Alessandro 93, 99
  Angelo 95, 98
  Camillo VIII Massimiliano 99
  (coat of arms) 46, 48
  Domenico 95
  Fabrizio 99

family 92, 99
  Giovanni 93
  Girolamo 99
  Giuliano 95
  Lelio 99
  Luca 99
  Marcantonio 99
  Palazzo 16, 19, 21, 23, 33, 36, 92–101
  Paolo 99
  Pietro 93, 98
  Quintus Fabius 92
Massimo d'Aracoeli (coat of arms) 99
  Fabrizio 99
  Tiberio 99
Mastai (pope) 86
Mattei, Alessandro 128, 131
    Asdrubale 128
  (coat of arms) 46
  Girolamo 131
  Giuseppe 131
  Lorenzo 131
  Luigi 131
  Maria Anna 131
  Villa 36
Mattei Antici, Matteo 135
  Tommaso 135
Mattei di Giove (family) 23
  Palazzo 17, 18, 20, 27, 30, 40, 126–135
Mazarin, Girolama 269
  Jules, cardinal 47, 238, 261, 269, 312
Mazzini, Giuseppe 87
Mazzoni, Giovanni 312
  Giulio 21, 204
Medici, de', Alessandro 150, 165
  Carlo 165
  Catherine 187
  Chiara 174
  family 146
  Ferdinando 156, 164, 165
  Ferdinando II 165
  Francesco 164
  Giovanna 382
  Giulio 148, 150
  Villa 18, 19, 21, 24, 25, 36, 40, 156–167
Medici Riccardi, Palazzo 42, 255
Melangoli, Giardino dei (Garden of the Seville
    Oranges) 327
Melani, Alfredo 42
Mellini (coat of arms) 46, 48
Melville, Herman 26, 40
Memmo Foundation 196
Mengs, Raphael 32
Mercede, Via della 234
Meróde, Frédéric Xavier de 41
Metastasio, Pietro 380
Meuzingen, sisters of 74
Michetti, Niccolò 238
Mignanelli, Pietro Paolo 204
Milani, Aureliano 32, 334
Millini, Palazzo 343
Milvian Bridge 168
Minghetti, Galleria 42
Ministero dell'Aeronautica, Palazzo 43
  della Marina 43
  della Pubblica Istruzione, Palazzo 43
  delle Finanze, Palazzo 43
  di Grazia e Giustizia, Palazzo 43
Ministry of Foreign Affairs 152, 372, 382
Miollis, General 224, 336
Misteri della Fede, Sala dei (Room of the
    Mysteries of the Faith) 67
Molara (coat of arms) della 48
Mole of Hadrian 12
Monaldeschi, Rinaldo 118
Mondragone 176, 177
Montaigne, Michel de 26, 36
Montecitorio, Palazzo di 38, 40, 375, 377
Montefiascone, Rocco da 24
Monte Giordano 350
  Palazzo di, 350–357

Taverna di, Palazzo 33
Montenegro, Elena di 226
Montesquieu, baron di 36
Montepulciano, Giovanni Ricci di 136
Monterotondo, Palazzo di 354
Monti, Vincenzo 348, 380
Moore, Jacob 288
Moraldi, Giovanni Pietro 333, 377
Moroni, Gaetano 152
Muro Torto, Casino del 290, 292
Muse 25
  Casino delle 32
  Loggia delle 267
Musei Capitolini, Palazzo 77
Musei, Parco dei (Park of Museums) 294
Museo Nazionale Romano 303
Museo Nuovo (New Museum) 87
Musset, Alfred de 40
  Paul de 40
Mussolini, Benito 64, 382
Muti, Bobone 48
  (coat of arms) 46, 48
Muziano, Girolamo 354

N
Napoli, Roberto di 230
Narcissus Fountain 279
Nardé, Gabriele 308
Navona, Piazza 18, 32, 38, 47, 174, 338, 339,
    348, 365
Nazionale, Via 268
Negro, Silvio 73
Neptune 15, 26
Neri, Filippo 99
Nero, emperor 10, 11, 12
Neuville d'Halincourt, Charles de 187
Nevers, duke of 189
Nicholas, Chapel of 67, 71
Nicholas III 66, 67, 350
Nicholas V 67, 71, 79
Nicoletti, Francesco 336
Niobe 165
Nozze, Sala delle (Wedding Chamber) 105

O
Obiccioni (coat of arms) 48
Odescalchi, Baldassarre 248,
  Baldassarre II 254
  Baldassarre III 254
  (coat of arms) 46
  Livio 246, 247, 248
  Maria Flaminia 34, 380
  Palazzo 40, 42, 242–255
Odoardo, Cardinal 34, 114, 115
Ojetti, Raffaello 42, 255
Oliva, Paolo 348
Onorio V Caetani 189
Oppian (hills) 10, 11
Orazi e Curiazi, Sala degli 82
Ordeaschi, Francesca 102
Order of St. John of Jerusalem 387
Orlandi, Clemente 316
Oro, Salone d' 380
Orologio, Casino dell' (Clock Lodge) 289, 291
Orsini, Camilla 259
  (coat of arms) 46, 48
  family 350
  Gabriele 49
  Giordano 350
  Mario 49
  Palazzo 338
  Villa 296
Orti Farnesiani 24
Orvieto 71
Ossoli, Palazzo 20
Ottavi (coat of arms) 48
Oultremont of Warfusé, Émile, 382
Oval Fountain 279
Overbeck, Friedrich 33
Ovid 10

P
Paesi, Camera dei 380
Palafrenieri, Sala dei 71
Palatine (hills) 10, 12, 24, 110
Palestrina (civil war) 243
Palestrina, Pier Luigi da 349
Pallai 104
Pallavicini, Giulio 272
  Lazzaro 269
Pallavicini Rospigliosi, Casino 30
  Domenico Clemente 272
  Giovanni Battista 269, 272
  Maria Camilla 269, 272
  Niccolò Maria 272
  Palazzo 18, 20, 26, 40, 264–273, 298
Palombara (coat of arms) 46
Pamphili, Benedetto 333, 336, 386
  Camillo 332, 338, 339, 348, 377
  Camillo Junior 333, 334
  Costanza 338
  Giovanni Battista 333, 338, 339, 343
  Girolamo 338
  Innocent X 27, 47
  Maria 338
  Palazzo 18, 32, 36, 338–349
  Pamphilio 338, 343
  Villa 38
Pamphili Maidalchini, Olimpia 27, 244, 338,
    343, 344, 348
Pannartz, Arnold 93
Pannini, Gian Paolo 33
Panvinio (historian) 93
Paolina, Cappella (Pauline Chapel) 222, 224,
    (or Regia), Sala 28
Papareschi (coat of arms) 46
Paparoni (coat of arms) 46
Papazzurri (coat of arms) 46, 48
Papi, Sala dei (Hall of the Popes) 74
Paradisi, Domenico 194
Paramenti, Sala dei 28
Pariolo (district known as Vigna Vecchia) 274
Parione (district) 268
Parlamento, Palazzo del 41
Parma 115, 152
  duke of 112, 114
Parnasus 25, 26, 159
Pasquale II 53
Pasquino, Piazza 338
Patarina 77
Patrimony of St. Peter 48
Patrizi (coat of arms) 46
Paul II 54, 56, 58, 59, 64, 385
Paul III 10, 13, 24, 28, 47, 64, 113, 114, 121,
    152, 204, 214
Paul IV 72, 172
Paul V 24, 222, 256, 259, 264
Paul VI 67, 74
Percier, Charles 24
Pertini, Sandro 226
Perin del Vaga 28, 98
Peruzzi, Baldassarre 28, 98, 102, 104, 174, 354
Petrarca, Francesco (Petrarch) 77, 230
Petroni, Palazzo 315
Philip II 259
Philip V of Spain 119, 194
Pia, Porta 14, 47, 226
  Strada (Via) 14, 214, 222, 305
Piacentini, Marcello 43, 152, 196
  Pio 42, 43
Pianetti, Paolo 24
Piattaia, Sala della 27
Piazza, Cosimo 259
Piemonte, Via 296
Pierleoni (coat of arms) 46
Pietro, apostle 12
Pigna quarter 314
Pigneto (estate) 146
Pilotta, Via della 26, 238
Pinaroli, Giovan Battista 299
Pinciana, Porta 244, 274

Via, 156, 275, 296
Pinturicchio, 67
Piombo, Raphael del 104
   Sebastiano del 104, 337
Piranesi, Giambattista 21, 47
Pirro (Pyrrhus) 98
   Palazzo di 98, 99
Pitigliano, Palazzo di 356
Pittori, Giovan Battista 356
Pius II Piccolomini, 46
Pius III Piccolomini, 46, 70
Pius IV 19, 47, 64, 70, 72, 172
   Casina di 21, 23, 36
Pius V Ghislieri 24, 55, 72, 215
Pius VI 166, 168, 222, 299
Pius VII 72, 224
Pius VIII 224
Pius IX 86, 180, 224, 226, 241, 261, 382
Pius X 72
Pius XI 73, 196
Pius XII 73, 74, 196
Planca Incoronati, Antonietta 95
Plebiscito, Via del 60, 315, 326, 334
Podesti, Giulio 41
Poland 47
   Marie of 180
Poli, dukes of 15
   Palazzo 14, 15
Polignac, cardinal di 177
Poligrafico dello Stato, Palazzo del 43
Polyclitus 99
Pomarancio 131, 177
Pontificio Collegio Spagnolo 181
Pontificio, Palazzo 14, 222
   State 36
Ponzio, Flaminio 222, 256, 264, 274
Popolo, Porta del 290
Porcari, Giuliano 46
Portinaio, Casa del 292
Portocarrero, G. F., Cardinal 387
Posi, Paolo 238
Posta Centrale, Palazzo della 42
Potenziani Grabinski, Giovanni 213
   Villa 226
Poussin, Nicolas 38, 40, 344
Pranzi, Casino dei 299, 303
Prati di Castello, Piazza dei 40
Primoli, Palazzo 42
Propaganda Fide 159, 195
   Palazzo 17, 20
Prospettive, Sala delle 28, 29, 107, 121
Psyche, Loggia di 29, 36, 38
Publicola, Publius Valerius, Consul 48
Pupazzi, Fontana dei (Fountain of Puppets) 288

Q
Quattracci (coat of arms) 48
Quattro Fontane, Via delle 305, 312
IV Novembre, Via 238,
Quattro Stagioni, Sala delle 382
Quirinal (hill) 14, 17, 26, 233, 242, 244, 305
   Palazzo del 27, 29, 33, 34, 40, 72, 214–229
Quirini, Angelo Maria 64
Quirinus, Romulus 214

R
Rabirius (architect) 12
Rainaldi, Carlo 20, 26, 87, 260
   Giacomo 81, 146
   Girolamo 26, 87, 275, 343
Rainaldo e Armida, Sala di 32
Rane, Fontana delle 43
Ranuccio the Elder 28, 112
Raphael, Sanzio 11, 28, 36, 38, 39, 40,
   71, 72, 102, 148, 337, 359
   Casina di 294
   Loggia of 29, 36, 39, 152
Ravenna 71
Redentore (Redeemer), Sala del 74
Reder, Giovanni 194

Regia, Sala 28, 29, 72
   Scala 27
Regola (district) 11, 200
Reni, Guido 27, 30, 34, 40, 206, 267, 298
Rezzonico, Giovan Battista 386
Rhodes, 53, 56
   Casa dei Cavalieri di (House of the Knights
     of Rhodes) 52–57, 387
   Knights of 53, 54, 56, 57, 385
   Palazzetto dei Cavalieri di 27
Riano 196
Riario Altemps, Palazzo 27
Riario, Girolamo 174
   Pietro 233
   Raffaele 358
   Villa 358
Riario Sforza, Camilla 355
   Francesco 358
   Galeazzo 358
   Ottavio 174
Ricci (coat of arms) 46
   Palazzo 20, 21, 36
   Sebastiano 356
Ricci of Montepulciano, Don Giovanni 156
   Don Giulio 156
   Giovanni 156
Richard I 47
Richelieu, Alphonse de 115
Ripetta (port) 256, 259
Riviera, Jacobo della 310
Rochefoucauld, Adele 261
Roman Forum 77
Romano, Giulio 148
Roncalli, Nicola 261
Roncione, Giovanni 350
Rosa, Salvator 39, 321
Rose, Casino delle 294
Rospigliosi (coat of arms) 46
   Giulio 308
   Tommaso 82
Rossa (or dell'Amore), Sala 321
Rossano (fiefdom) 376
Rossi, Nicola 365
Rossini, Gioacchino 325
Rosso, Giovanni Gaetano 350
   Luigi 42
   Matteo 350
Rosso, Salone 99
Round Fountain 279
Rovere, Bianca della 174
   Francesco Maria della 327
   Francesco Maria I della 327
   Giuliano della 233
   Guidobaldo II della 327
   Julius II della 46
   Lucrezia della 233
Rubens, Pieter Paul, 40 194, 337
Rucellai, Ferdinando 187, 189
   Giovanni 354
   Luigi 187, 189
   Orazio 186, 187
   Piero 186
Rufinella, Villa della 146
Ruffini (coat of arms) 48
Ruskin, John 40
Ruspoli, Alessandro 195, 196
   Bartolommeo 195
   Carlo 196
   (coat of arms) 46
   Emanuele 196
   Eugenio 196
   Francesco Maria 194, 195
   Palazzo 18, 27, 29, 33, 40, 110, 186–199, 256
Russell, Odo William 382

S
Sacchetti, family 20, 46
   Giulio 146
   Luigi 312
   Palazzo 28, 29, 36, 40, 136–147, 156

Scipione 146
   Urbano 146
Sacconi, Giuseppe 42
   Palazzo 42
Sacred Hospice 196
Sade, marquis de 25, 26, 38
Salaria, Porta 26, 226, 300
Salvi, Nicola 15, 47, 248
Salviati (coat of arms) 46
   Francesco 28, 34, 114, 138
Sadoleto, Iacopo 104
San Bartholomew (massacre) 72
San Basilio (church) 56, 386
San Bernardo, Piazza 42
San Callisto, Palazzo 20
San Damaso (courtyard) 66, 72
Sangallo, Antonio da 12, 98, 112, 136, 148
San Gemini, Giovanni Antonio 176
San Giovanni (basilica) 299
   Porta, 165
San Giovanni della Pigna (church) 46
San Giovanni in Laterano (church) 386
   rectory of 378
Sanguigni (coat of arms) 46
San Lorenzo in Lucina, Palazzo 327
San Luigi dei Francesi, Palazzo 17
San Marco (church) 58, 64
   Palazzo 13
   Piazza 60
   quarter 61
San Martino ai Monti 56
San Martino al Cimino 348
Sannazzaro, Jacopo 150
San Nicola da Tolentino, Via 305
San Pancrazio, Porta 26
San Pantaleo, Piazza 92, 98
San Sebastianello, Salita di 156
San Stanislao (church) 47
Santa Congregazione del Buon Governo (Holy
   Congregation of Good Government) 382
Santacroce (coat of arms) 46, 48
Sant'Agnese (church) 344
Sant'Alessio (convent) 92
Santa Maria (church) 333
Santa Maria (monastic chapter) 326
Santa Maria della Vittoria (church) 47
Santa Maria dell'Orto (church) 47
Santa Maria del Priorato (church) 387
Santa Maria Maggiore 386
Sant'Ambrogio (St. Ambrose), Sala di 74
Sant'Andrea della Valle, Piazza 92
Sant'Angelo (district) 128
Sant'Apollinare, Piazza 174, 180
Santa Prassede, Archive of 48
Santarelli, Carlo 310
Sant'Eustachio (district) 148
Santi Apostoli, Piazza dei 242, 248, 377, 378
   Palazzo dei 245
   Vicolo dei 248
Santi Pietro e Paolo (St. Peter and Paul), Sala
   dei 74
Santo Stefano del Cacco, Via di 315
Saragat, Giuseppe 226
Sarto, Andrea del 40
Sartorio, Aristide 43
Savelli (coat of arms) 46, 48
Savoia Carignano, Maria Gabriella
   Carlo Emanuele I 354
   Caterina Antonietta 99
   Maurizio di 354
   Tommaso Francesco 354
   Vittorio Amedeo 354
Saxony, Christine of 99
   Marianne of 316
   Teschen, Albert of 166
Sayn-Wittgenstein, Ludwig of 382
Scala Santa 299
Scalfaro, Oscar Luigi 226
Schnorr, Julius 33
Schor, Giovanni Paolo 26, 245, 261

Schweynheim, Conrad 93
Sciarra Colonna (portal) 110
Sciarra, Palazzo 40
Scienze e delle Arti Liberali, Sala delle 70
Scotti, Luisa 366
Scultori (Sculptors), Sala degli 74
Sdrucciolo, Via dello 377
Secret Garden 279
Segnatura, Sala della 71
Segni, Antonio 226
Semidei, Sala dei (Room of the Demigods) 29
Senatorio, Palazzo 13, 40, 77, 79, 86
Septimus Severus, Arch of 291
Serenissima 64
Seripando, Giorgio 387
Serlio 19
Serlupi (coat of arms) 46
Sermattei della Genga, Annibale 224
Sermoneta 194
Settimiana, Porta 358, 366
Severus (architect) 12
Sfondrati, Paolo Emilio 358
Sforza, Bosio II 112
    Caterina 174
    Giovanni 67
Sforza-Cesarini, Palazzo 42
Sibille, Sala delle (Hall of the Sibyls) 69
Sidney Morgan, Lady 39
Siena, Piazza di 289, 291
Silvester I 28
Sistine Chapel 36, 67, 222
Sistine Palace 28, 66, 72
Sixtus IV 46, 67, 79, 174, 233
Sixtus V 24, 66, 71, 72, 220
Sobieski, Maria Casimira 247, 248
    Sala 72
Società Musicale Romana (Roman Musical
    Society) 349
Society of Jesus 166
Soderini (coat of arms) 46
    Francesco 174
Solari, Giovanbattista 99
Spada, Alessandro 213
    Bernardino 204, 211, 212
    (coat of arms) 46
    Clement 213
    Fabrizio 212
    Giuseppe 213
    Maria 213
    Orazio 211
    Palazzetto 20
    Palazzo 19, 21, 22, 27, 34, 36, 40, 200–213
    Paolo 204
    Virgilio 206
Spada Veralli Potenziani, Ludovico 213
Spagna, Piazza di 47
Specchi, Alessandro 82
Specchi, Galleria degli 32, 334
    Sala degli 32, 321
Speroni, Alessandro 316
Spinelli, Baldassarre 387
Spinola, Gian Domenico 377
St. Antimo 56
St. Catherine (church) 242
    Sala di, 74
St. George 86
St. John the Baptist, church of, 53, 56

St. Johns of Acre 53
St. Peter's (church) 66, 248, 275
    dome 386
    fabric of 211, 376
    piazza 74
    treasury of 350
Stamperia Orientale 159
Stefaneschi (coat of arms) 46
Stendhal 22, 40, 299
Stern, Giovanni 34, 380
    Raphael 224
Stolberg, Friedrich Leopold 134
Stoppani, Palazzo 40
Strozzi, Uberto 354
Stuart family 47
Stuart, Mary 261
Stucchi, Galleria degli 204
Suetonius, Gaius 10, 11
Svizzeri, Sala degli (Hall of the Swiss Guards)
    71
Sweden, Christina of, 115, 165, 172, 247, 248,
    358, 359, 360
    Gustavus III of 64
Swiss Guards 74, 220, 222

T
Taine, Ippolito 21, 40, 300
Targone, Pompeo 358
Tassi, Agostino 32, 222, 226, 267, 298, 331,
    343
Tasso, Torquato 33, 354
Tebaldeschi (coat of arms) 48
Tedallini, Adriano 372
Teofili, house of the 338
Terranova, Tommaso Marino di 138
Tesino, valley of the 212
Thun and Hohenstein, Grand Master of 387
Tiber island 189
Tiber, River 11, 13, 79, 104, 106, 107, 108, 110,
    138, 148, 168, 171, 258, 387
Tiepolo, Lorenzo 64
Tintoretto 337
Titian 337, 359
Tivoli 112, 165
Tolentino 48
Tor di Nona 189, 350, 360
Torlonia (coat of arms) 46
    Giovanni 370
    Palazzo 40
Torre delle Milizie (Military Tower) 230
Torre, Raimondo della 256
Tour Maubourg, ambassador 240
Trajan, Forum of 54
Trastevere 13, 358, 365
Trevi, Fountain of 47, 244
    Piazza di, 14, 15, 47
Trinità dei Monti 165, 247, 299
Triton Fountain 304
Trono, Sala del (Throne Room) 121, 224, 238
Tunis 152
Tuxany, Leopold of 64
Tuscolo counts of 230

U
Udine, Giovanni da 29, 34, 148
Umberto I 292
Umberto II 226

Universal Exhibition 43
United States embassy 303
Unterberger, Carlo 321
Urban III 36
Ursina, Cornelia 176

V
Valesio 21
Valvassori, Gabriele 21
Vanvitelli, Luigi 248
Vasanzio, Giovanni 264, 267, 274, 275
Vasari, Giorgio 13, 28, 72, 102, 136, 148, 171,
    354
Vasi, Giuseppe 18, 26,
Vatican 19, 27, 28, 29, 36, 40, 47, 60, 66, 73,
    74, 152, 165, 172, 173, 215, 226, 234, 312
Vecchiarelli, Palazzo 18
Veit, Philipp 33
Velázquez, Diego 27, 165, 337
Veneto, Via 296, 303
Venezia (Venice) 64
    Palazzo 17, 19, 28, 29, 36, 40, 58–65, 382
    Piazza 13, 58
XXIV Maggio Via 238, 264
Venti, Torre dei (Tower of the Winds) 215
Veralli, Maria 211
Verde (or dell'Inverno), Sala 321
Vernet, Horace 167
Verospi, Palazzo 40
Versailles 38
Vetera (coat of arms) 48
Vicars of Christ 47
Vicenza 54
Vico, Giovanni di 350
Vidoni, Girolamo 377
Vienna 194, 196, 212, 247
Vignanello 196
Vignola 24, 113, 171, 256
Vinci, Leonardo 180
Viola, G. B. 298
Virgil 54
Visconti, Ennio Quirino 380
Vitelli, Vitellozzo 204
Viterbo 77
Vittorio Emanuele, Corso 92, 93
    piazza 41
Vittorio Emanuele II 42, 226, 254, 303
Vittorio Emanuele III 226
Volterra, Daniele da 21, 114

W
Widmanstadt, Johann Albert 150
Wolkonsky, Peter 382

Z
Zagarolo (fiefdom) 243, 299
    Pierfrancesco di 243
Zola, Emile 26, 40, 146
Zoological Gardens 284, 292
Zuccari, casa degli 248
    Federico 21, 114
    Taddeo 28, 114, 171
Zucchi, Jacopo 29, 164, 187

PHOTOGRAPHIC CREDITS

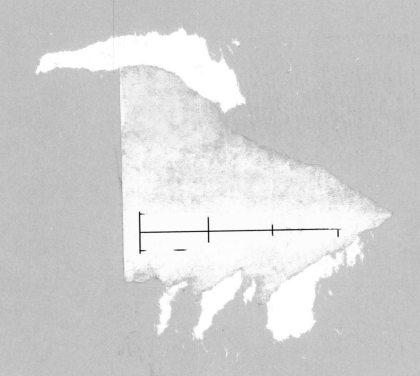

3 x 5/08 (10/14)